WRITTEN BY
IAN EDGINTON

ART BY
CHRISTOPHER SHY

DEAD SPACE™
LIBERATION

For Dead Space Liberation:
    Producers — Cate Latchford
                        Chuck Beaver

For Dead Space:
    VP / EP — Steve Papoutsis
    Creative Director — Ben Wanat
    Art Director — Alex Muscat

Special thanks to:
    Beth Pielert
    Dino Ignacio
    Ellana Fortuna
    Erika Peterson
    Frank Gibeau
    John Riccietello
    Justin Porter
    Laura Miele
    Matt Bendett
    Monique Miller
    Patrick Soderlund
    Peter Moore
    Steve Pointon

www.deadspace.com

EA   VISCERAL

FOR STUDIO RONIN

EDITED BY Nose Osaka

PRODUCTION MANAGER Emmalee Pearson

DEAD SPACE™ LIBERATION
ISBN: 9781781165539

Published by Titan Books,
A division of Titan Publishing Group Ltd.,
144 Southwark St., London, SE1 0UP

A CIP catalogue record for this title is available from the British Library.

First edition: February 2013

10 9 8 7 6 5 4 3 2 1

Printed in the USA.

What did you think of this book? We love to hear from our readers. Please email us
at: readerfeedback@titanemail.com, or write to us at the above address.

To receive advance information, news, competitions, and exclusive offers online,
please sign up for the Titan newsletter on our website: www.titanbooks.com

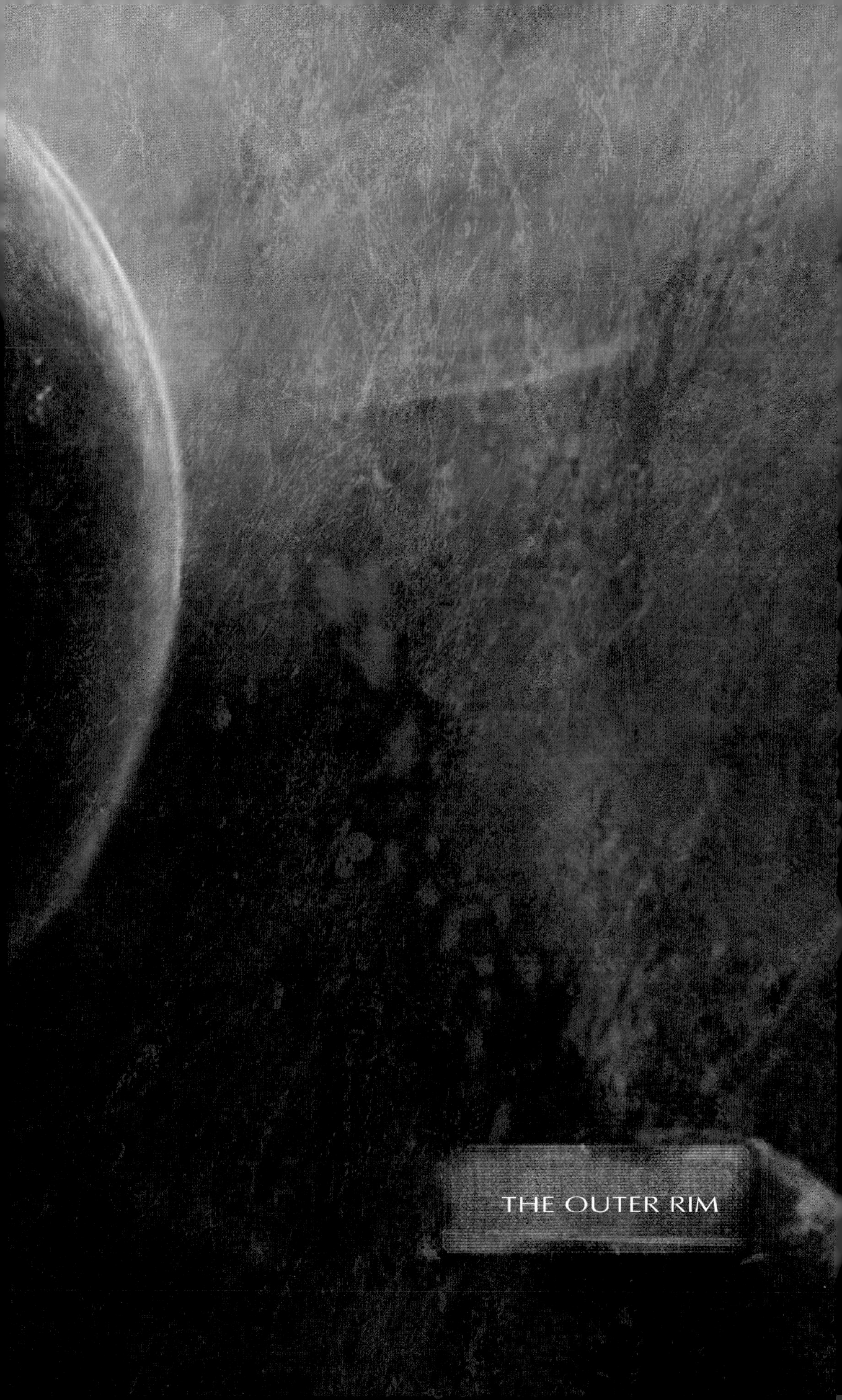
THE OUTER RIM

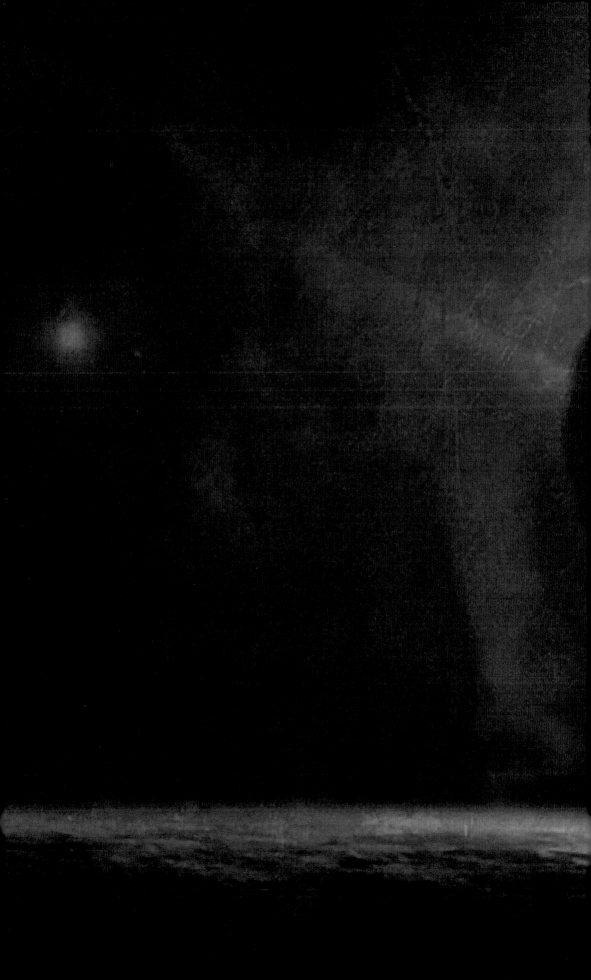

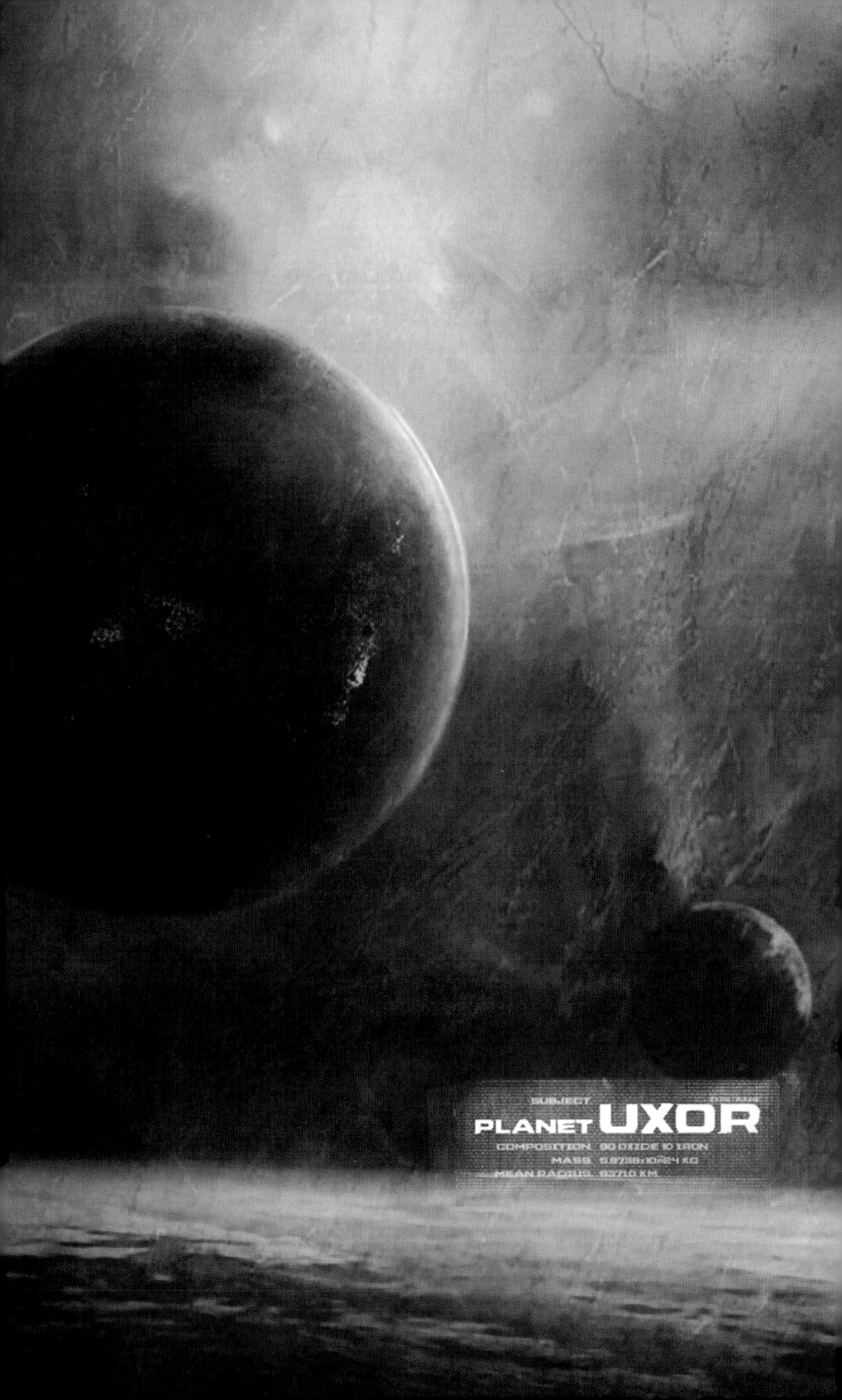
SUBJECT.
PLANET UXOR
COMPOSITION. 90 OXIDE 10 IRON
MASS. 5.9736x10^24 KG
MEAN RADIUS. 6370.0 KM

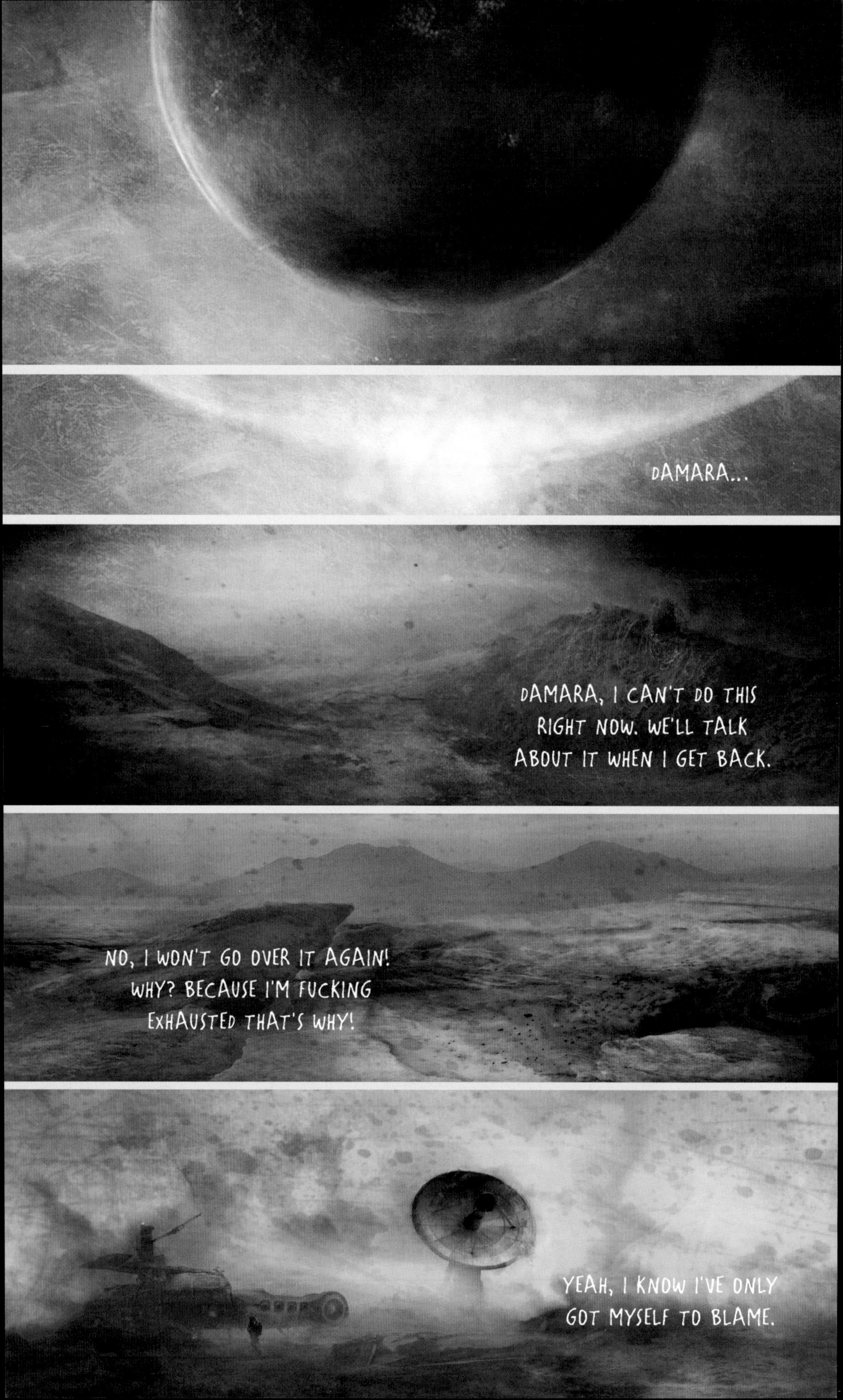
DAMARA...
DAMARA, I CAN'T DO THIS RIGHT NOW. WE'LL TALK ABOUT IT WHEN I GET BACK.
NO, I WON'T GO OVER IT AGAIN! WHY? BECAUSE I'M FUCKING EXHAUSTED THAT'S WHY!
YEAH, I KNOW I'VE ONLY GOT MYSELF TO BLAME.

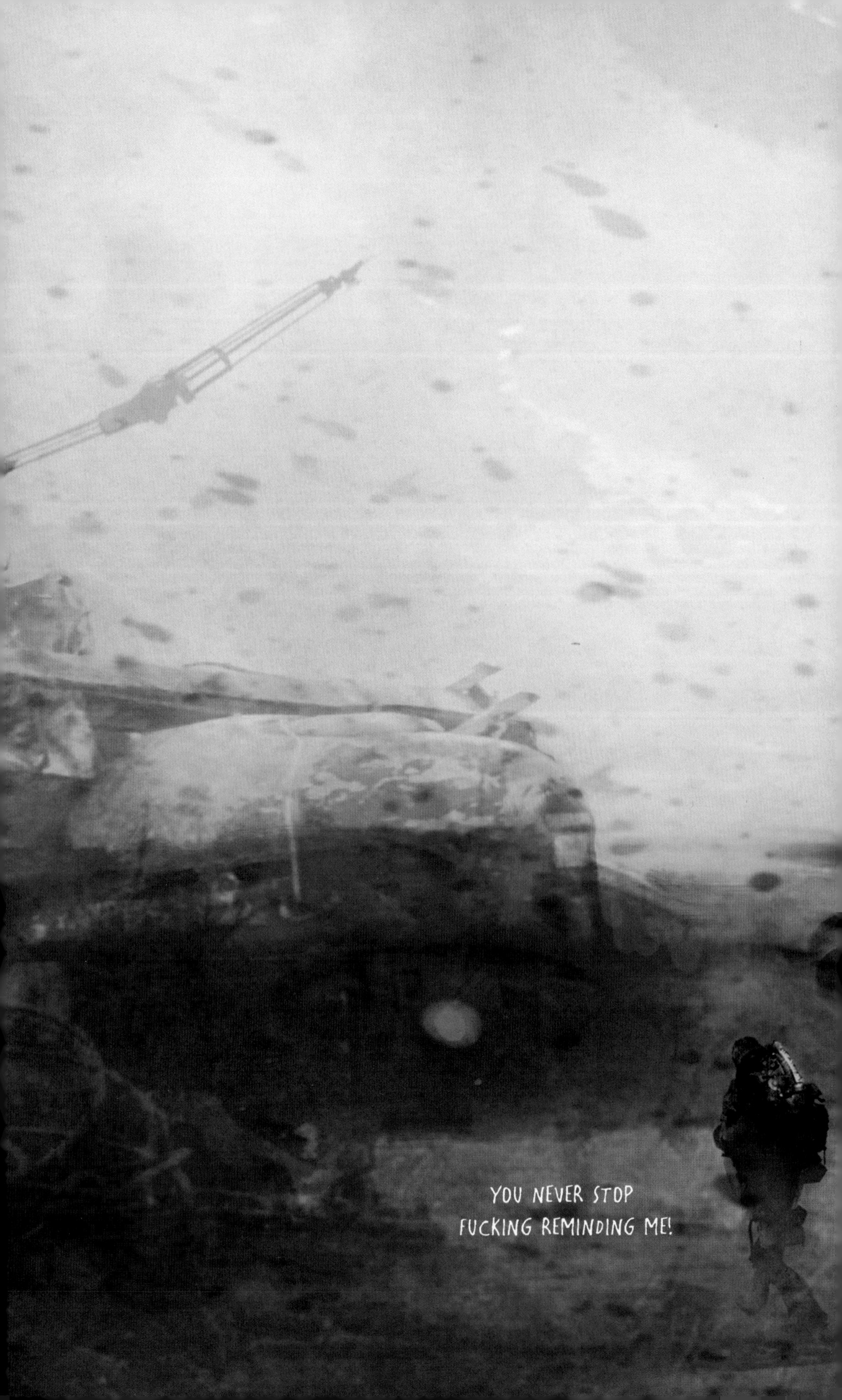
YOU NEVER STOP
FUCKING REMINDING ME!

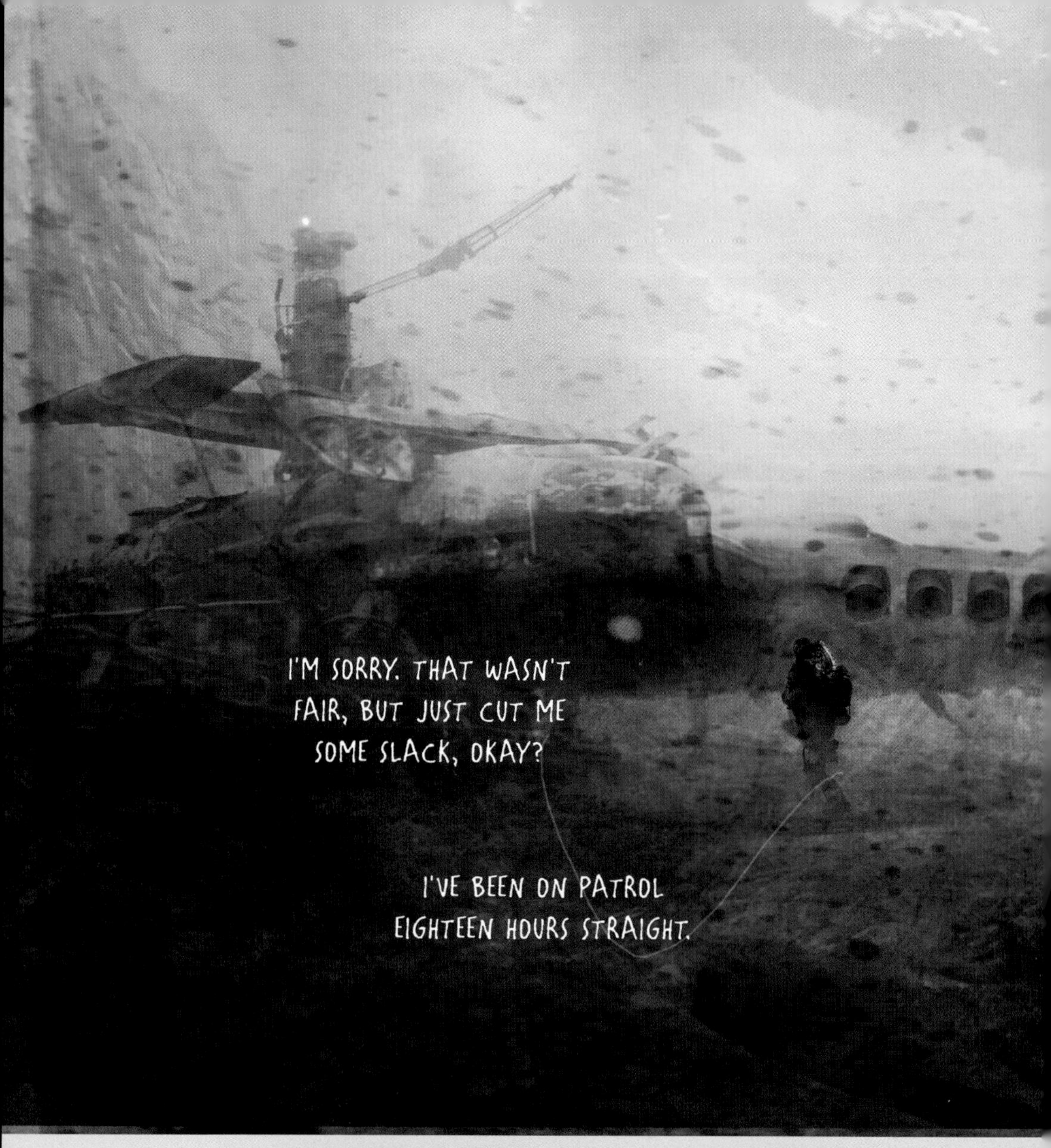
I'M SORRY. THAT WASN'T FAIR, BUT JUST CUT ME SOME SLACK, OKAY?
I'VE BEEN ON PATROL EIGHTEEN HOURS STRAIGHT.

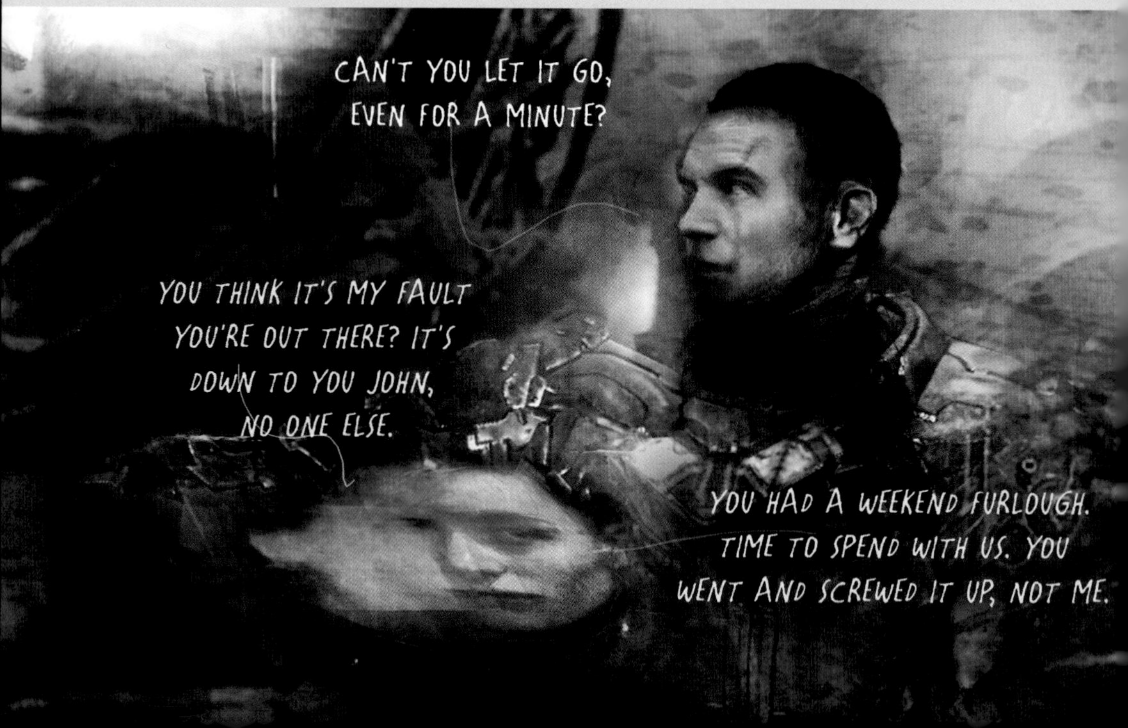
CAN'T YOU LET IT GO, EVEN FOR A MINUTE?
YOU THINK IT'S MY FAULT YOU'RE OUT THERE? IT'S DOWN TO YOU JOHN, NO ONE ELSE.
YOU HAD A WEEKEND FURLOUGH. TIME TO SPEND WITH US. YOU WENT AND SCREWED IT UP, NOT ME.

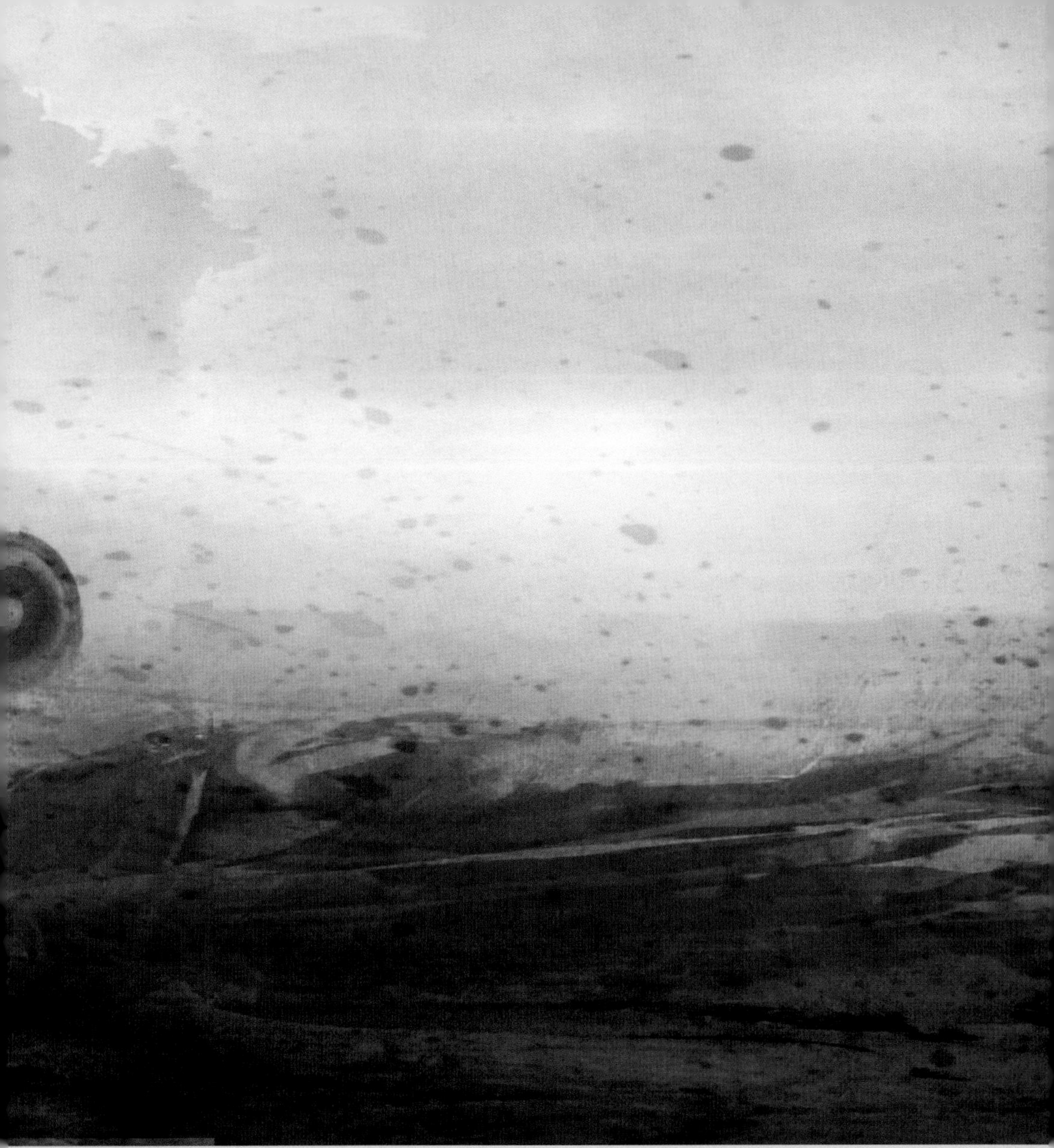

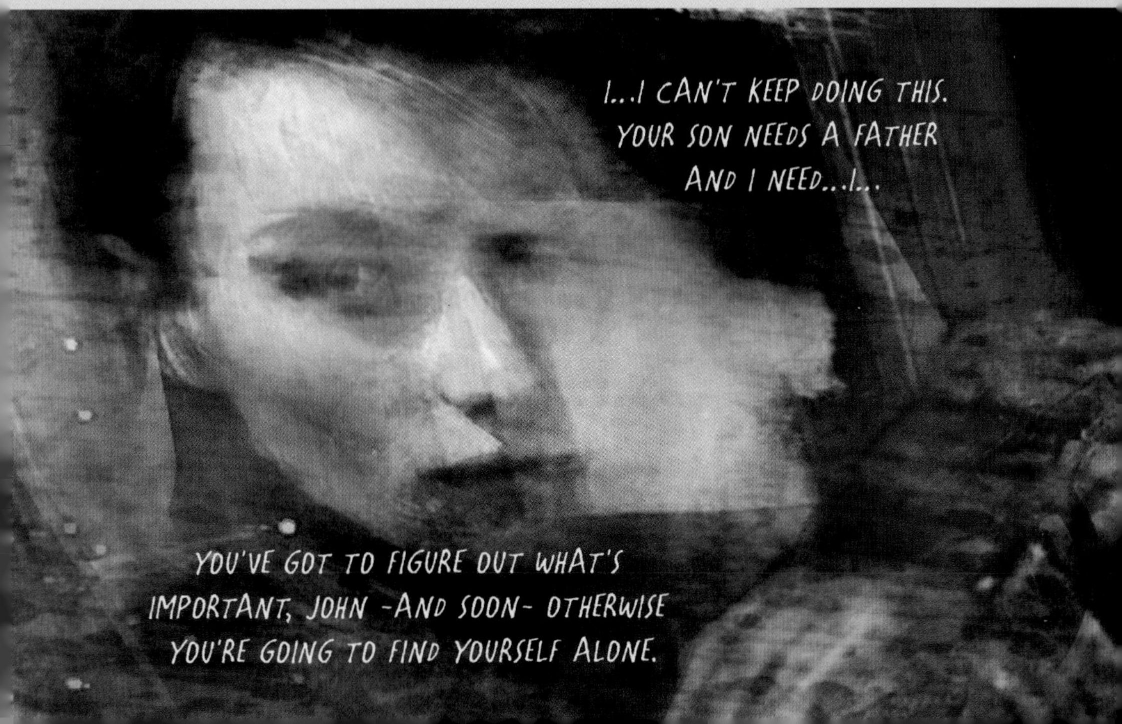
I...I CAN'T KEEP DOING THIS. YOUR SON NEEDS A FATHER AND I NEED...I...
YOU'VE GOT TO FIGURE OUT WHAT'S IMPORTANT, JOHN -AND SOON- OTHERWISE YOU'RE GOING TO FIND YOURSELF ALONE.

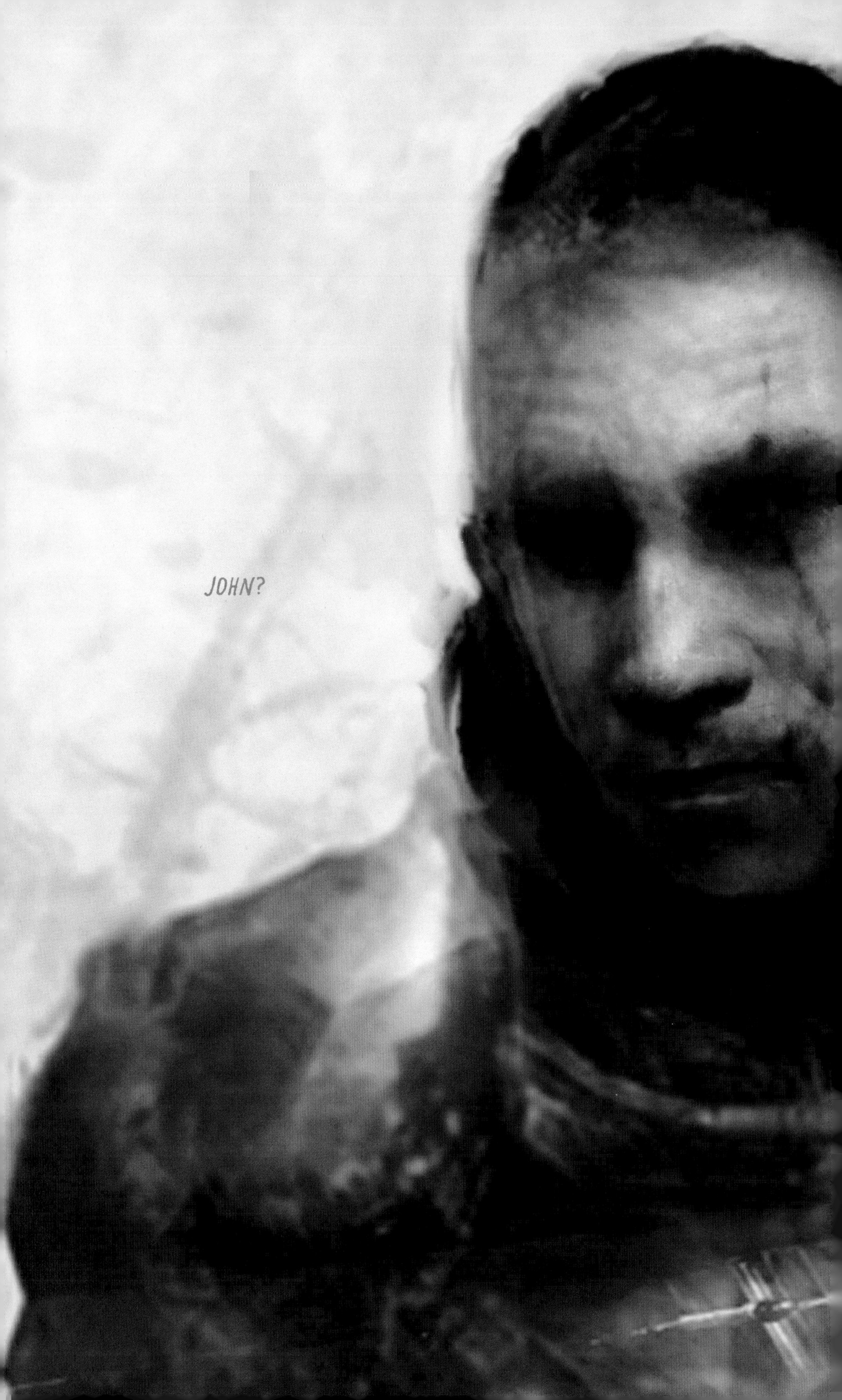
JOHN?

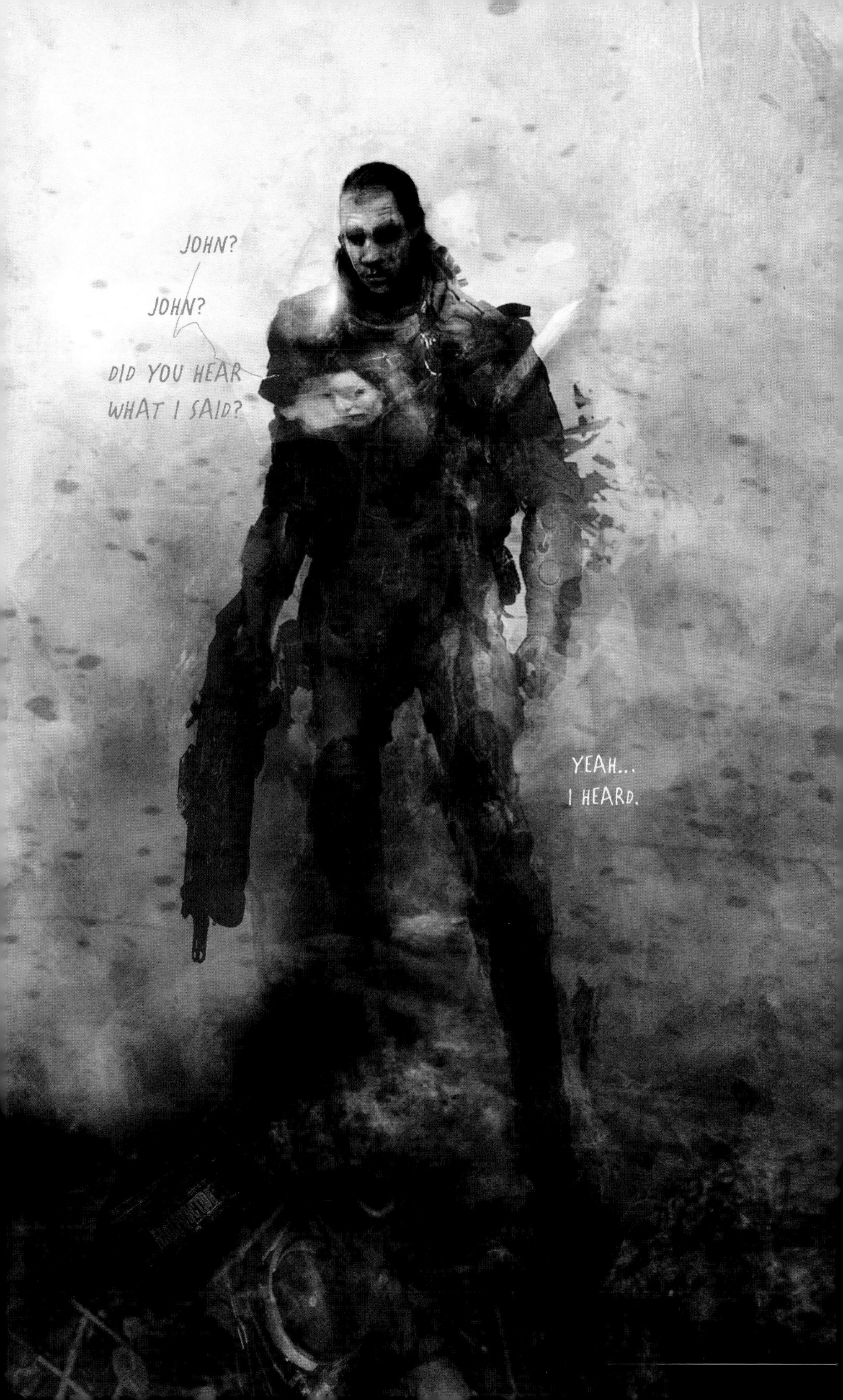
JOHN?
JOHN?
DID YOU HEAR WHAT I SAID?
YEAH... I HEARD.

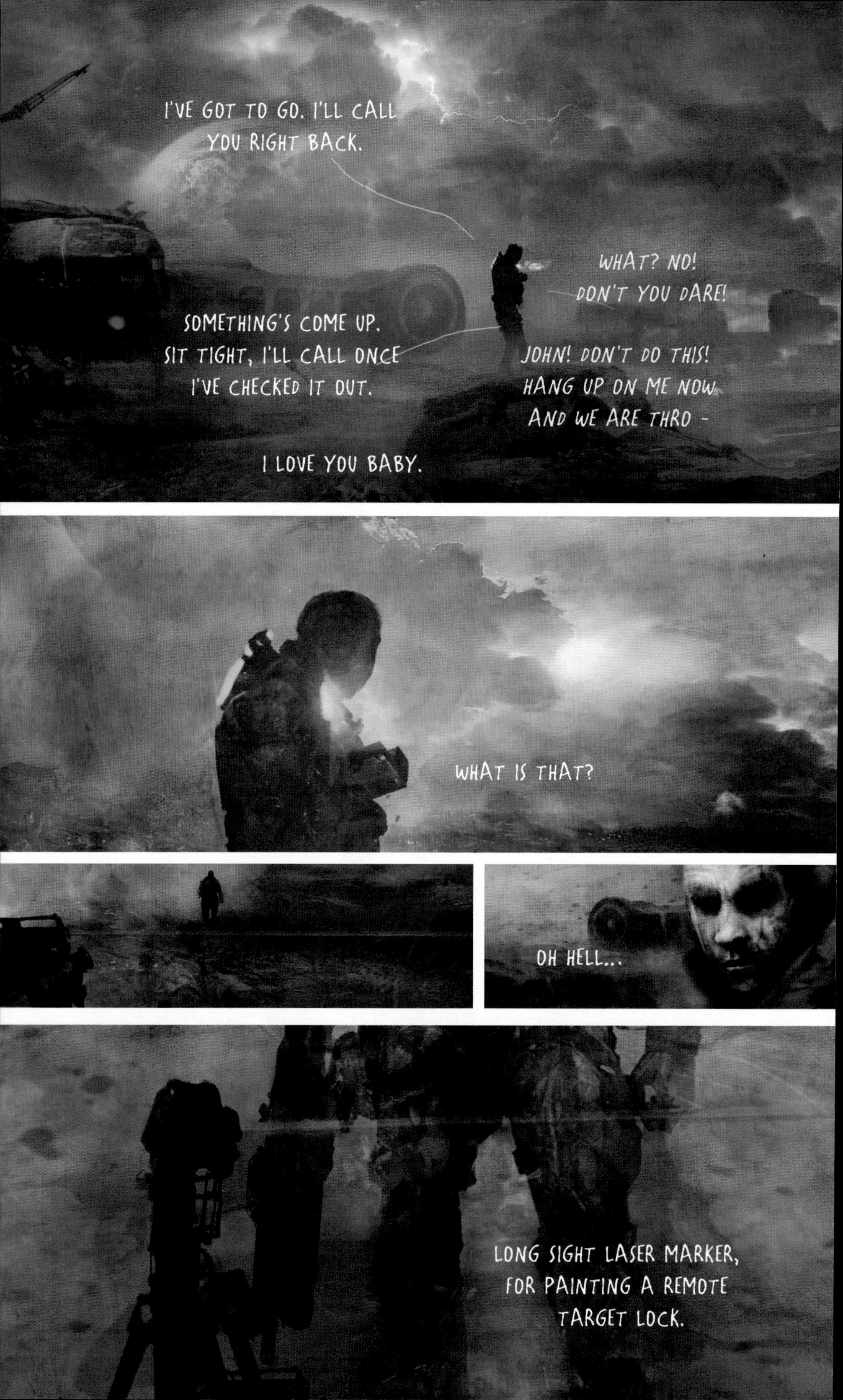
I'VE GOT TO GO. I'LL CALL YOU RIGHT BACK.
WHAT? NO! DON'T YOU DARE!
SOMETHING'S COME UP. SIT TIGHT, I'LL CALL ONCE I'VE CHECKED IT OUT.
JOHN! DON'T DO THIS! HANG UP ON ME NOW AND WE ARE THRO -
I LOVE YOU BABY.
WHAT IS THAT?
OH HELL...
LONG SIGHT LASER MARKER, FOR PAINTING A REMOTE TARGET LOCK.

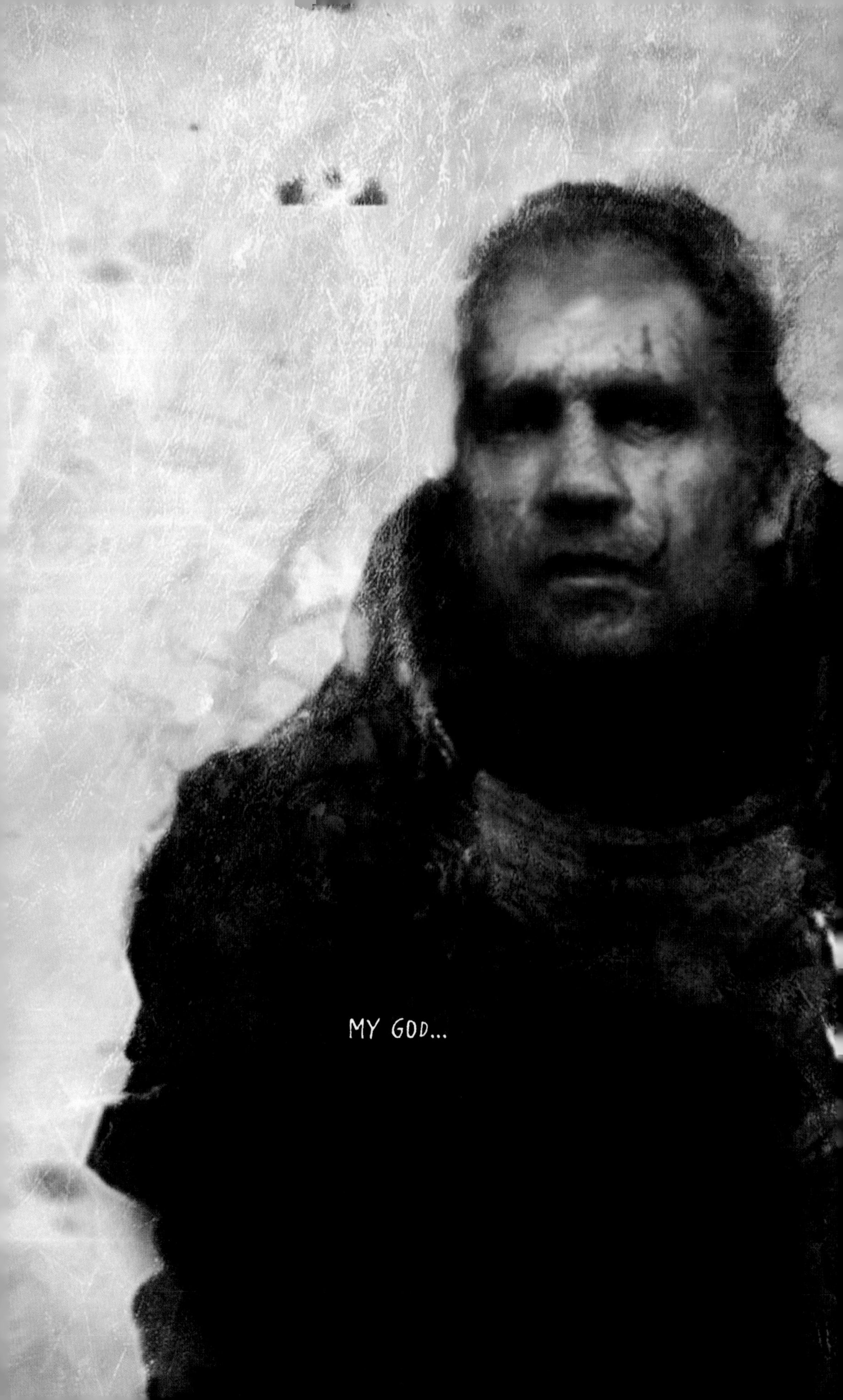
MY GOD...

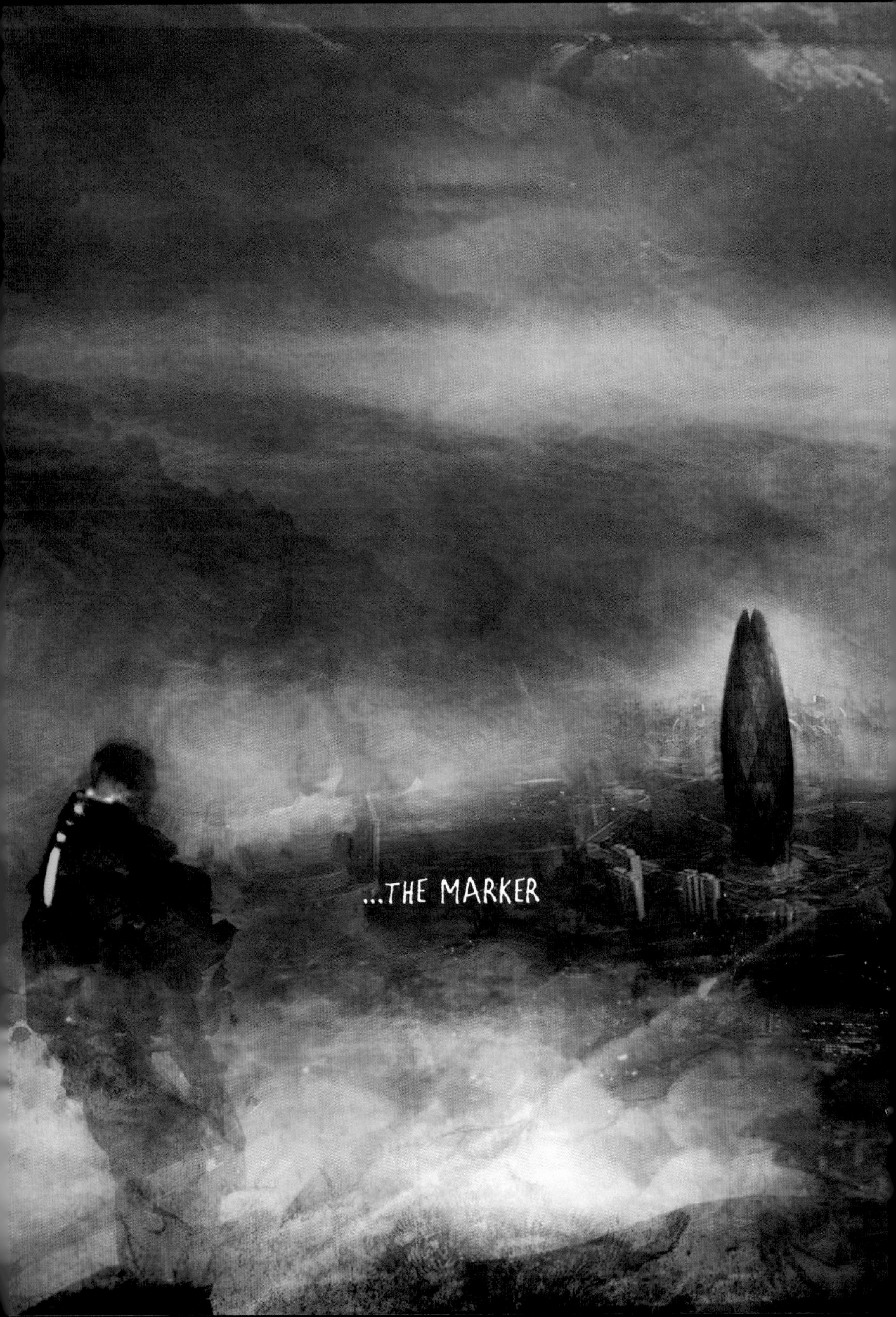
...THE MARKER

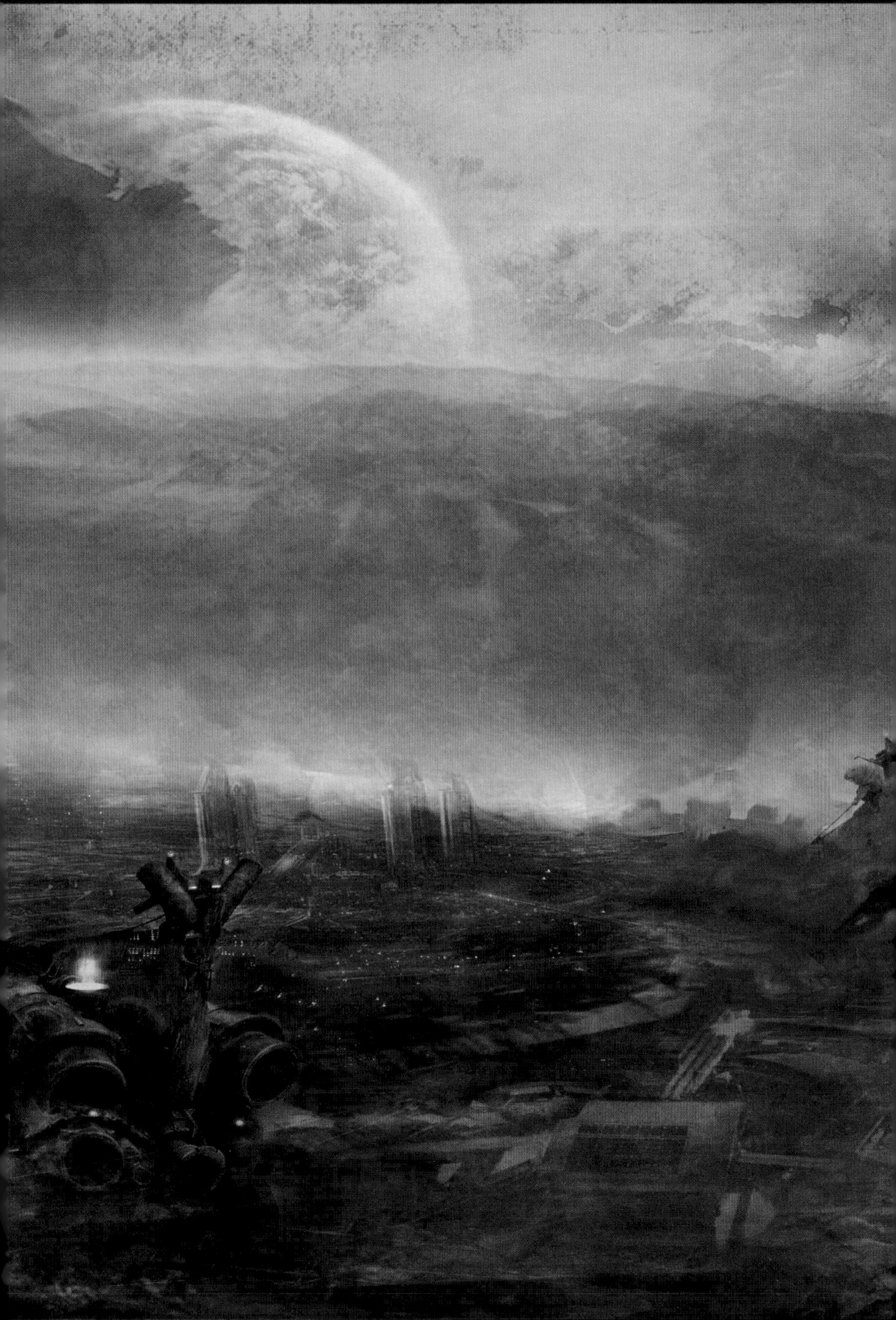

DAMARA!
YOU THINK YOU CAN JUST -
SHUT UP AND LISTEN! GRAB DYLAN AND GO DOWN TO THE BLAST SHELTER!
JOHN, WHAT'RE YOU -
GO, NOW! BEFORE IT'S --
-- TOO LATE!
DAMARA!

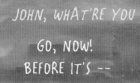

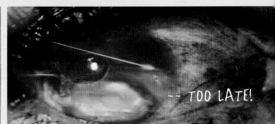

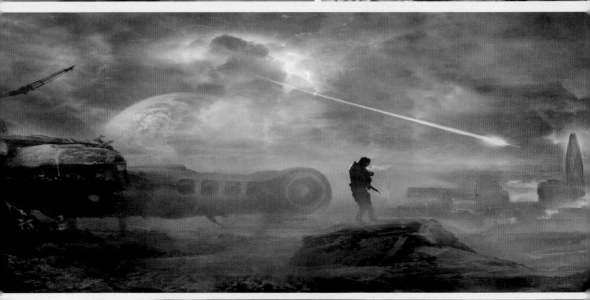

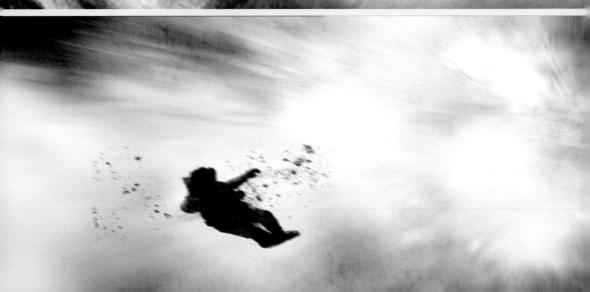

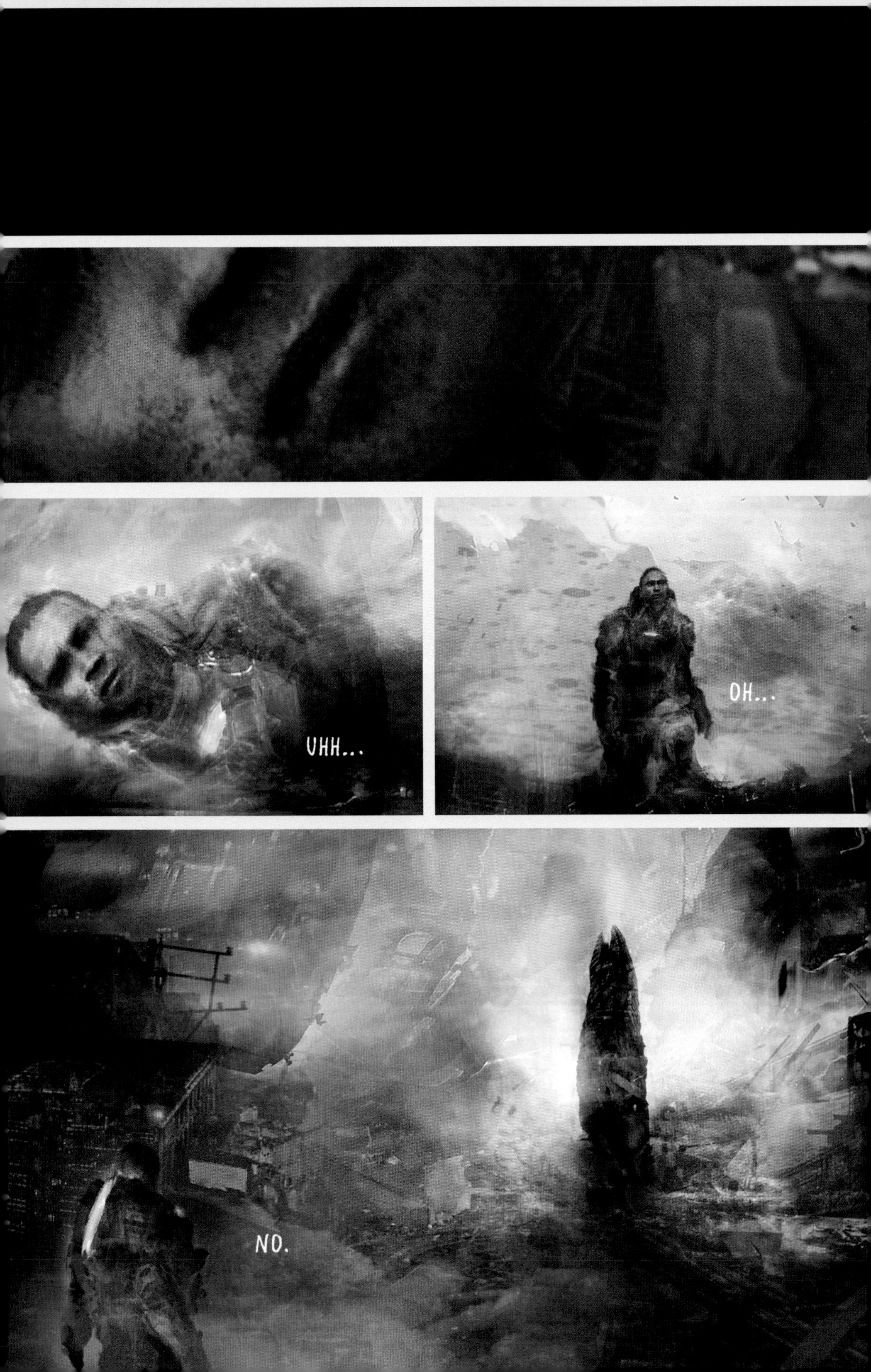
UHH...
OH...
NO.

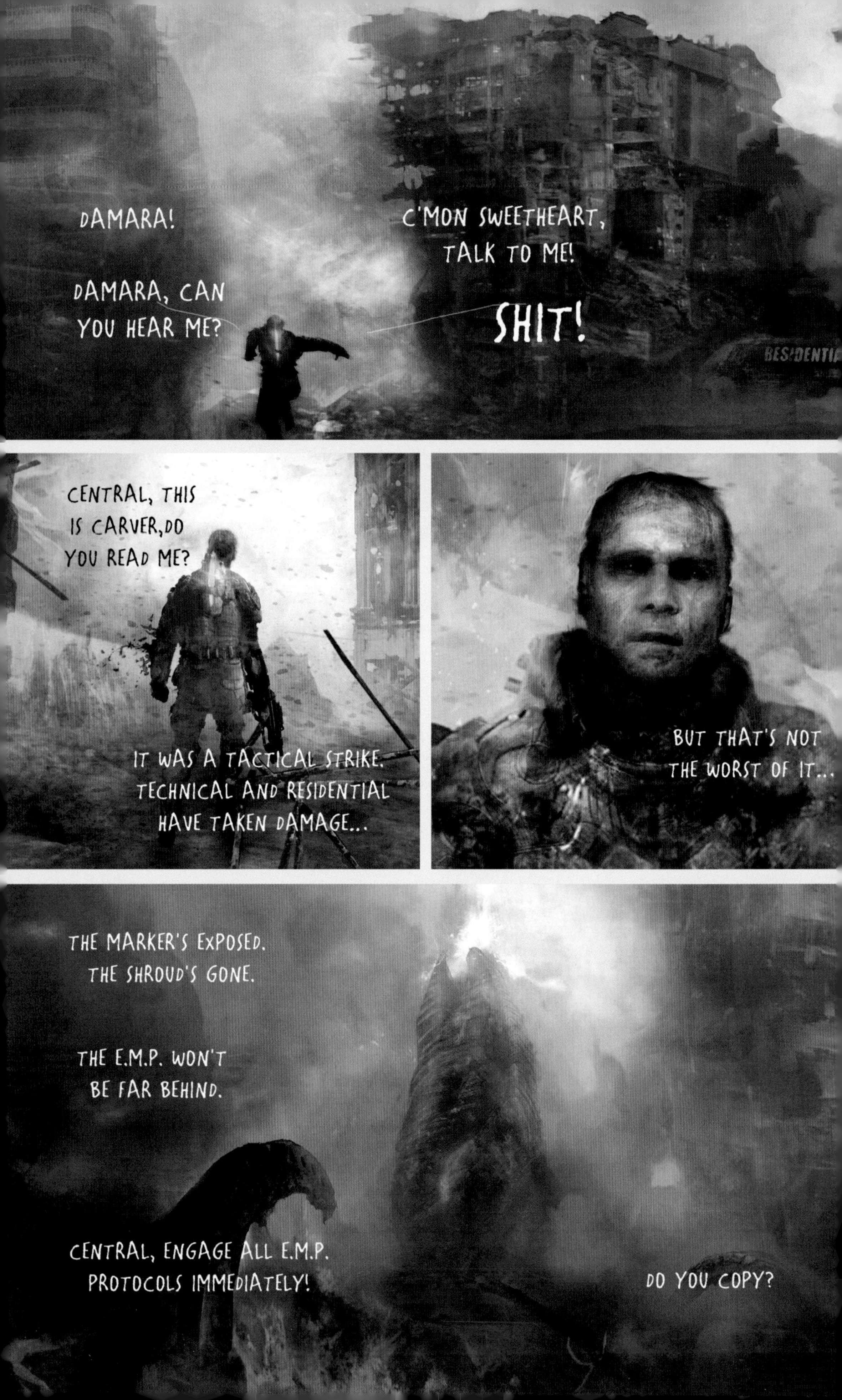
DAMARA!
DAMARA, CAN YOU HEAR ME?
C'MON SWEETHEART, TALK TO ME!
SHIT!
CENTRAL, THIS IS CARVER, DO YOU READ ME?
IT WAS A TACTICAL STRIKE. TECHNICAL AND RESIDENTIAL HAVE TAKEN DAMAGE...
BUT THAT'S NOT THE WORST OF IT...
THE MARKER'S EXPOSED. THE SHROUD'S GONE.
THE E.M.P. WON'T BE FAR BEHIND.
CENTRAL, ENGAGE ALL E.M.P. PROTOCOLS IMMEDIATELY!
DO YOU COPY?

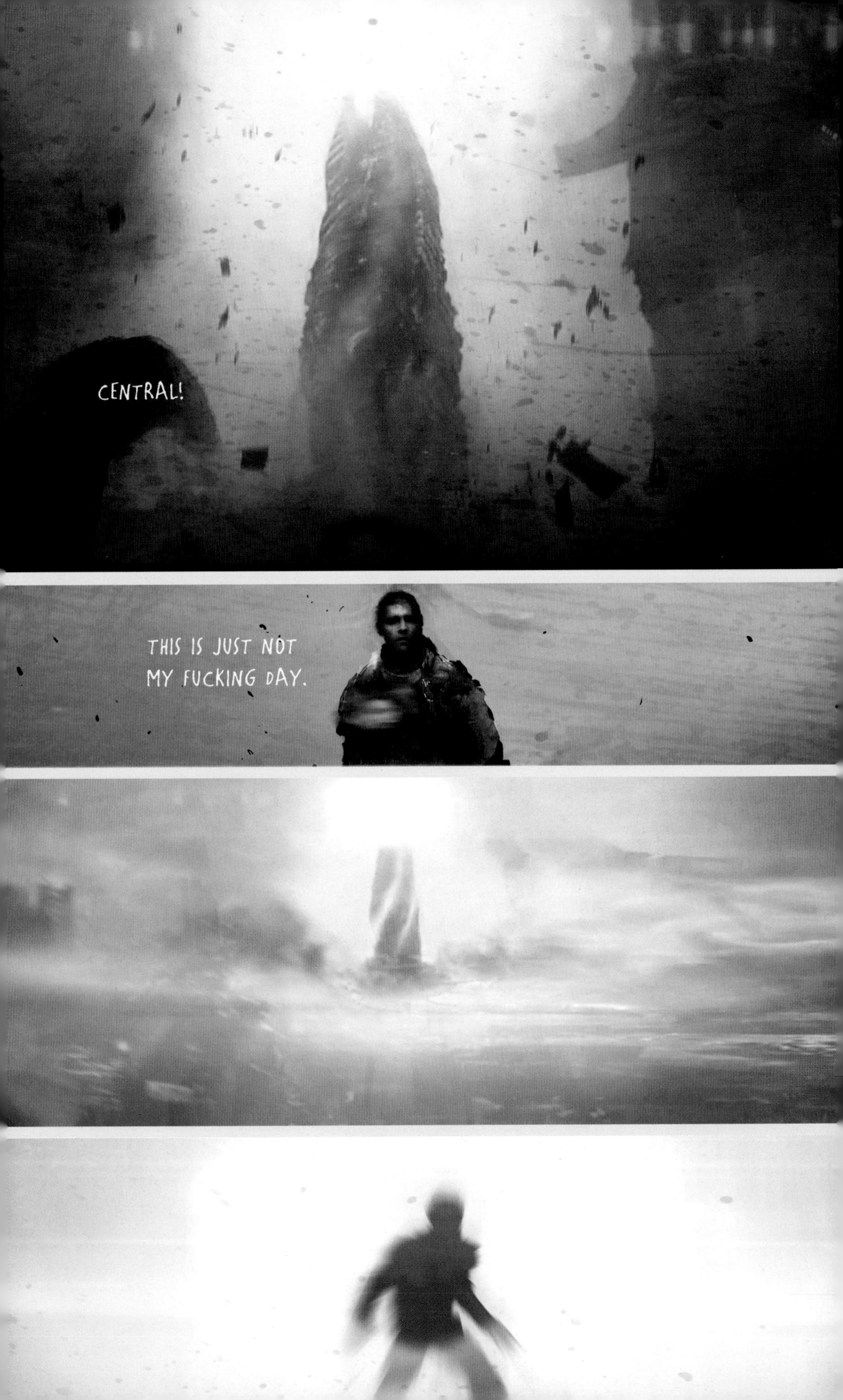
CENTRAL!
THIS IS JUST NOT MY FUCKING DAY.

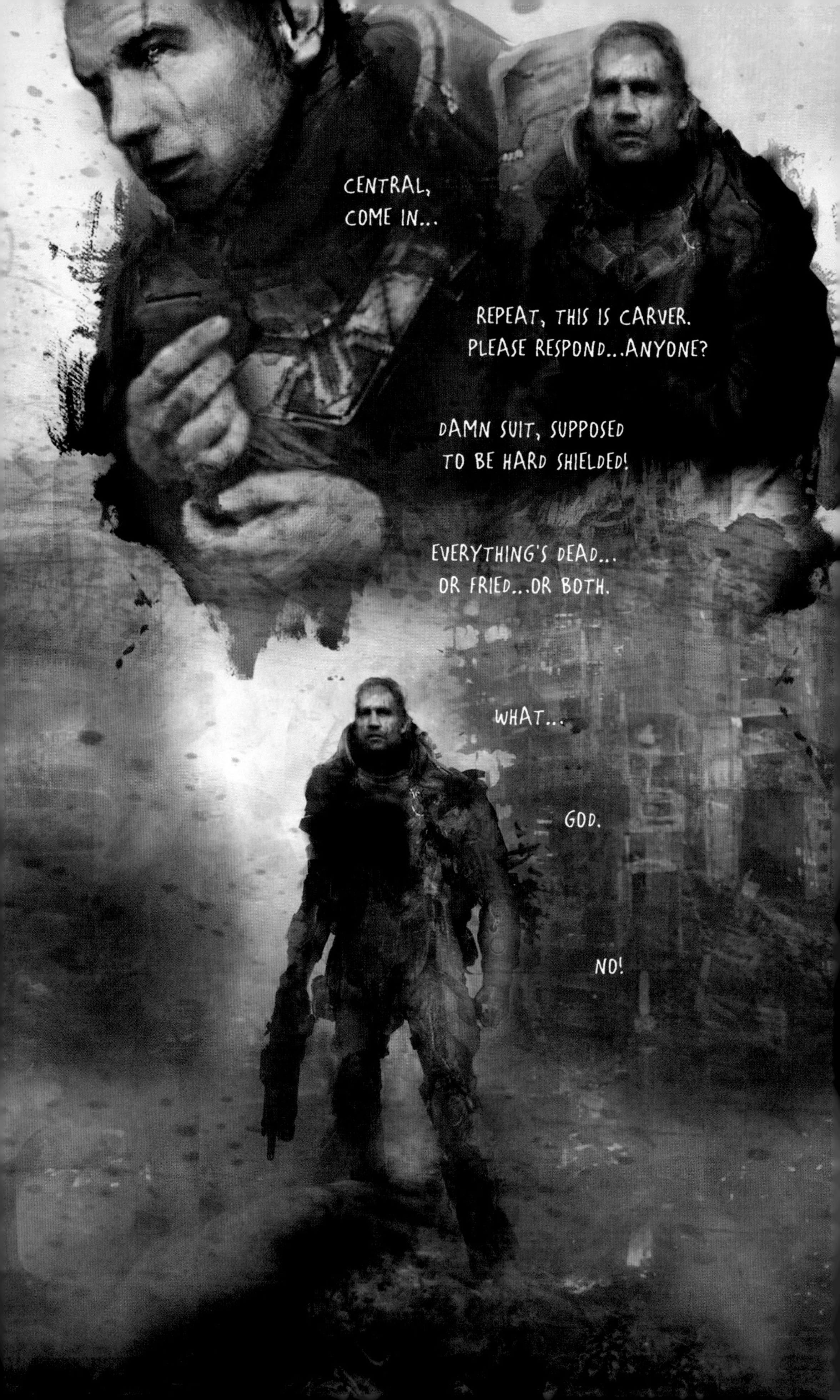
CENTRAL, COME IN...
REPEAT, THIS IS CARVER. PLEASE RESPOND...ANYONE?
DAMN SUIT, SUPPOSED TO BE HARD SHIELDED!
EVERYTHING'S DEAD... OR FRIED...OR BOTH.
WHAT...
GOD.
NO!

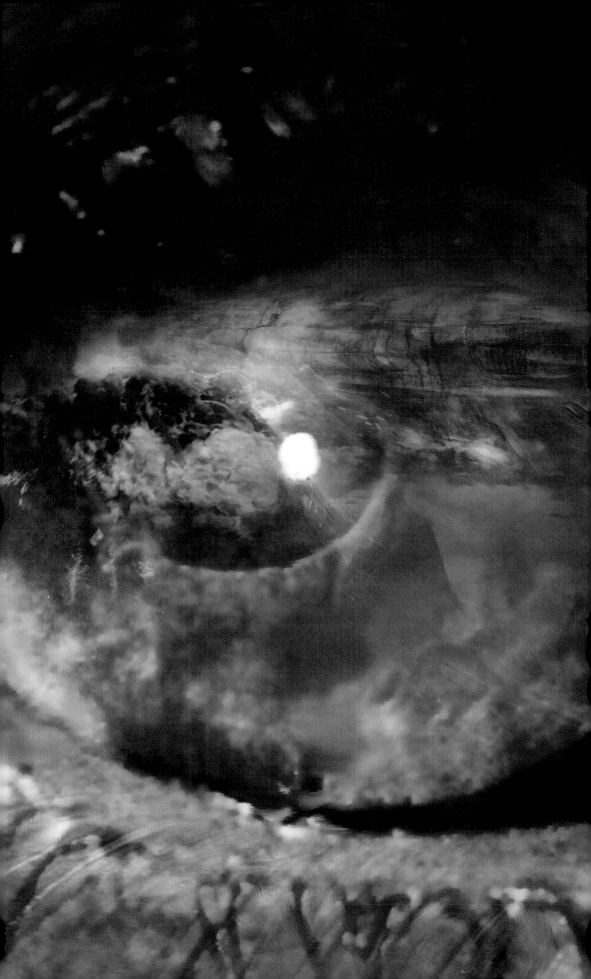

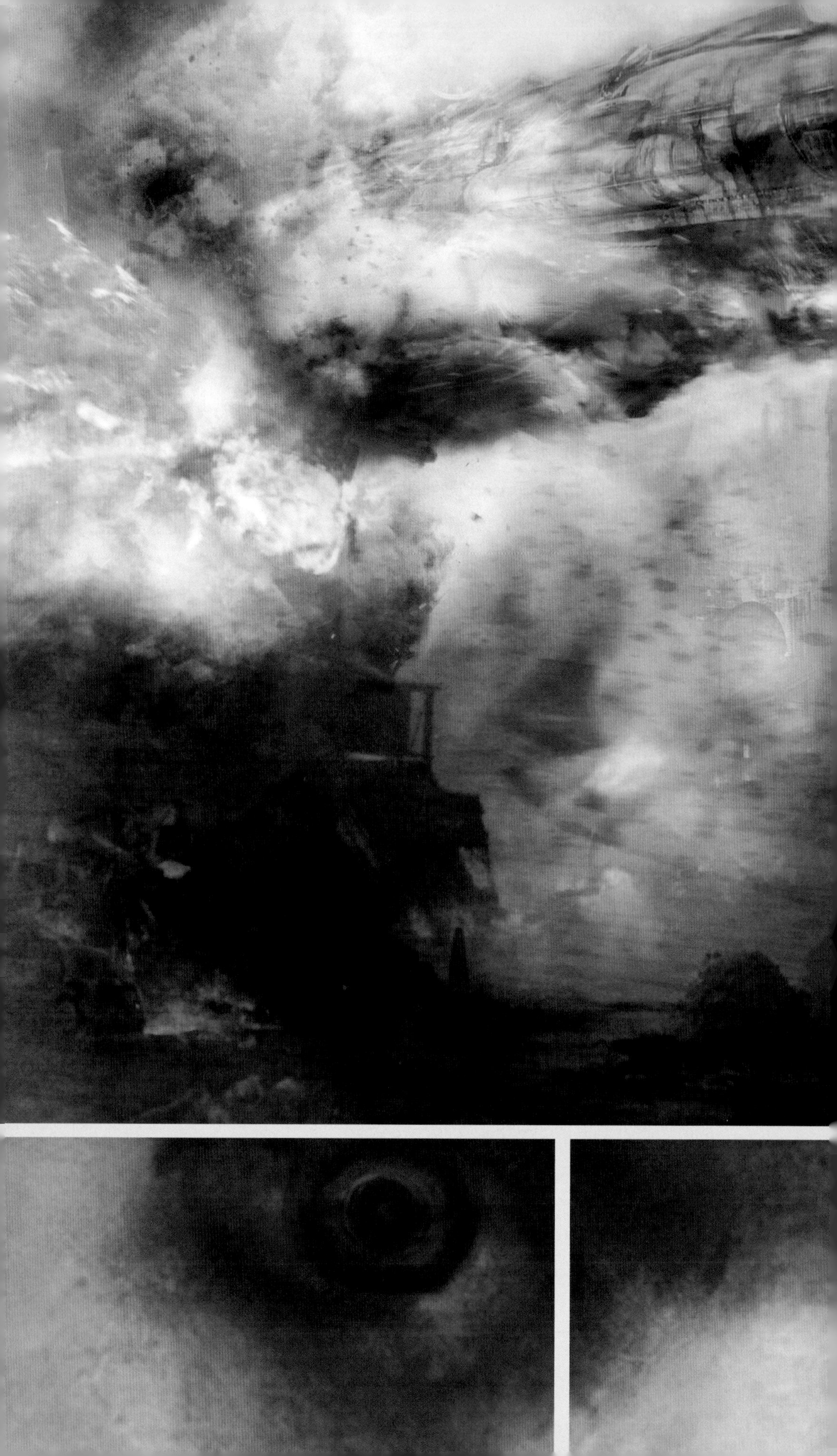

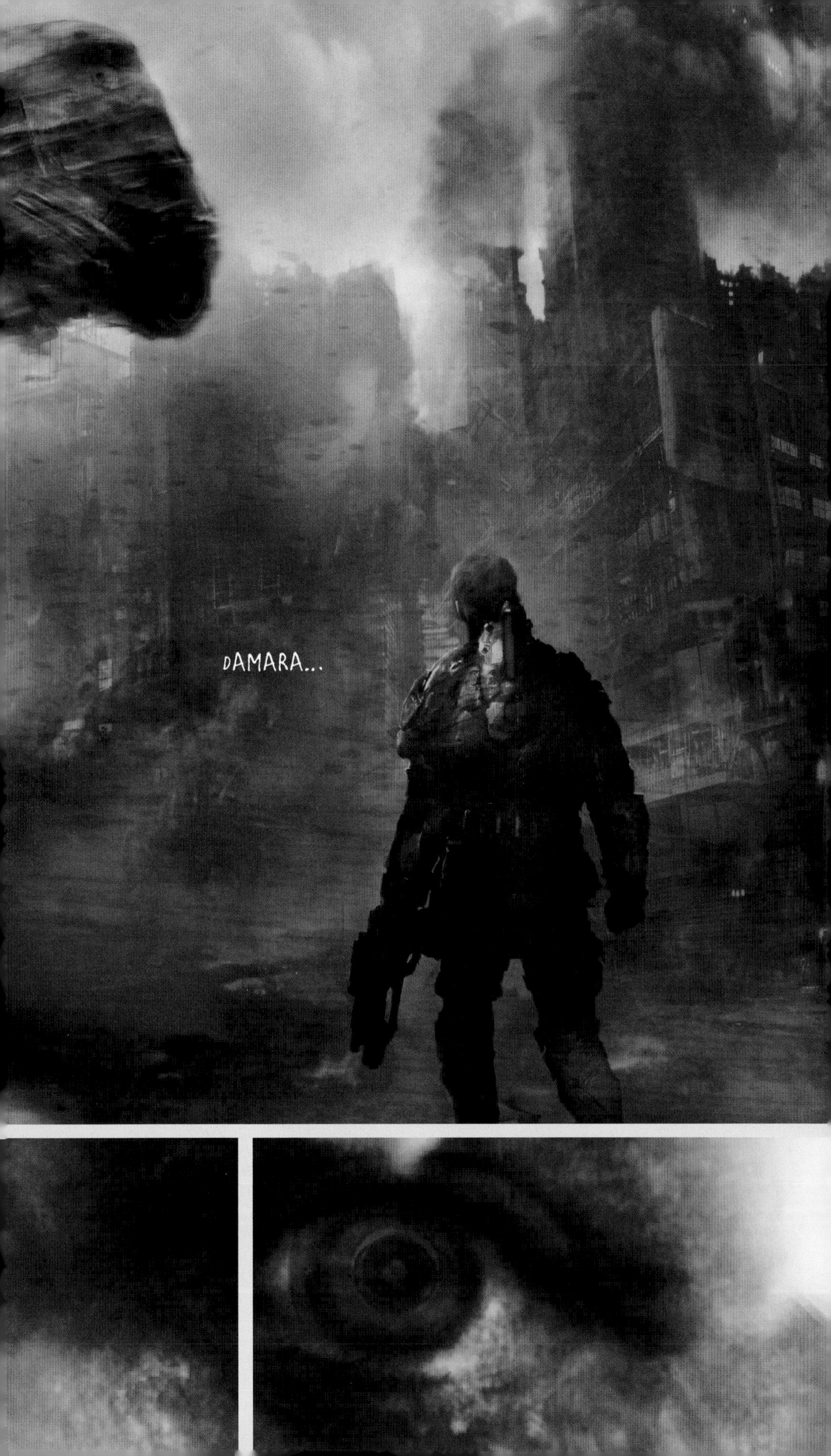
DAMARA...

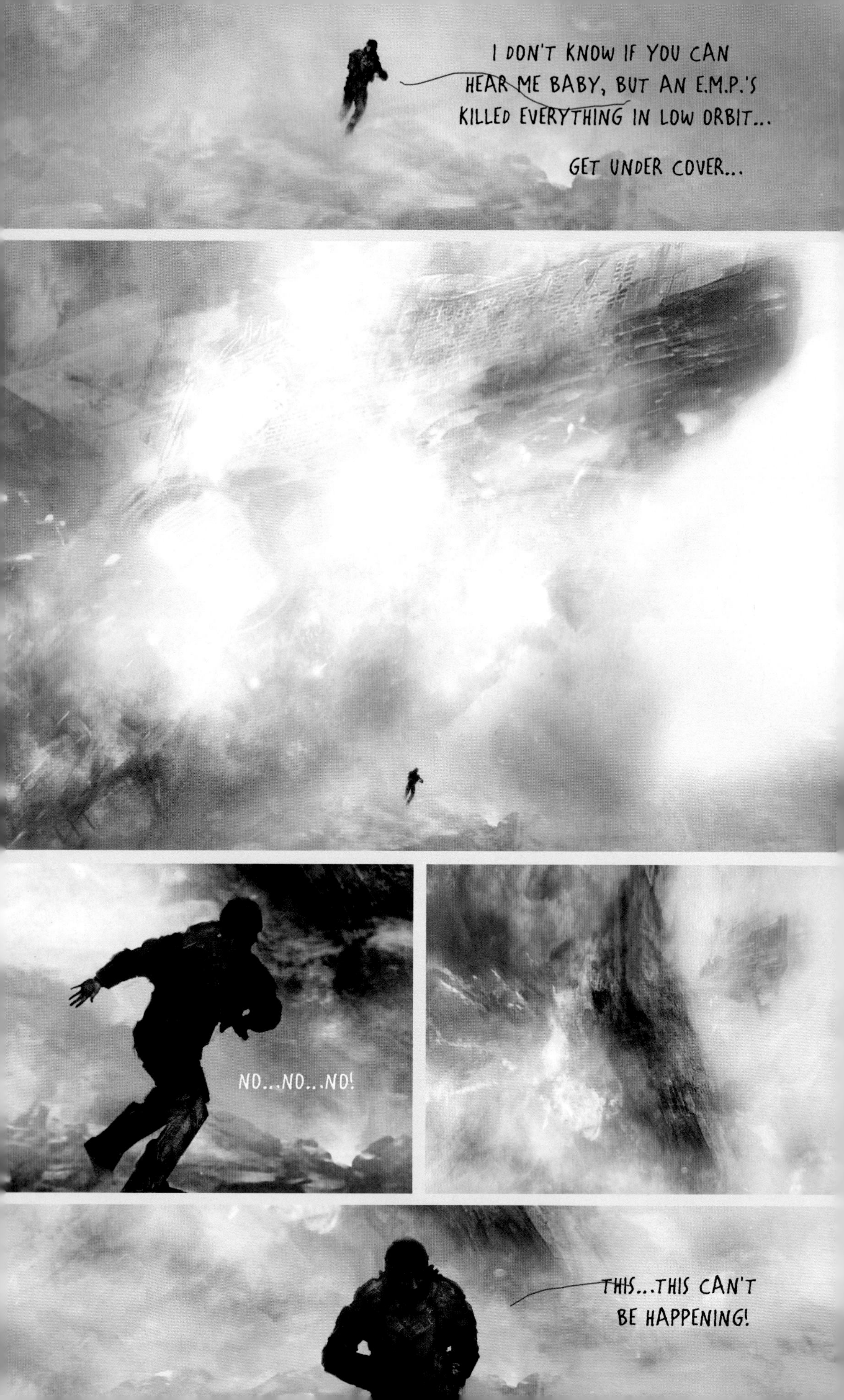
I DON'T KNOW IF YOU CAN HEAR ME BABY, BUT AN E.M.P.'S KILLED EVERYTHING IN LOW ORBIT...
GET UNDER COVER...
NO...NO...NO!
THIS...THIS CAN'T BE HAPPENING!

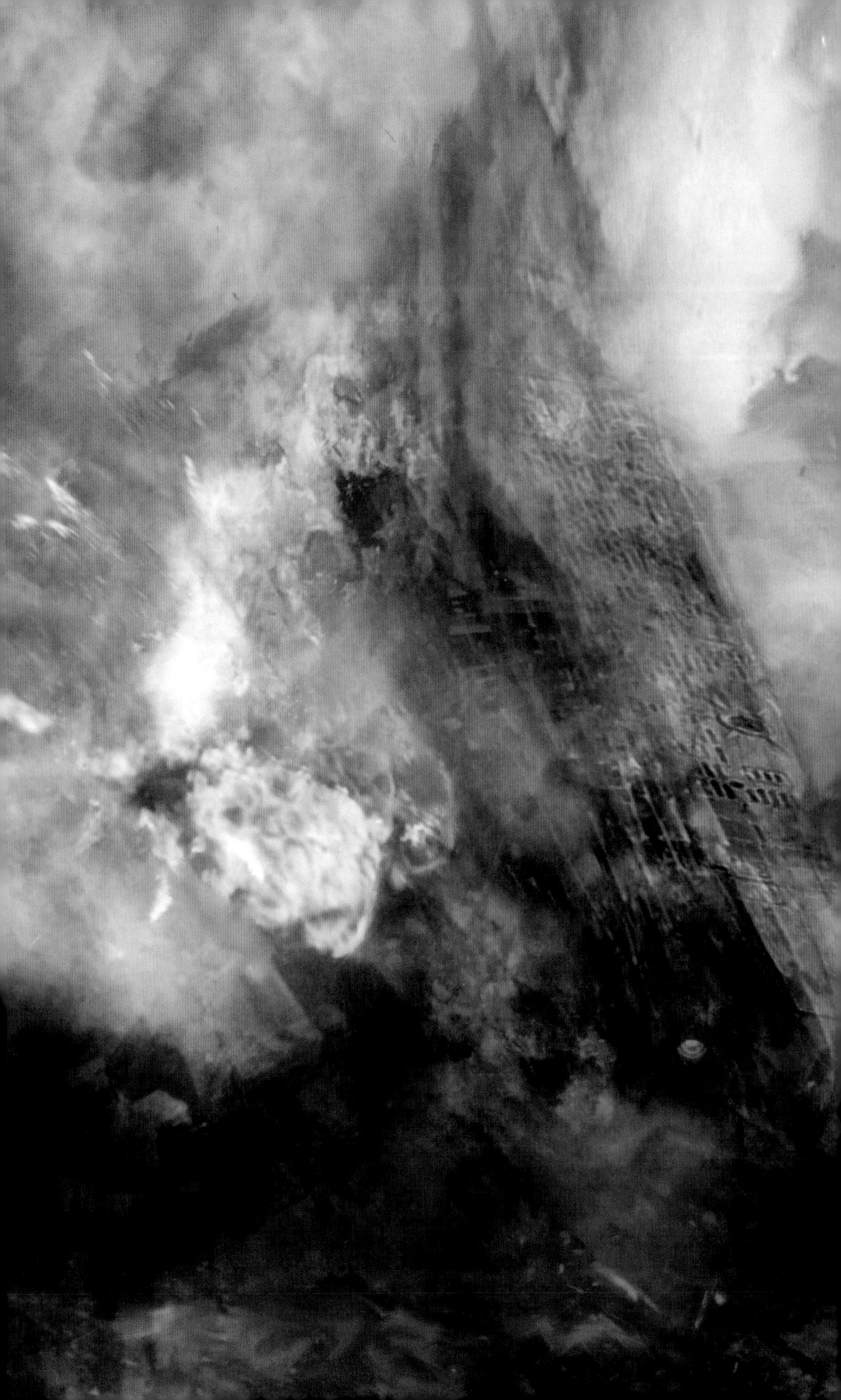

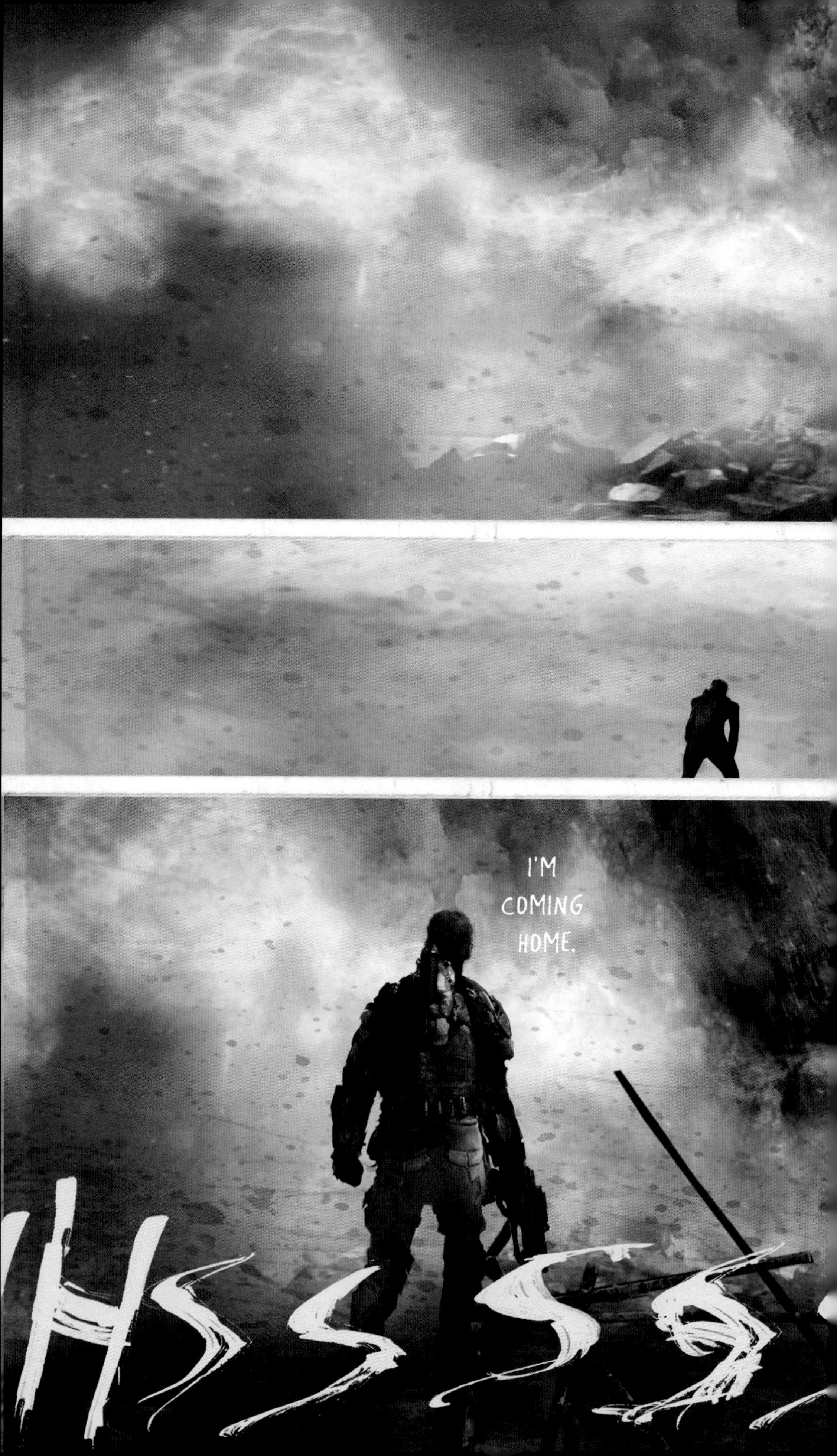
I'M COMING HOME.
HSSS

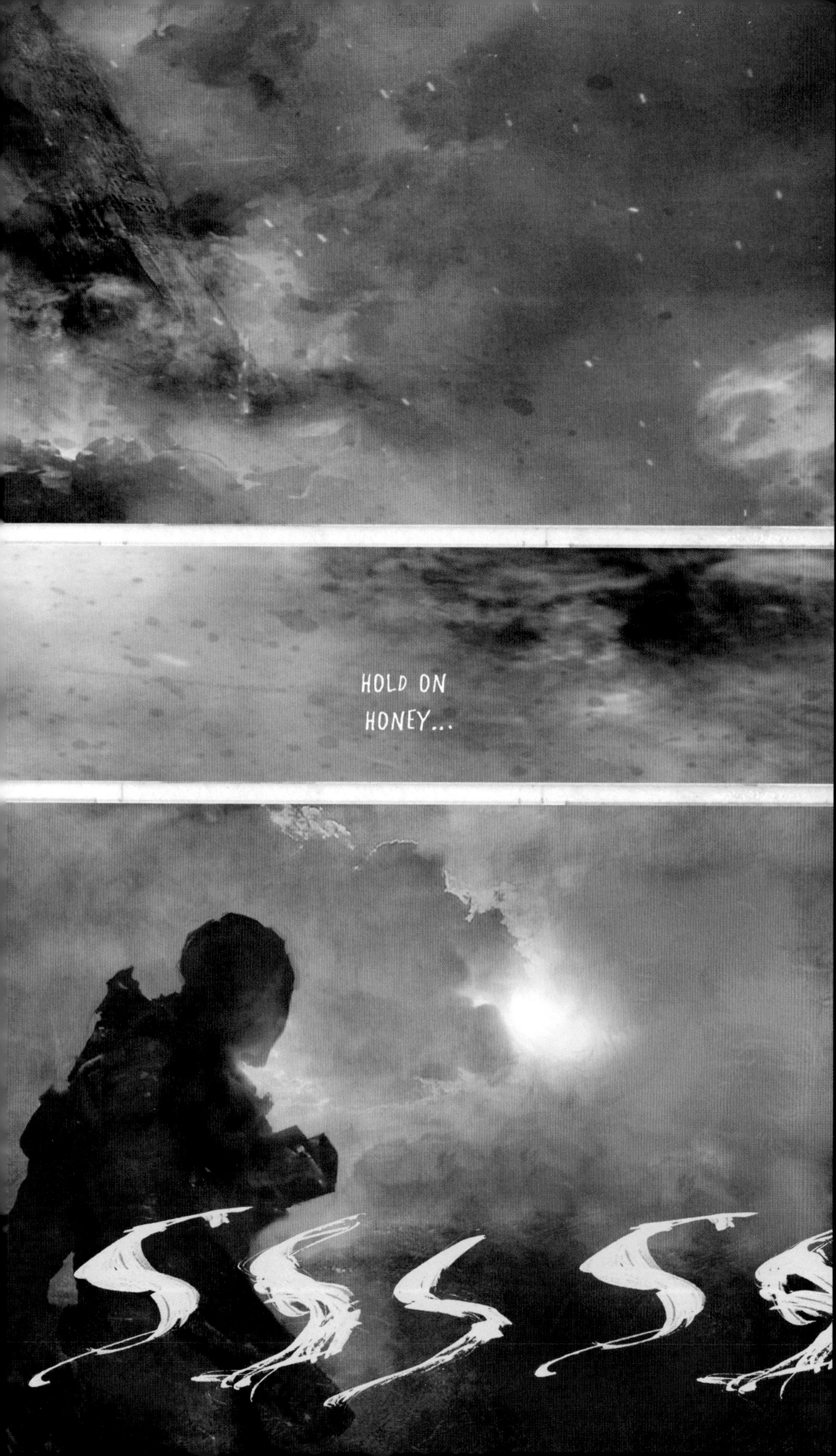
HOLD ON
HONEY...
SSSSS

SYSTEM REBOOT
JESUS!
CORE NOW ONLINE
90 PERCENT
ABOUT FUCKING TIME!
REBOOT : COMPLETE
WARNING
NO SHIT!

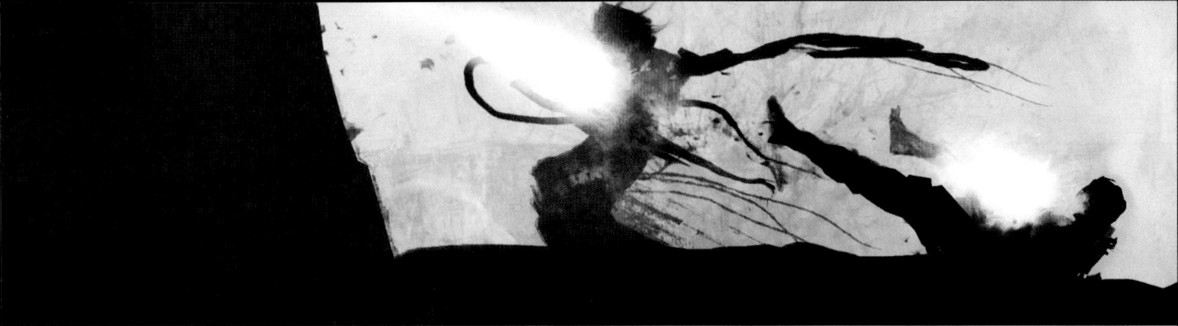

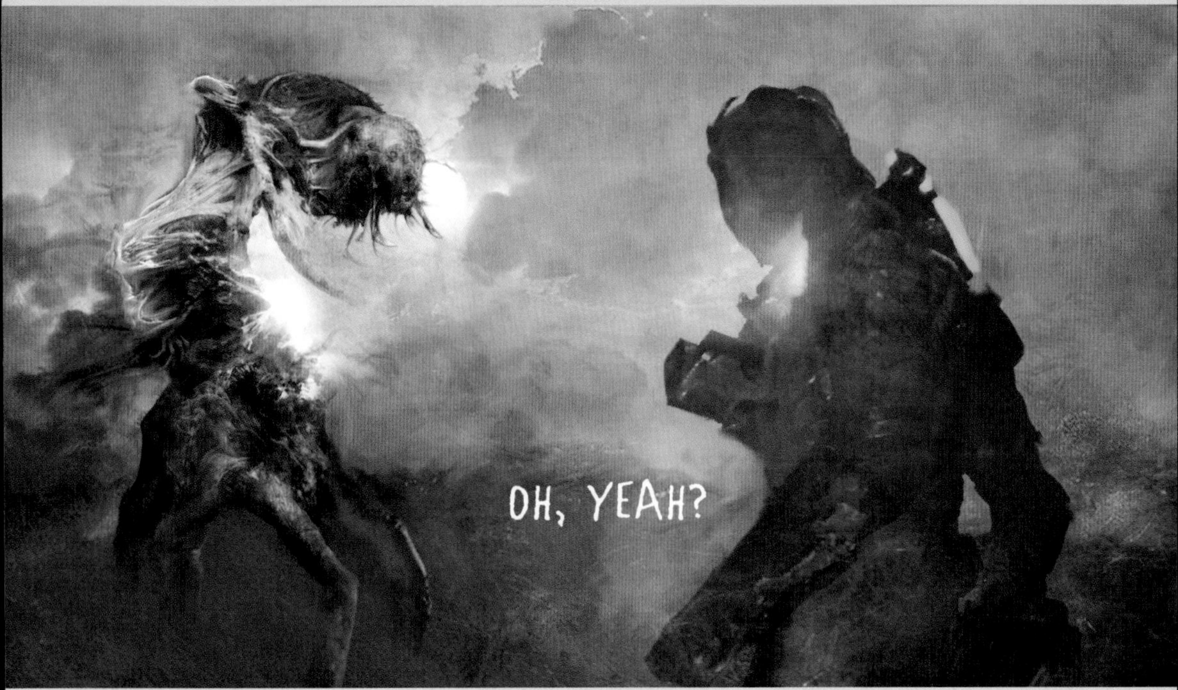
OH, YEAH?

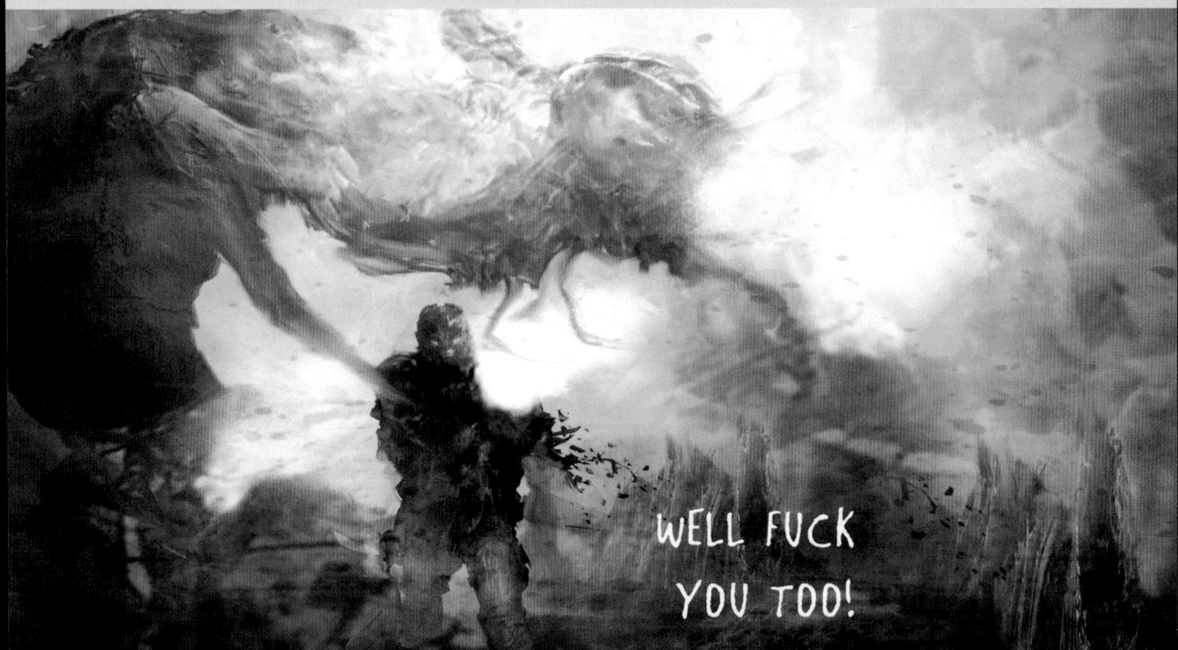
WELL FUCK
YOU TOO!

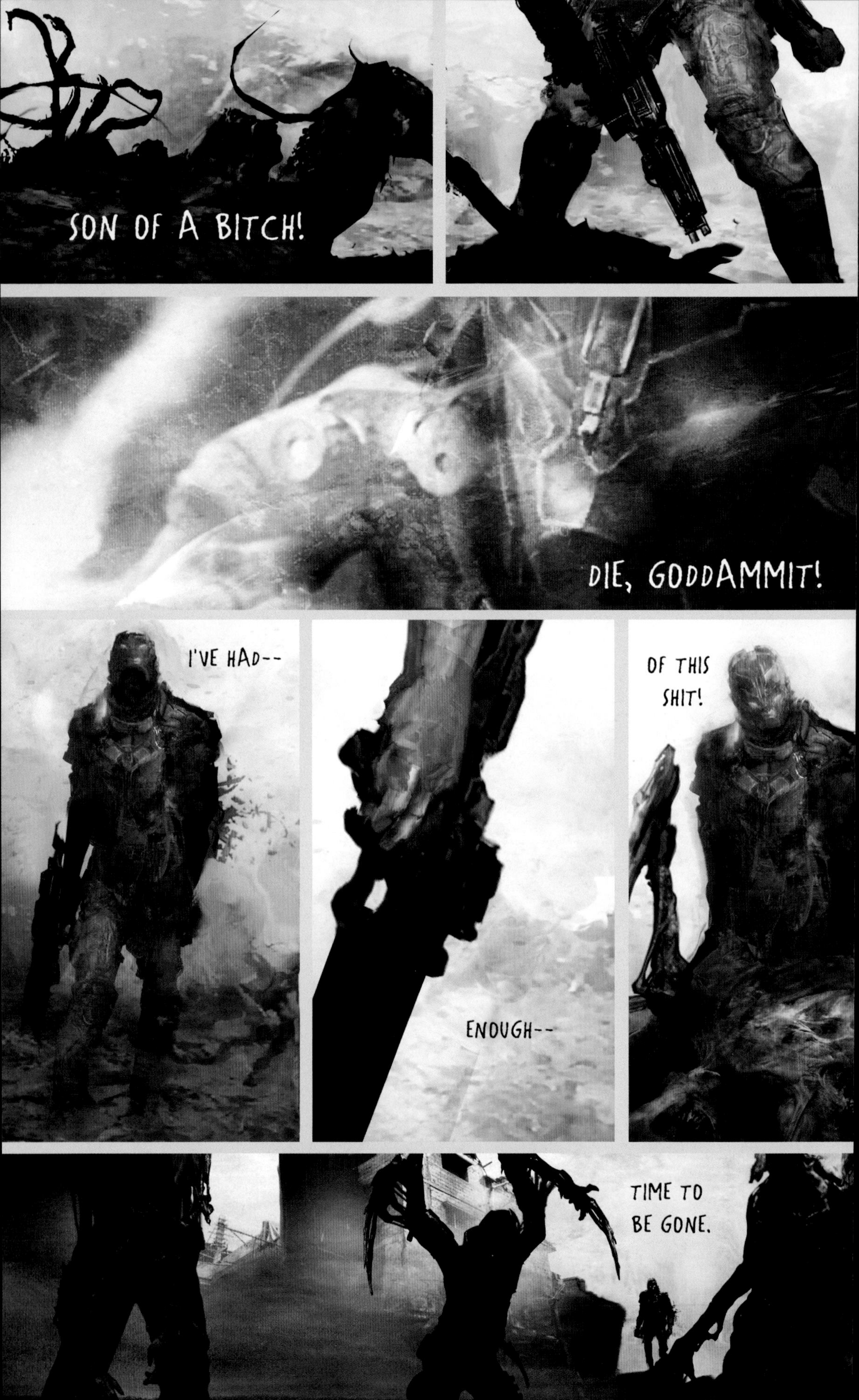
SON OF A BITCH!
DIE, GODDAMMIT!
I'VE HAD--
ENOUGH--
OF THIS SHIT!
TIME TO BE GONE.

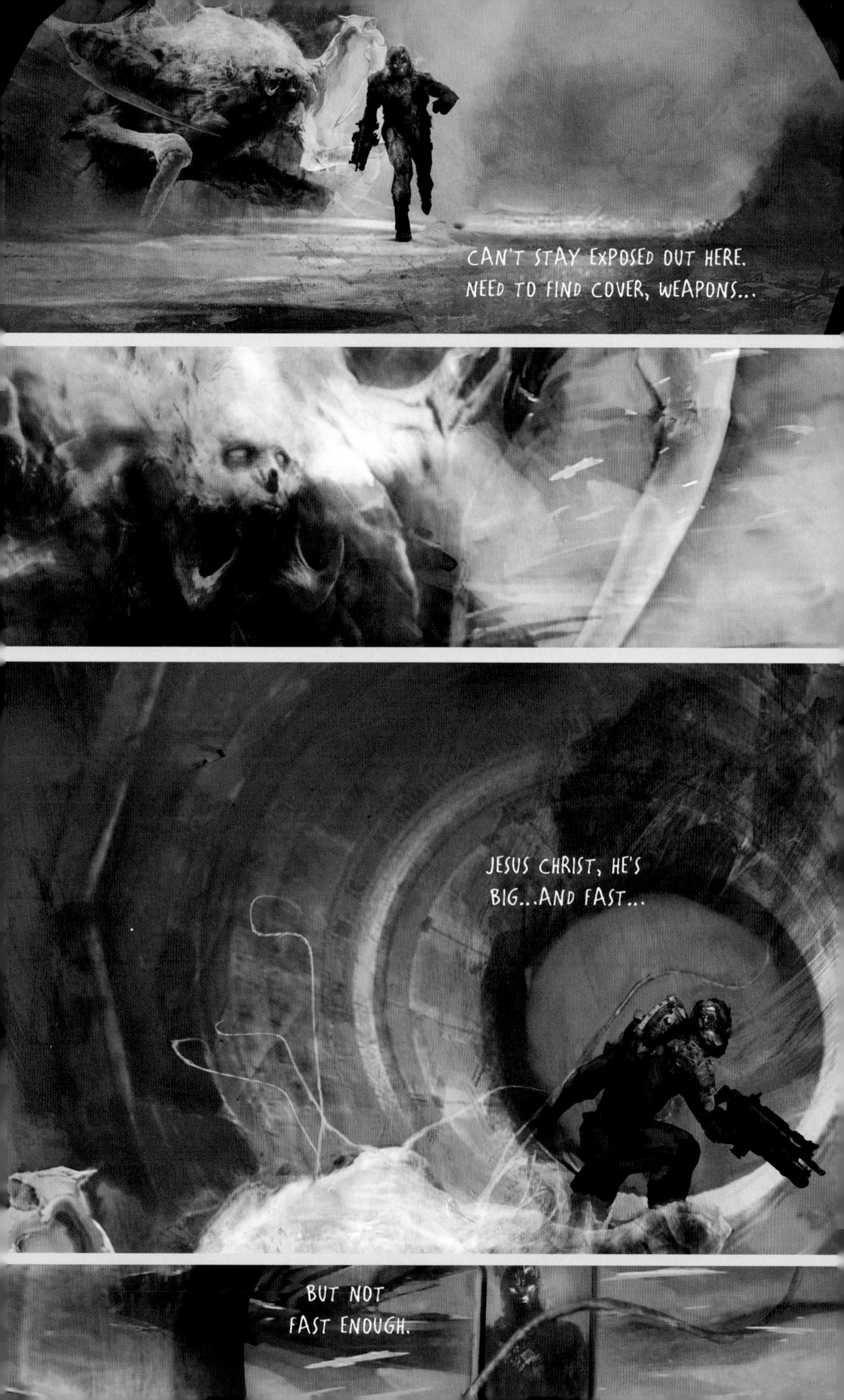
CAN'T STAY EXPOSED OUT HERE. NEED TO FIND COVER, WEAPONS...
JESUS CHRIST, HE'S BIG...AND FAST...
BUT NOT FAST ENOUGH.

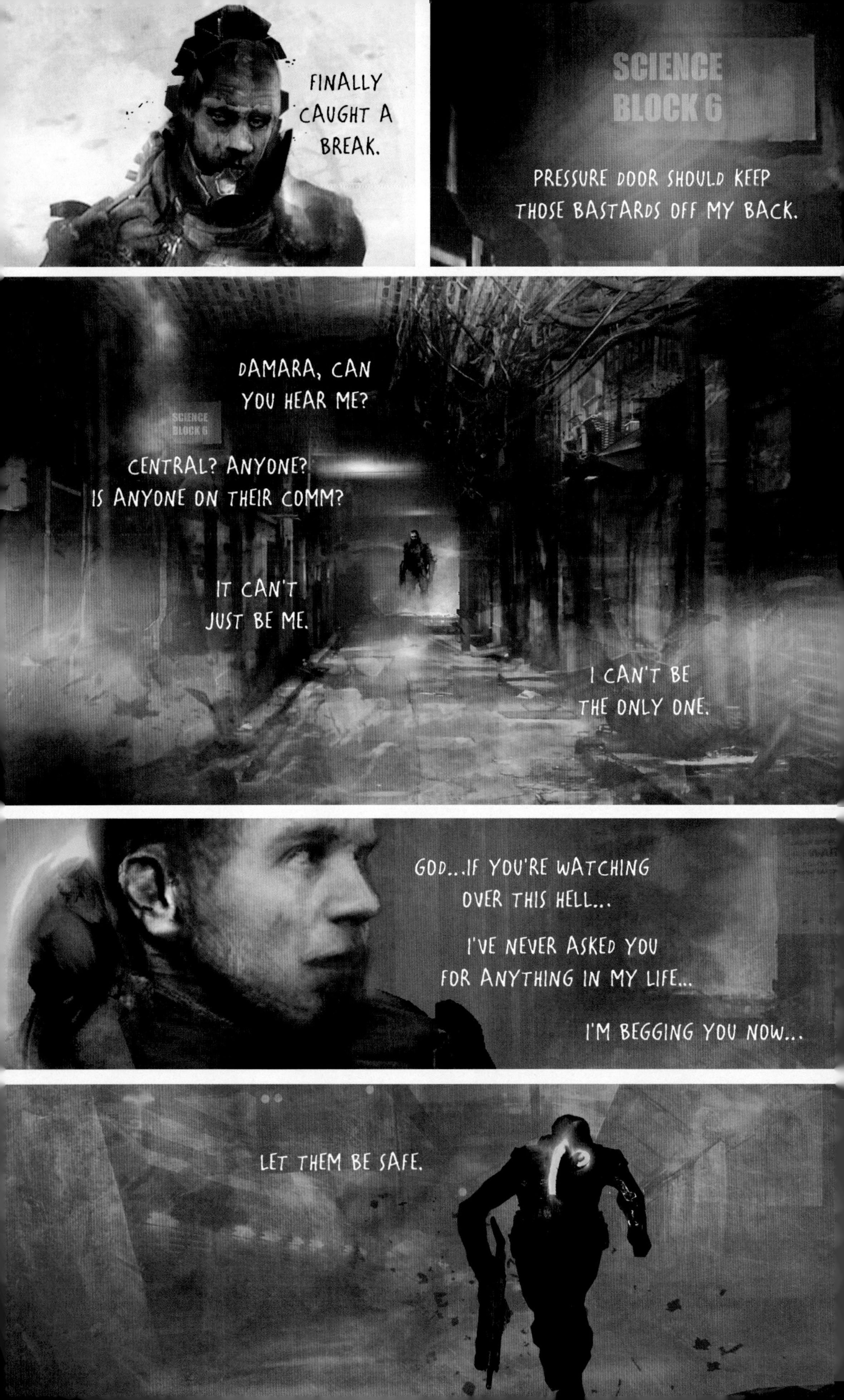
FINALLY CAUGHT A BREAK.
SCIENCE BLOCK 6
PRESSURE DOOR SHOULD KEEP THOSE BASTARDS OFF MY BACK.
DAMARA, CAN YOU HEAR ME?
SCIENCE BLOCK 6
CENTRAL? ANYONE? IS ANYONE ON THEIR COMM?
IT CAN'T JUST BE ME.
I CAN'T BE THE ONLY ONE.
GOD...IF YOU'RE WATCHING OVER THIS HELL...
I'VE NEVER ASKED YOU FOR ANYTHING IN MY LIFE...
I'M BEGGING YOU NOW...
LET THEM BE SAFE.

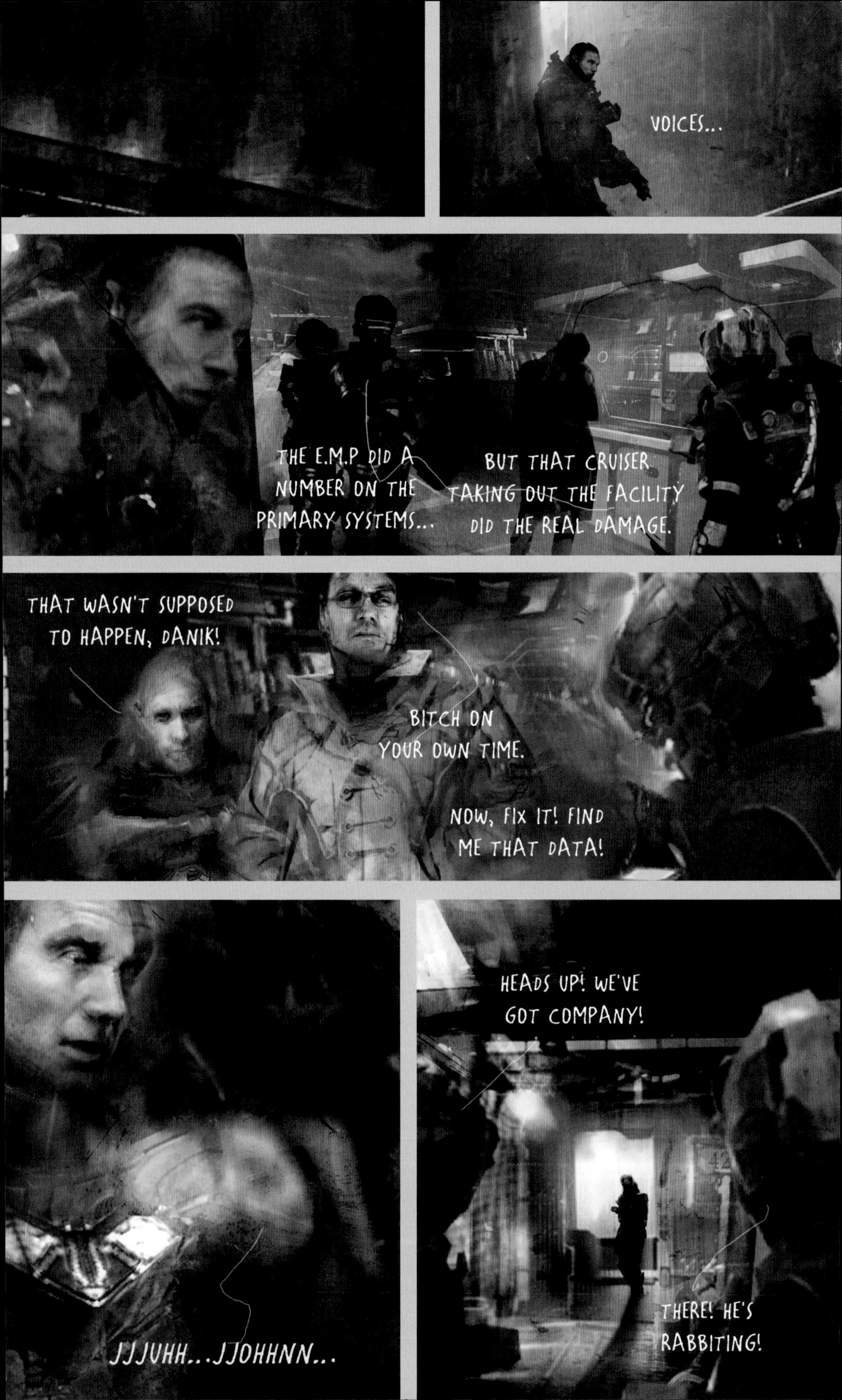
VOICES...
THE E.M.P DID A NUMBER ON THE PRIMARY SYSTEMS...
BUT THAT CRUISER TAKING OUT THE FACILITY DID THE REAL DAMAGE.
THAT WASN'T SUPPOSED TO HAPPEN, DANIK!
BITCH ON YOUR OWN TIME.
NOW, FIX IT! FIND ME THAT DATA!
JJJUHH...JJOHHNN...
HEADS UP! WE'VE GOT COMPANY!
THERE! HE'S RABBITING!

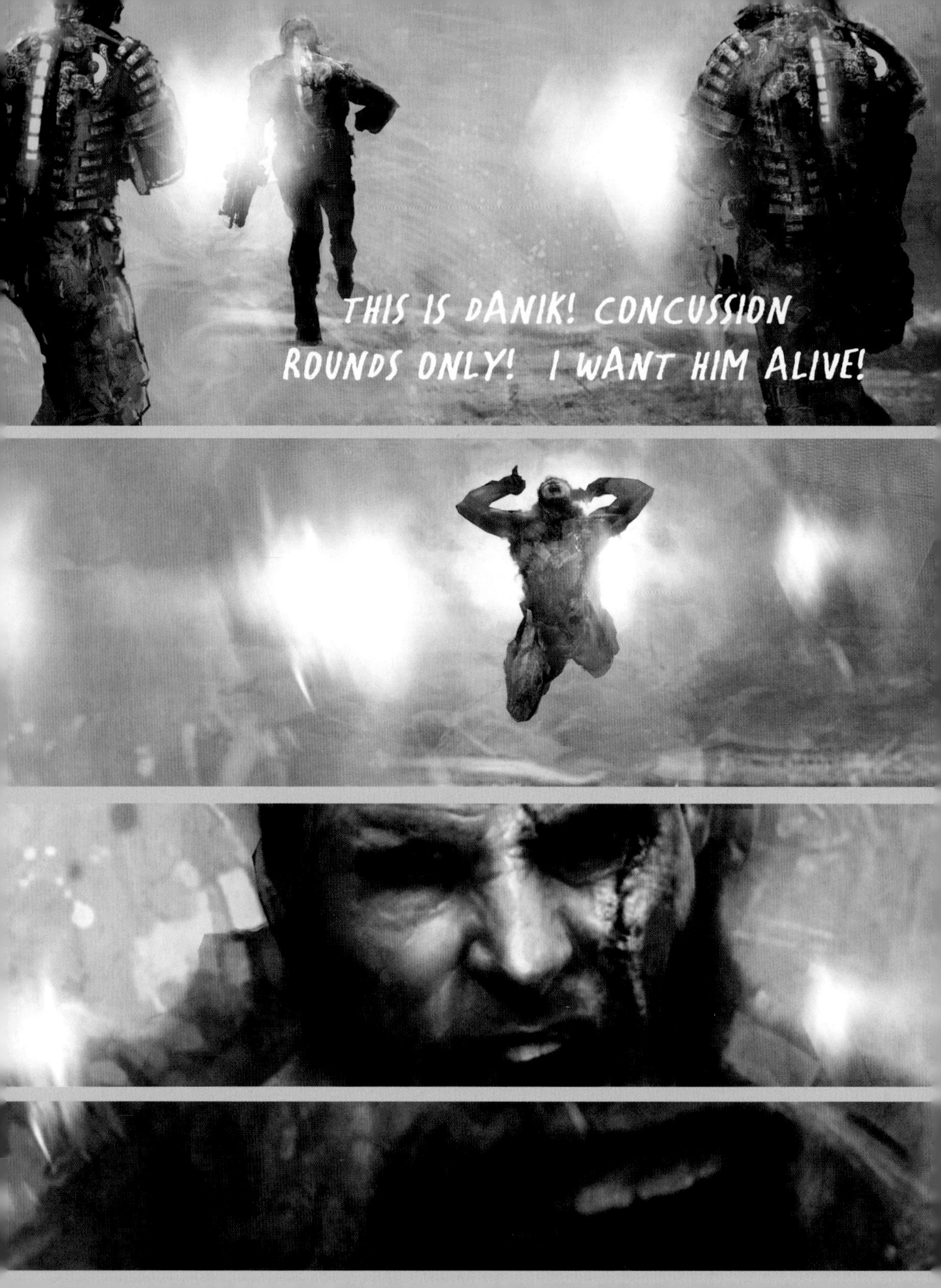
THIS IS DANIK! CONCUSSION ROUNDS ONLY! I WANT HIM ALIVE!

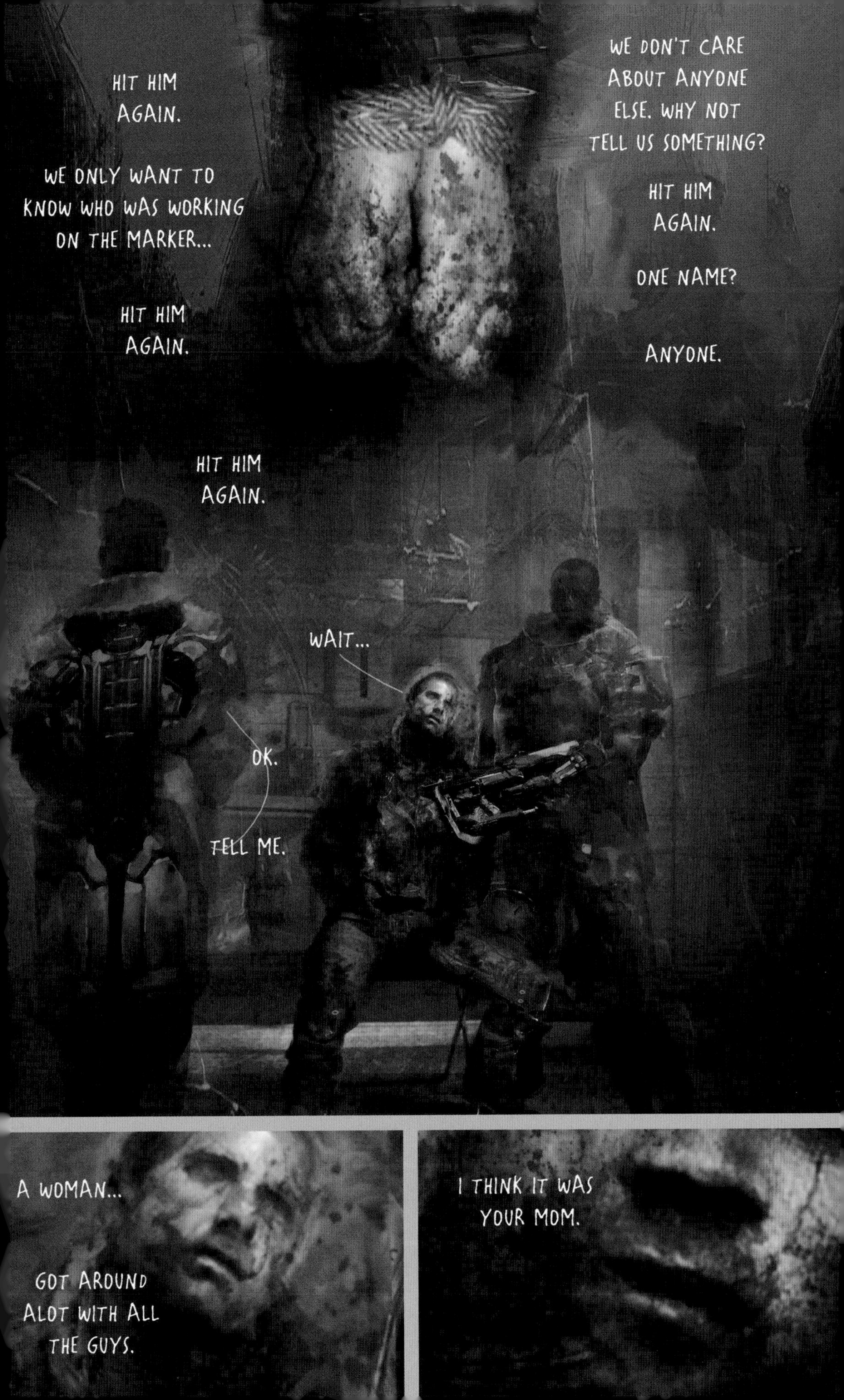
HIT HIM AGAIN.
WE ONLY WANT TO KNOW WHO WAS WORKING ON THE MARKER...
HIT HIM AGAIN.
WE DON'T CARE ABOUT ANYONE ELSE. WHY NOT TELL US SOMETHING?
HIT HIM AGAIN.
ONE NAME?
ANYONE.
HIT HIM AGAIN.
WAIT...
OK.
TELL ME.
A WOMAN...
GOT AROUND ALOT WITH ALL THE GUYS.
I THINK IT WAS YOUR MOM.

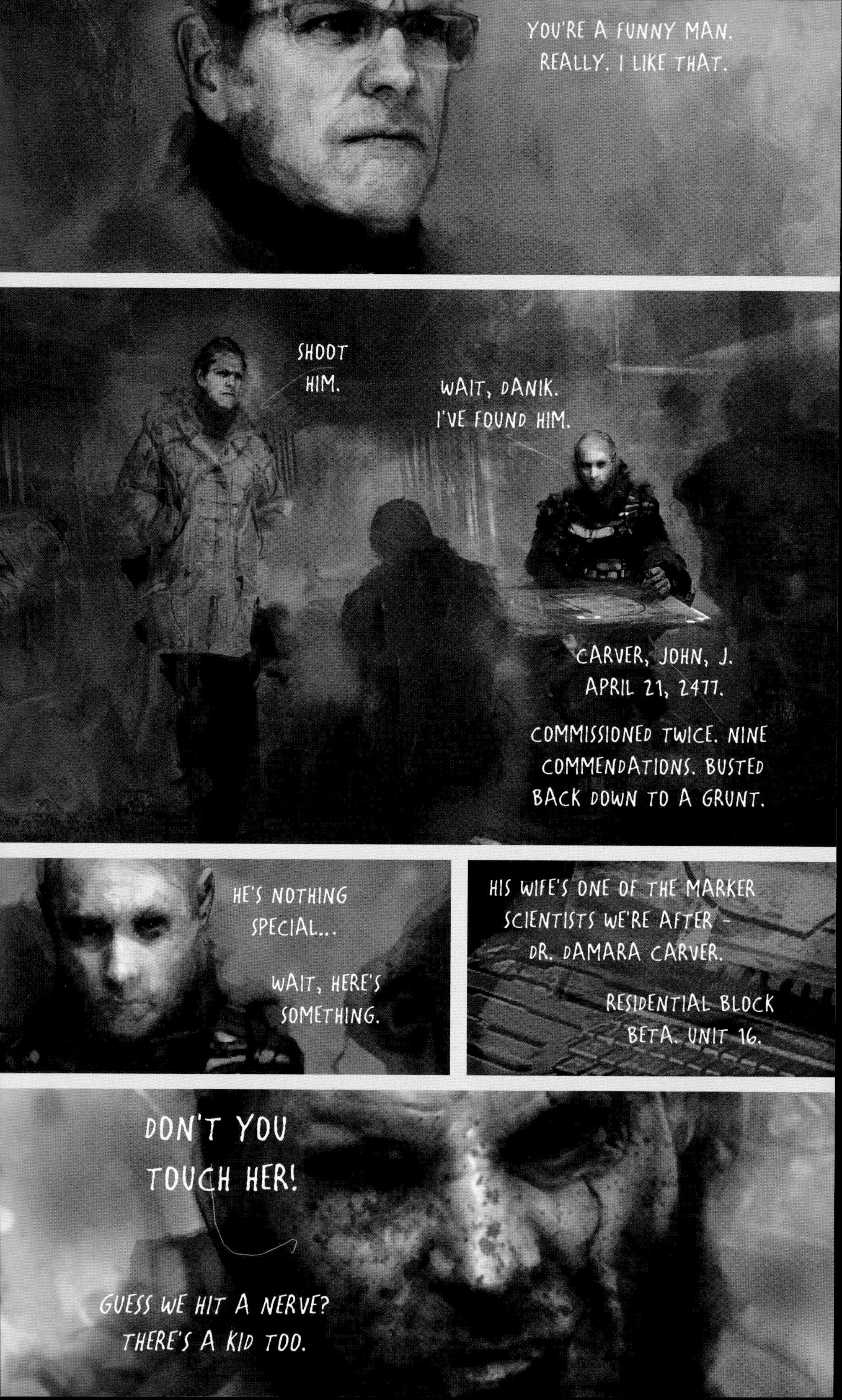
YOU'RE A FUNNY MAN. REALLY. I LIKE THAT.
SHOOT HIM.
WAIT, DANIK. I'VE FOUND HIM.
CARVER, JOHN, J. APRIL 21, 2477.
COMMISSIONED TWICE. NINE COMMENDATIONS. BUSTED BACK DOWN TO A GRUNT.
HE'S NOTHING SPECIAL...
WAIT, HERE'S SOMETHING.
HIS WIFE'S ONE OF THE MARKER SCIENTISTS WE'RE AFTER - DR. DAMARA CARVER.
RESIDENTIAL BLOCK BETA. UNIT 16.
DON'T YOU TOUCH HER!
GUESS WE HIT A NERVE? THERE'S A KID TOO.

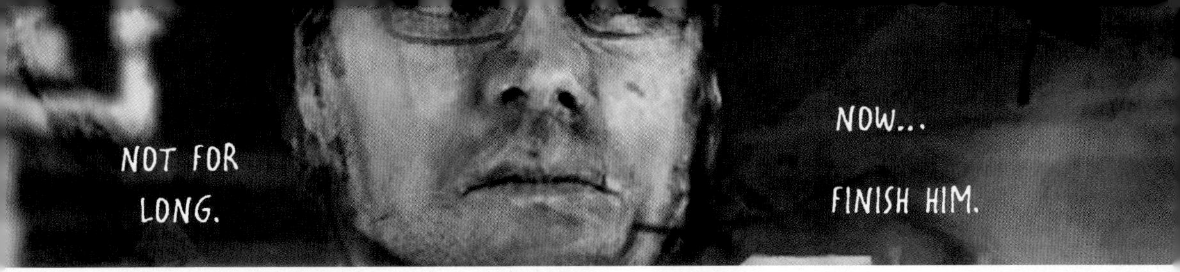
NOT FOR LONG.
NOW...
FINISH HIM.

I'M GOING TO KILL YOU...
I'LL RIP YOUR FUCKING HEART OUT!

GYAHH!

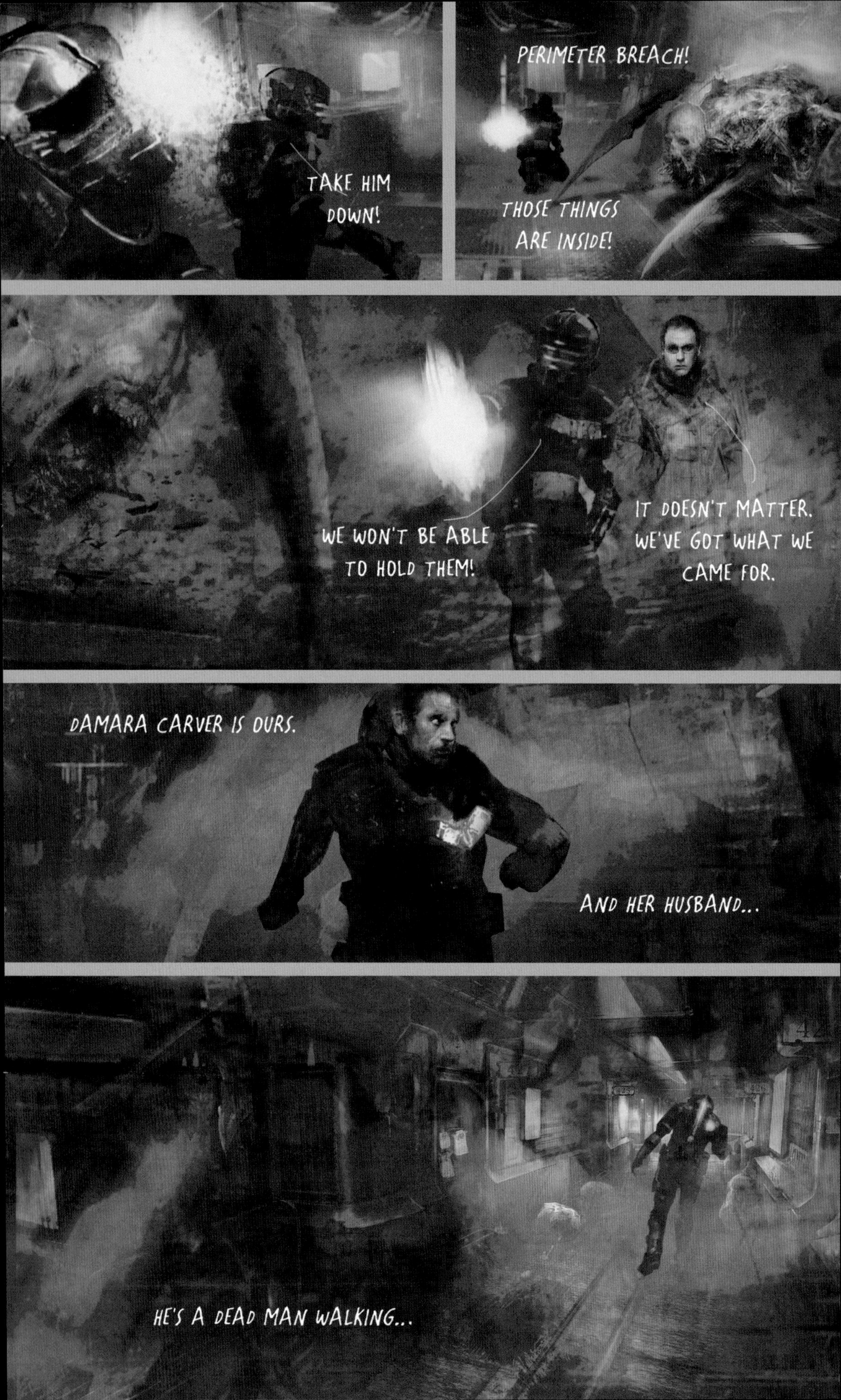
TAKE HIM DOWN!
PERIMETER BREACH!
THOSE THINGS ARE INSIDE!
WE WON'T BE ABLE TO HOLD THEM!
IT DOESN'T MATTER. WE'VE GOT WHAT WE CAME FOR.
DAMARA CARVER IS OURS.
AND HER HUSBAND...
HE'S A DEAD MAN WALKING...

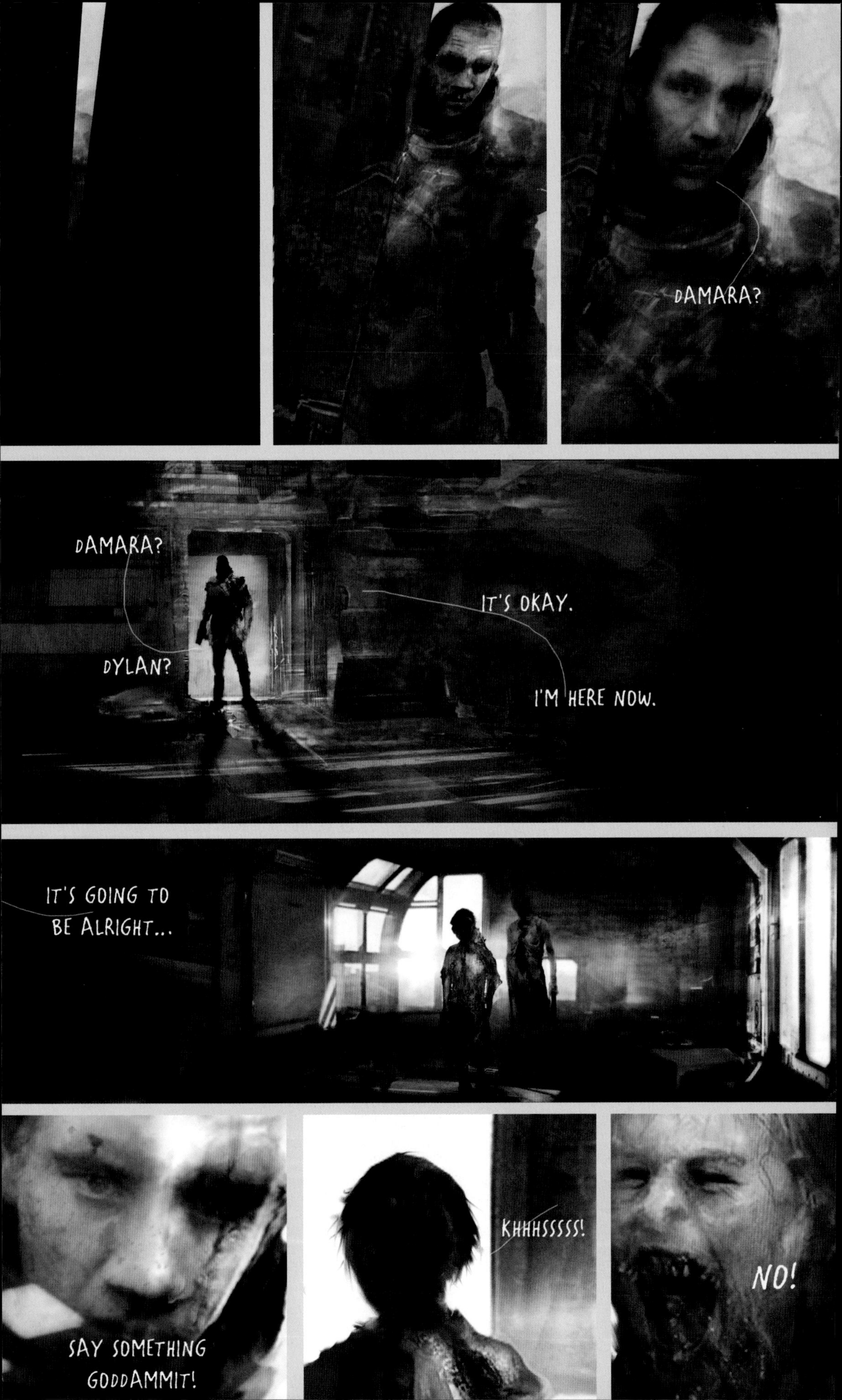
DAMARA?
DAMARA?
DYLAN?
IT'S OKAY.
I'M HERE NOW.
IT'S GOING TO BE ALRIGHT...
SAY SOMETHING GODDAMMIT!
KHHHSSSSS!
NO!

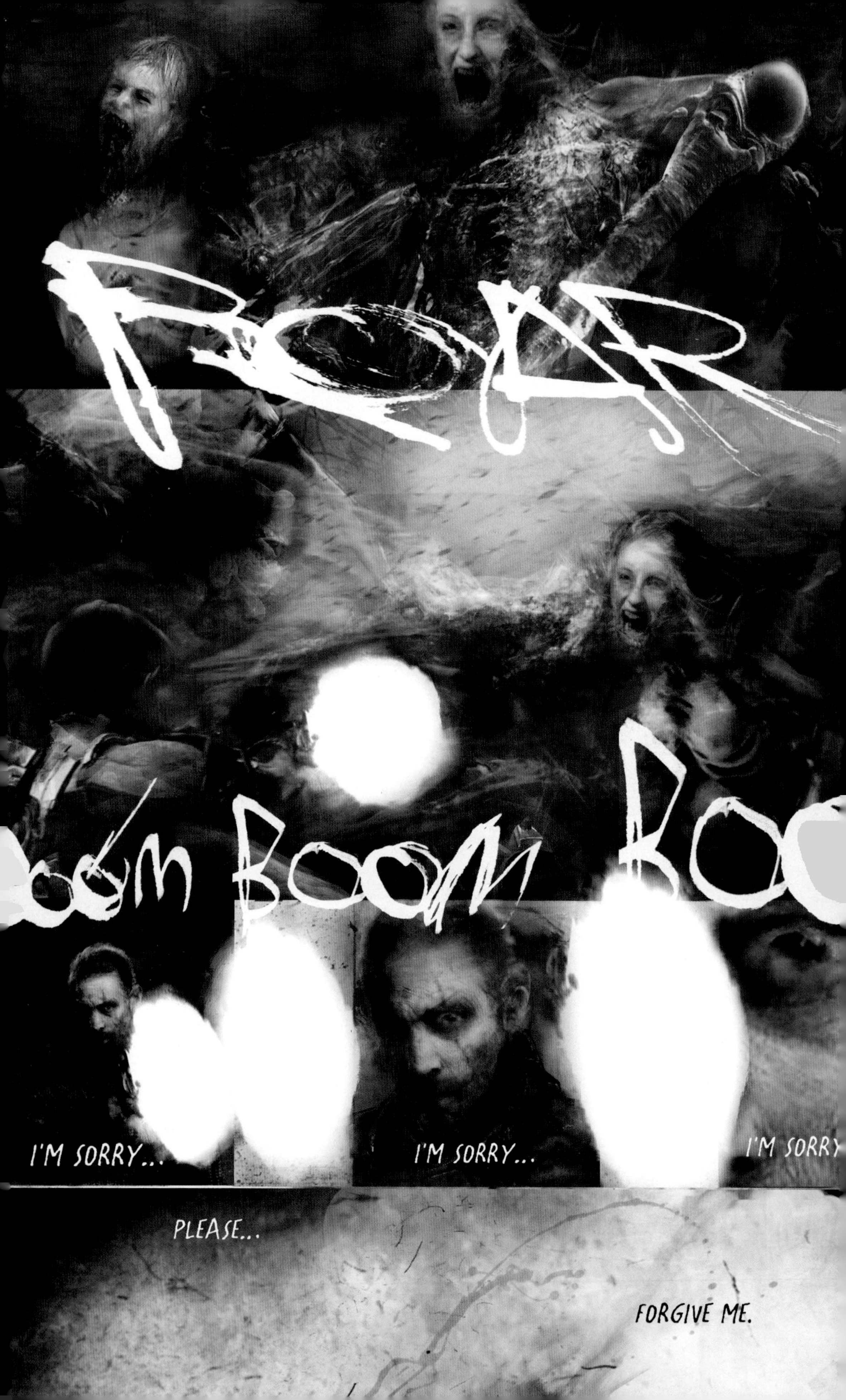
ROAR
BOOM BOOM BOO
I'M SORRY...
I'M SORRY...
I'M SORRY
PLEASE...
FORGIVE ME.

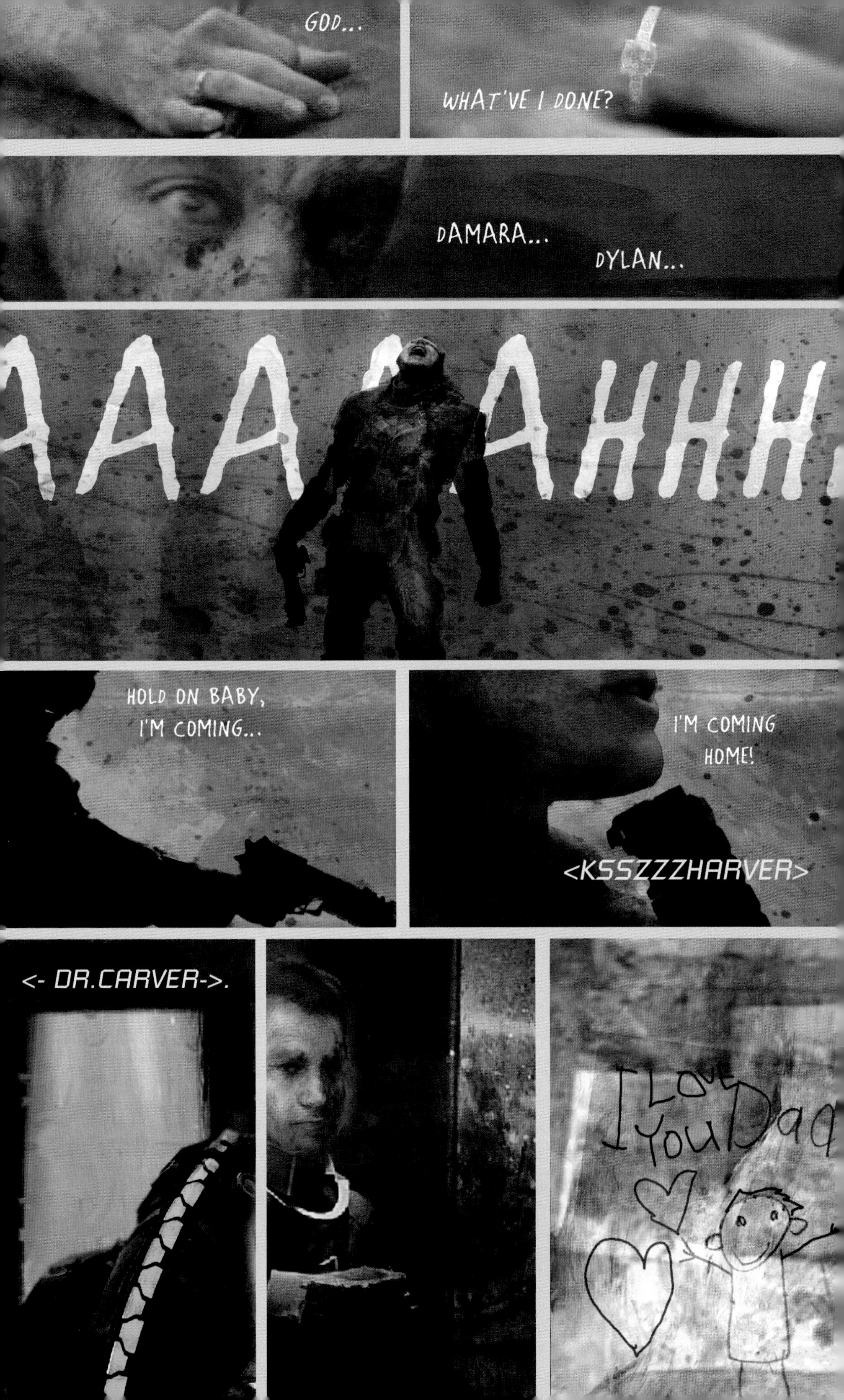
GOD...
WHAT'VE I DONE?
DAMARA...
DYLAN...
AAAAAHHH!
HOLD ON BABY, I'M COMING...
I'M COMING HOME!
<KSSZZZHARVER>
<- DR.CARVER->.
I LOVE YOU DAD

<- DR.CARVER PLEASE RESPOND ->.
<DR.CARVER... DAMARA. I KNOW YOUR COMM'S OPEN >.
<PLEASE, PICK UP.>
WHAT THE HELL?
AH, CLEVER.
SPEAK.
<WHO IS THIS? WHERE'S DR. CARVER.>
SHE...SHE'S DEAD. THEY'RE ALL DEAD.
<THE DATA STICK, IS IT THERE?>
YES.

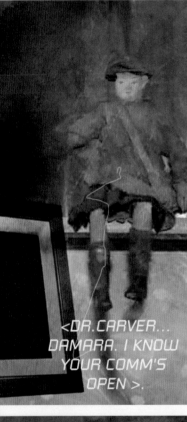

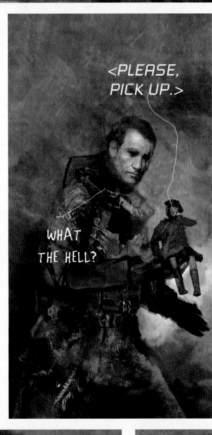

<WAIT. GOD! JOHN? JOHN CARVER, IS THAT YOU?>

WHO WANTS TO KNOW?

<IT'S ELLIE LANGFORD.>

<I'M HERE WITH CAPTAIN ROBERT NORTON. YOU WERE STATIONED TOGETHER AT HAVEN PRIME.>

<I MET YOU AT A PARTY. MY BIRTHDAY.>

<DAMARA HAD JUST FOUND OUT SHE WAS PREGNANT WITH DYLAN.>

ELLIE...?

IS IT REALLY YOU?

<WHAT'RE YOU DOING HERE?>

DAMARA CONTACTED ME. IN HER MARKER RESEARCH, SHE'D FOUND SOMETHING UNEXPECTED. SHE DISCOVERED THAT MARKER TAMPERING WENT WAY BACK, PAST EARTH-GOV TO THE OLD SOVEREIGN COLONIES ADMINISTRATION.

SHE WAS INVESTIGATING A MASSIVE HISTORICAL COVER-UP.

SHE'D AMASSED A GOLDMINE OF SECRETS.

THAT'S WHY DANIK AND HIS PEOPLE ARE HERE. THEY'RE DESPERATE TO FIND IT.

YEAH, I NOTICED.

WE'VE GOTTA GET OFF-WORLD. EXCEPT THE E.M.P'S TRASHED ANYTHING AIRWORTHY.

NOT A PROBLEM. ROBERT'S SHIP, THE EUDORA'S IN HIGH ORBIT.

HE CAN COME GET US.

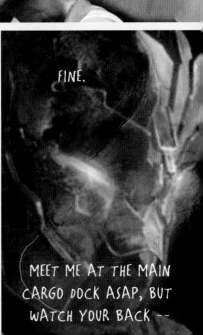

FINE.

MEET ME AT THE MAIN CARGO DOCK ASAP, BUT WATCH YOUR BACK --

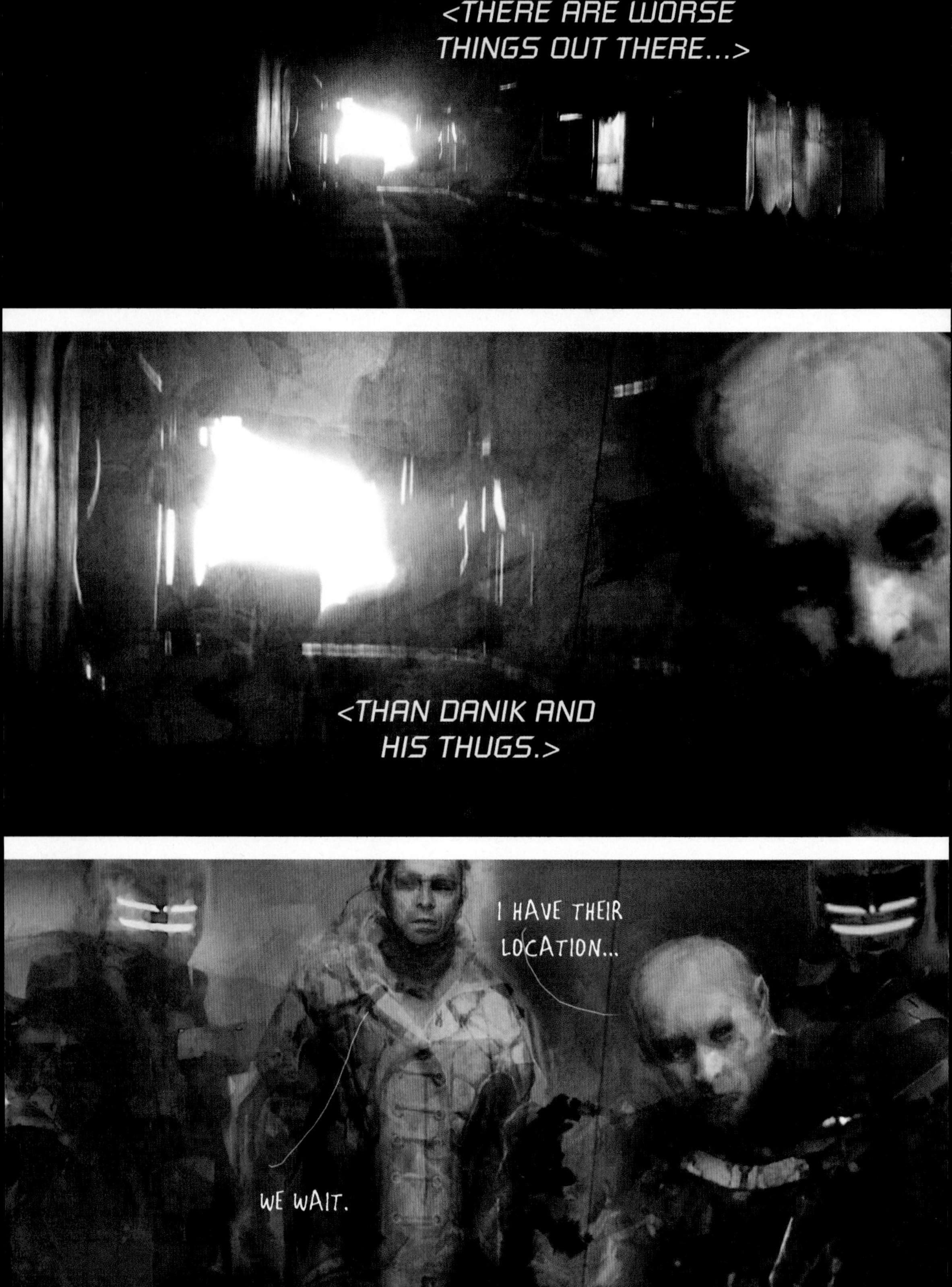
<THERE ARE WORSE THINGS OUT THERE...>
<THAN DANIK AND HIS THUGS.>
I HAVE THEIR LOCATION...
WE WAIT.

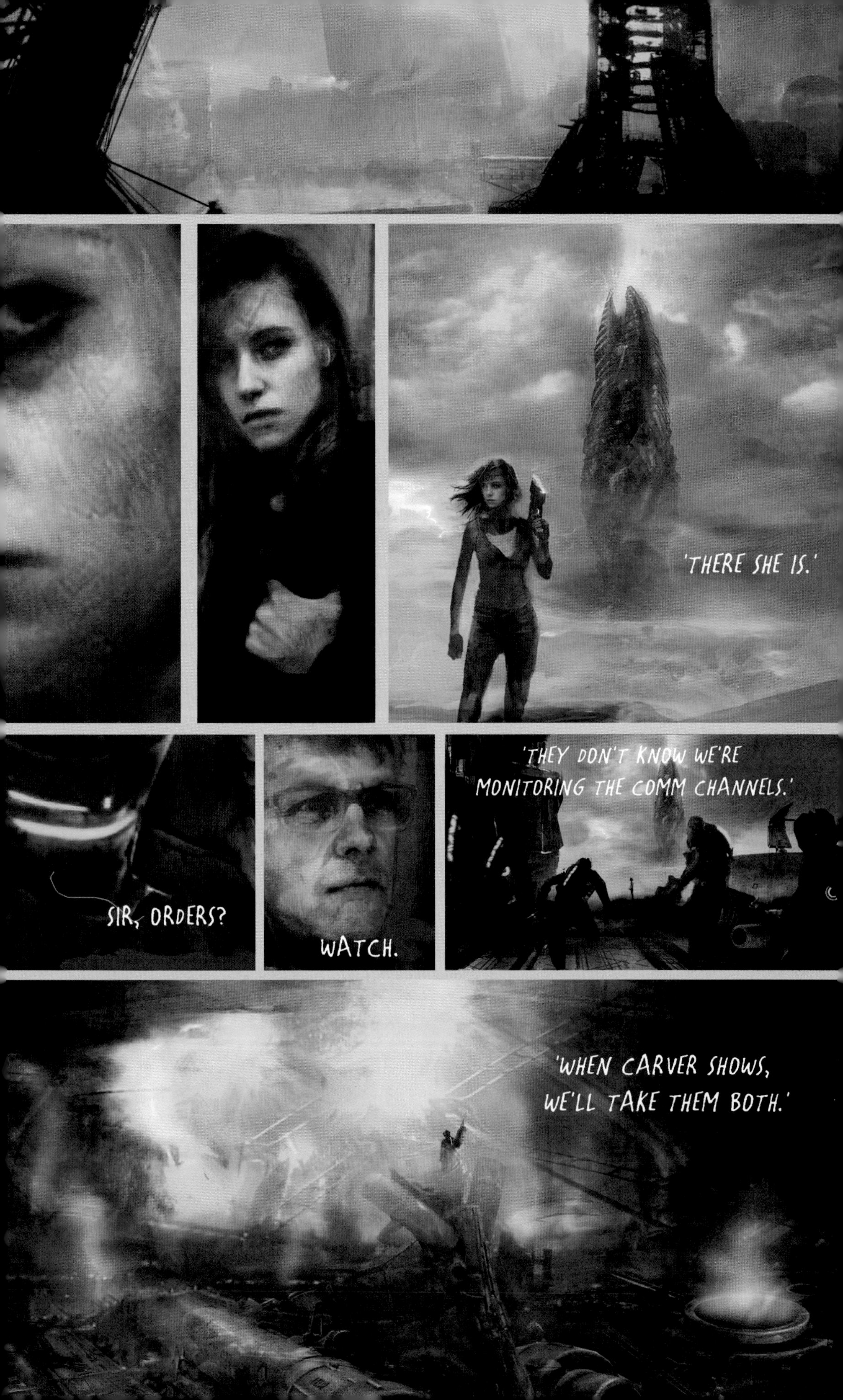
'THERE SHE IS.'
SIR, ORDERS?
WATCH.
'THEY DON'T KNOW WE'RE MONITORING THE COMM CHANNELS.'
'WHEN CARVER SHOWS, WE'LL TAKE THEM BOTH.'

<CARVER, IT'S ELLIE. I'M AT THE RENDEZVOUS, WHERE THE HELL ARE YOU?>

I'M HERE.

<WHERE, I DON'T SEE YOU?>

I SEE YOU.

IT'S A TRAP. I THOUGHT THEY MIGHT BE LISTENING IN.

THEY'RE MOVING UP ON YOUR FLANK.

<YOU USED ME AS BAIT? YOU BASTARD!>

SIT TIGHT.

I'VE GOT THIS COVERED.

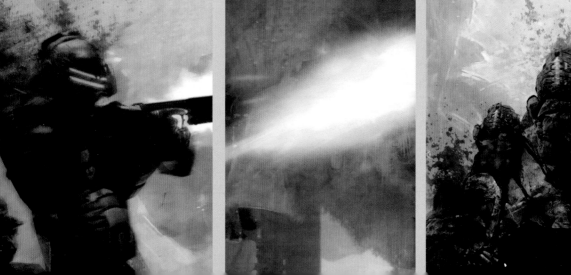

ELLIE—

GET READY TO MOVE OUT!

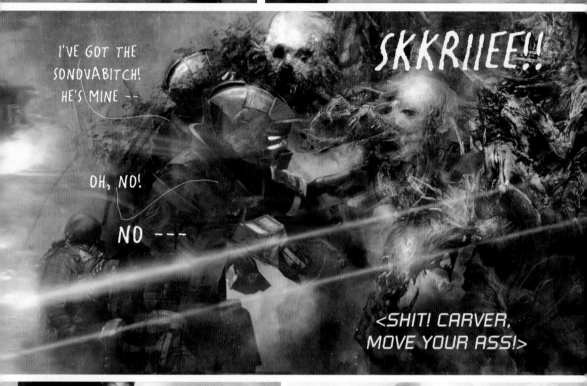

I'VE GOT THE SONOVABITCH! HE'S MINE --

SKKRIIEE!!

OH, NO!

NO ---

<SHIT! CARVER, MOVE YOUR ASS!>

<YOUR PARTY JUST PICKED UP SOME GATECRASHERS!>

I'M ON MY WAY!

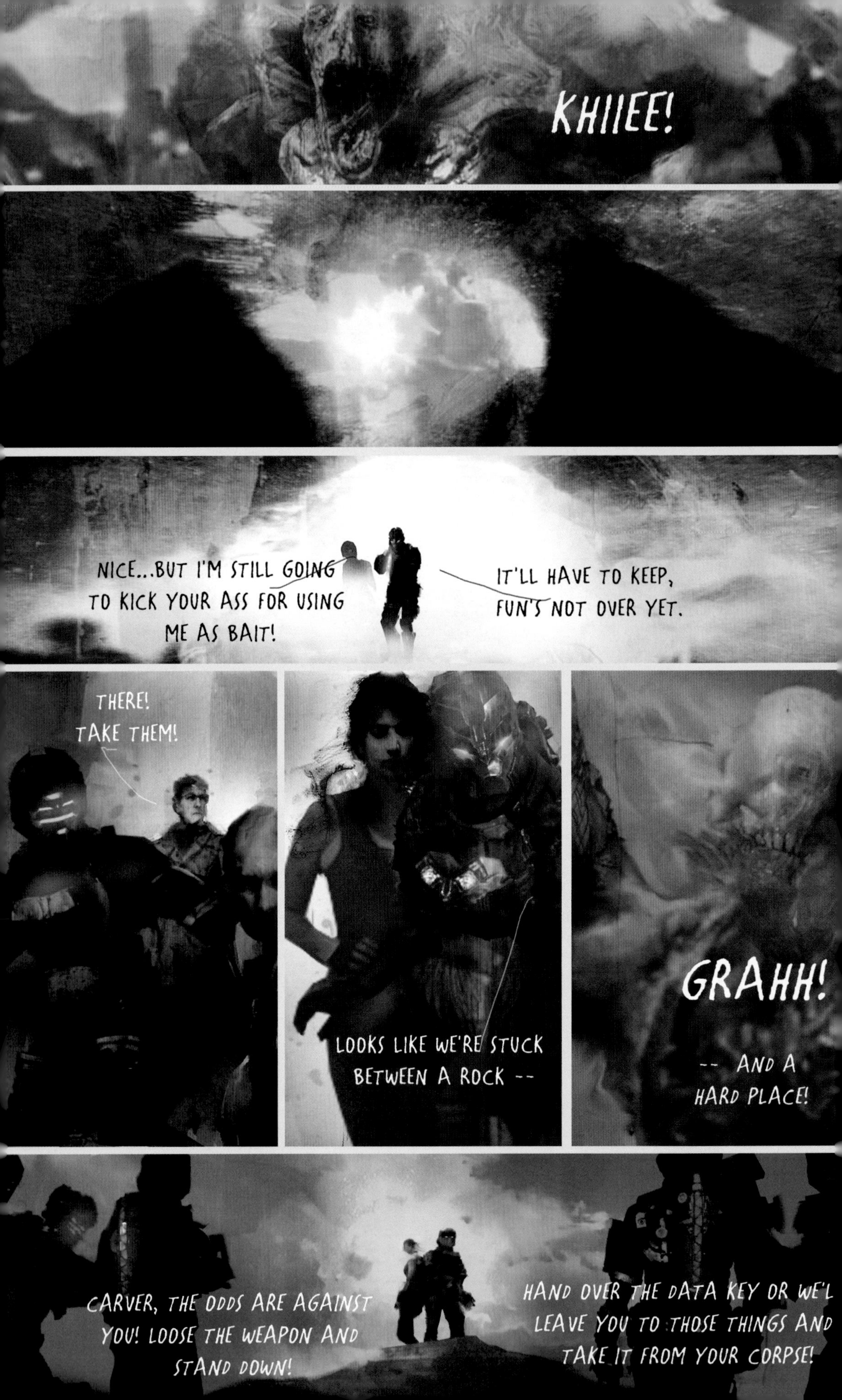
KHIIEE!
NICE...BUT I'M STILL GOING TO KICK YOUR ASS FOR USING ME AS BAIT!
IT'LL HAVE TO KEEP, FUN'S NOT OVER YET.
THERE! TAKE THEM!
LOOKS LIKE WE'RE STUCK BETWEEN A ROCK --
GRAHH!
-- AND A HARD PLACE!
CARVER, THE ODDS ARE AGAINST YOU! LOOSE THE WEAPON AND STAND DOWN!
HAND OVER THE DATA KEY OR WE'L LEAVE YOU TO THOSE THINGS AND TAKE IT FROM YOUR CORPSE!

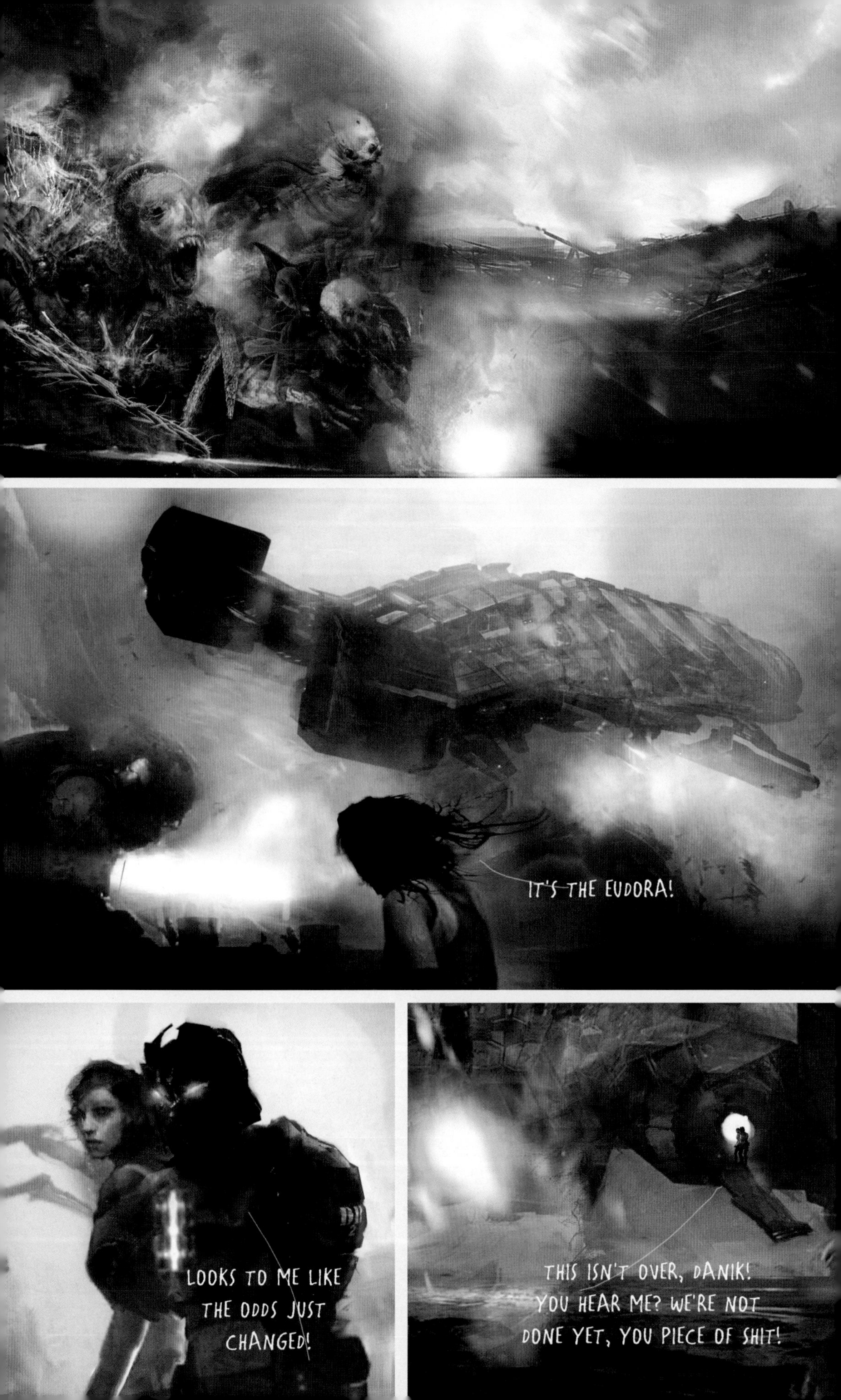
IT'S THE EUDORA!
LOOKS TO ME LIKE THE ODDS JUST CHANGED!
THIS ISN'T OVER, DANIK! YOU HEAR ME? WE'RE NOT DONE YET, YOU PIECE OF SHIT!

YOU GOT THAT RIGHT.

SEE YOU SOON.

YOU GET WHAT WE CAME FOR?

THE DATA'S SECURE—

SO TELL ME, WHY'S EVERYONE DEAD?

TELL ME WHY I HAD TO KILL MY WIFE AND CHILD?

THAT'S ON A NEED TO KNOW BASIS, SOLDIER...

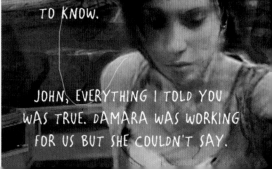

HE DESERVES TO KNOW.

JOHN, EVERYTHING I TOLD YOU WAS TRUE. DAMARA WAS WORKING FOR US BUT SHE COULDN'T SAY.

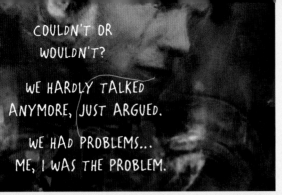

COULDN'T OR WOULDN'T?

WE HARDLY TALKED ANYMORE, JUST ARGUED.

WE HAD PROBLEMS... ME, I WAS THE PROBLEM.

WE APPROACHED DAMARA BECAUSE OF HER EXPERTISE IN DATA RECOVERY.

I KNOW YOU'RE SKEPTICAL. PERHAPS IT MIGHT HELP IF YOU HEARD FROM HER FIRST HAND —

AS A DATA ARCHAEOLOGIST, SHE WAS ABLE TO LOCATE, RETRIEVE AND REBUILD INFORMATION FROM COUNTLESS REDUNDANT SYSTEMS.

MY NAME IS DOCTOR DAMARA CARVER --

-- AND IF YOU ARE SEEING THIS, THEN I AM MOST LIKELY DEAD.

FOR THE SAKE OF THE HUMAN RACE, IT IS VITAL THE INFORMATION IN THESE FILES DOES NOT FALL INTO UNITOLOGIST HANDS.

I'VE DISCOVERED RESEARCH ON THE MARKERS THAT PRE-DATES EARTHGOV BY SOME TWO CENTURIES.

DURING THE EARLIER GOVERNMENT, THE SOVEREIGN COLONIES LOCATED A SINGLE, MASTER SIGNAL THAT CONTROLLED ALL THE OTHERS.

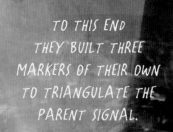

TO THIS END THEY BUILT THREE MARKERS OF THEIR OWN TO TRIANGULATE THE PARENT SIGNAL.

THEY SUCCEEDED, BUT SOON AFTER PURPOSEFULLY PURGED ALL DATA FROM THEIR SYSTEMS.

HOWEVER, I'VE MANAGED TO RECONSTRUCT A SIGNIFICANT PORTION.

THAT'S MY GIRL...

THE LOCATION OF THE TRIANGULATION STATION — THE PTOLEMY ARRAY IS IN THESE FILES.

I...I'VE FOUND IT HARD CONCEALING MY WORK FROM MY HUSBAND. IF HE KNEW THE DANGER, HE'D TRY TO STOP ME.

IT'S MADE THINGS...DIFFICULT BETWEEN US. BUT I HAVE TO DO THIS...

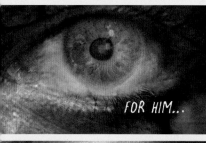

FOR HIM...

FOR OUR SON...

FOR ALL OUR CHILDREN. THIS IS DAMARA CARVER, SIGNING OFF.

IF YOU WANT TO HONOR HER MEMORY...

AND AVENGE HER. HELP US FINISH HER WORK.

FINE —

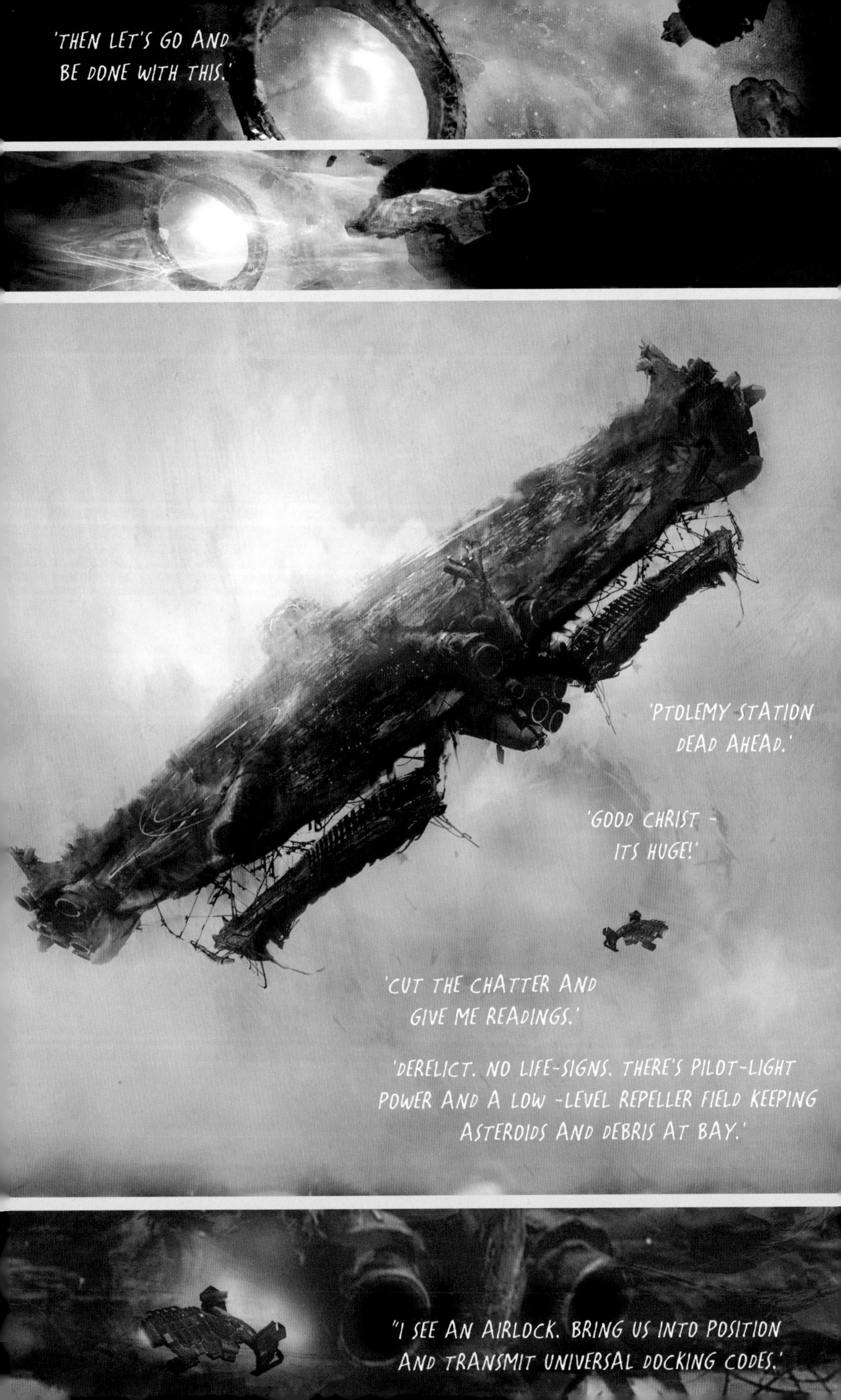
'THEN LET'S GO AND BE DONE WITH THIS.'
'PTOLEMY STATION DEAD AHEAD.'
'GOOD CHRIST - ITS HUGE!'
'CUT THE CHATTER AND GIVE ME READINGS.'
'DERELICT. NO LIFE-SIGNS. THERE'S PILOT-LIGHT POWER AND A LOW-LEVEL REPELLER FIELD KEEPING ASTEROIDS AND DEBRIS AT BAY.'
"I SEE AN AIRLOCK. BRING US INTO POSITION AND TRANSMIT UNIVERSAL DOCKING CODES.'

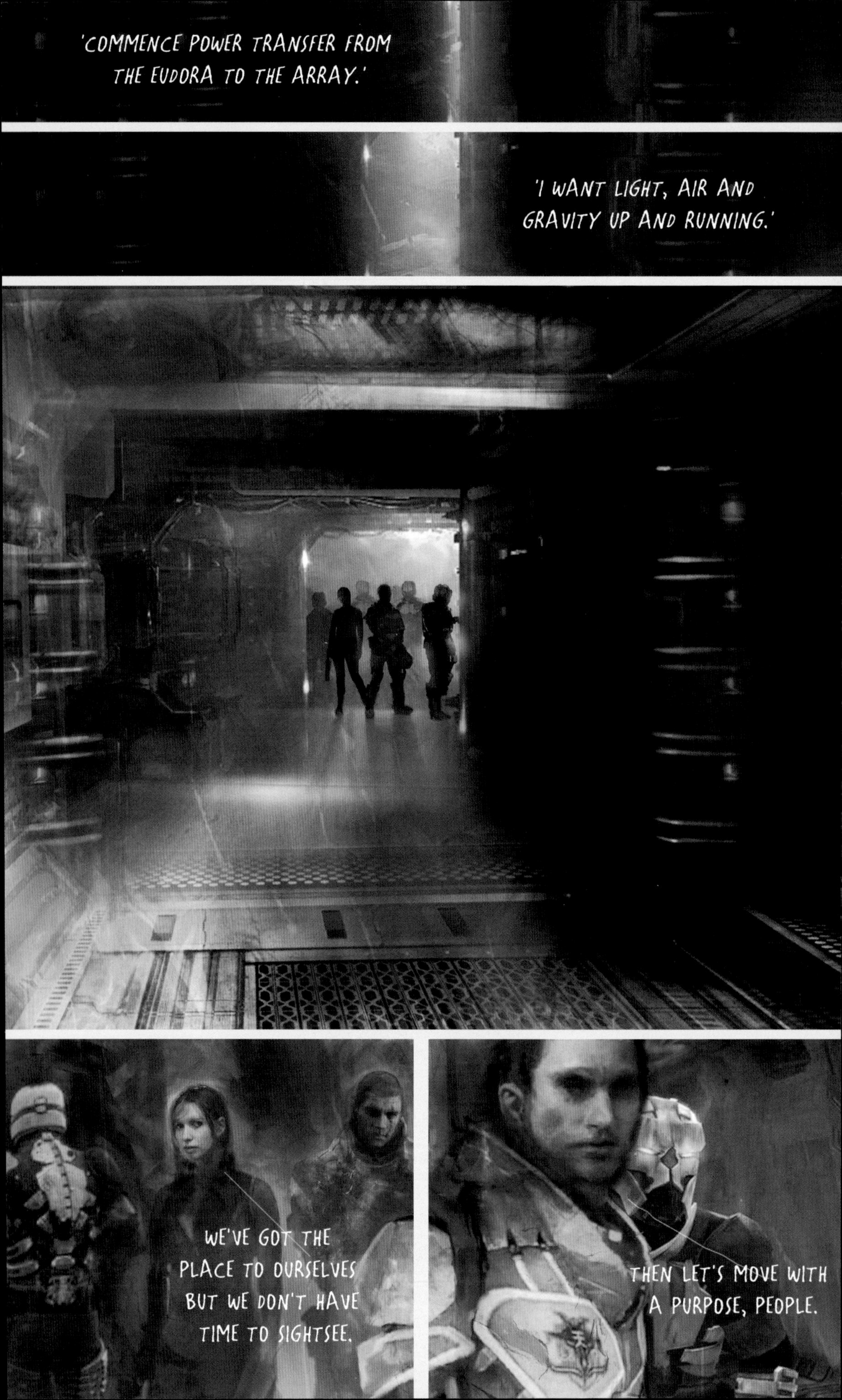
'COMMENCE POWER TRANSFER FROM THE EUDORA TO THE ARRAY.'
'I WANT LIGHT, AIR AND GRAVITY UP AND RUNNING.'
WE'VE GOT THE PLACE TO OURSELVES BUT WE DON'T HAVE TIME TO SIGHTSEE.
THEN LET'S MOVE WITH A PURPOSE, PEOPLE.

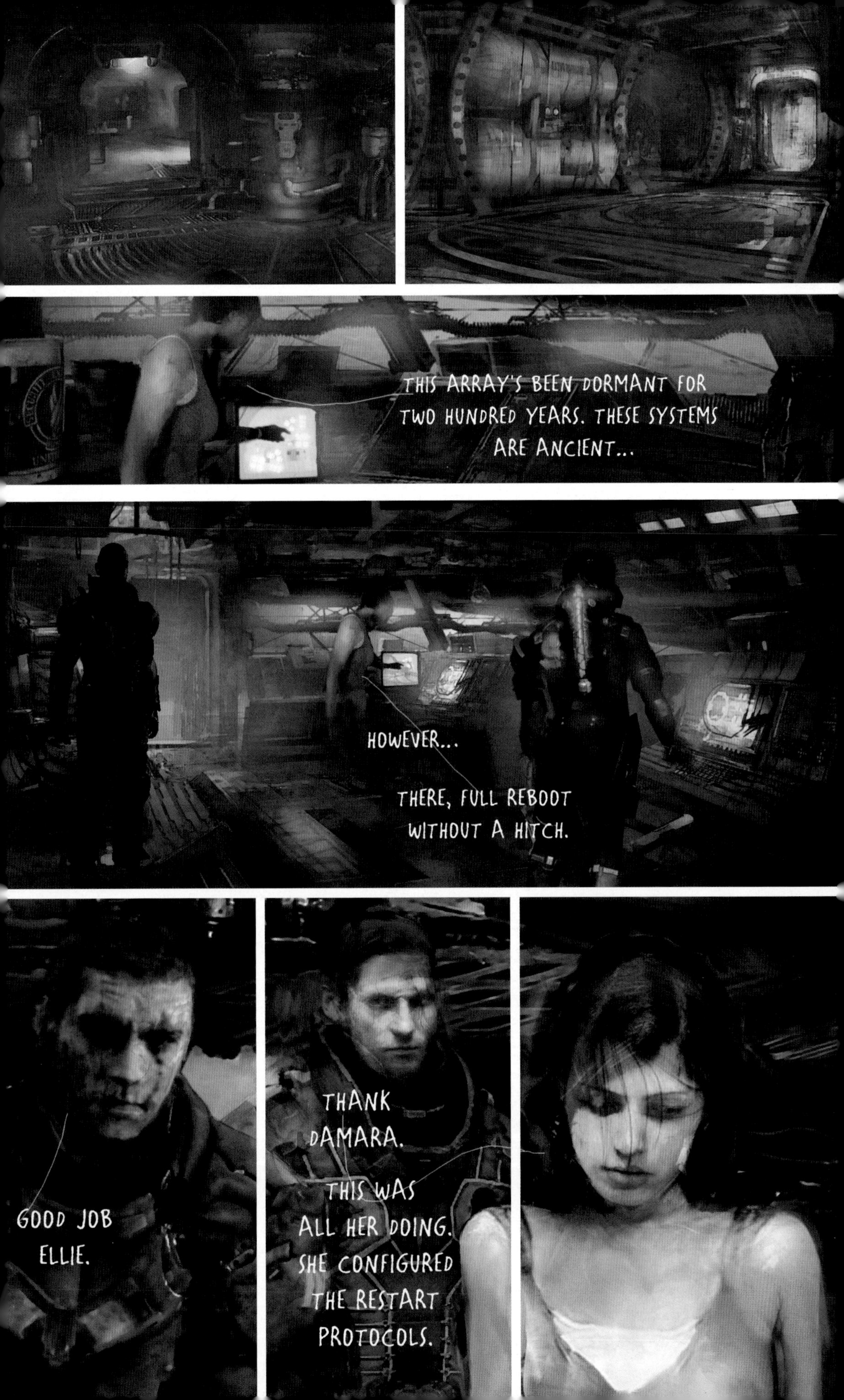
THIS ARRAY'S BEEN DORMANT FOR TWO HUNDRED YEARS. THESE SYSTEMS ARE ANCIENT...
HOWEVER...
THERE, FULL REBOOT WITHOUT A HITCH.
GOOD JOB ELLIE.
THANK DAMARA.
THIS WAS ALL HER DOING. SHE CONFIGURED THE RESTART PROTOCOLS.

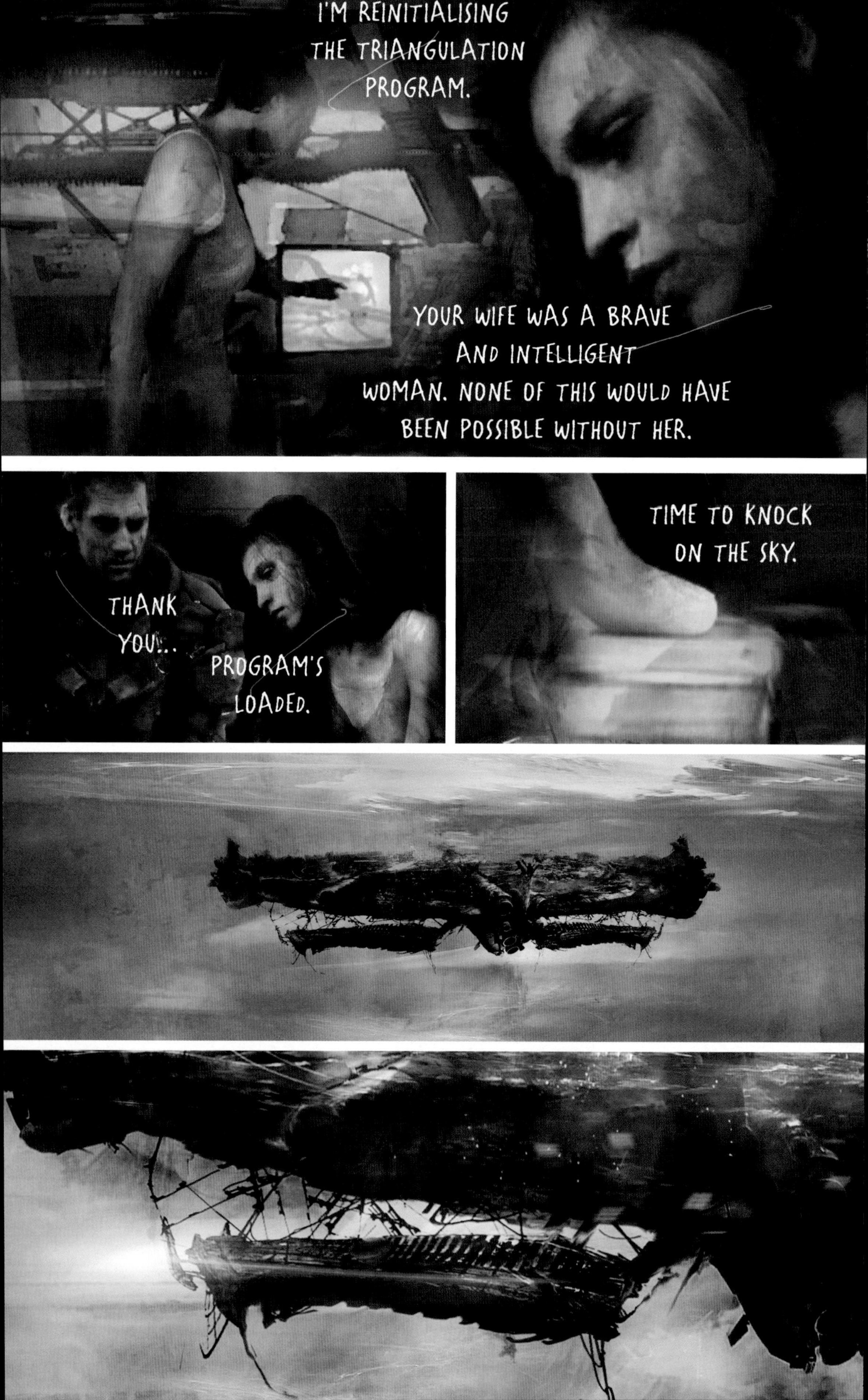

I'M REINITIALISING THE TRIANGULATION PROGRAM.
YOUR WIFE WAS A BRAVE AND INTELLIGENT WOMAN. NONE OF THIS WOULD HAVE BEEN POSSIBLE WITHOUT HER.
THANK YOU...
PROGRAM'S LOADED.
TIME TO KNOCK ON THE SKY.

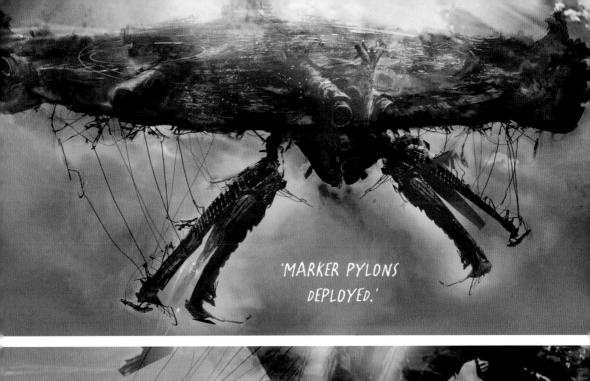

'MARKER PYLONS DEPLOYED.'

'MARKERS EXPOSED AND CHARGING.'

'WE HAVE TRIANGULATION!'

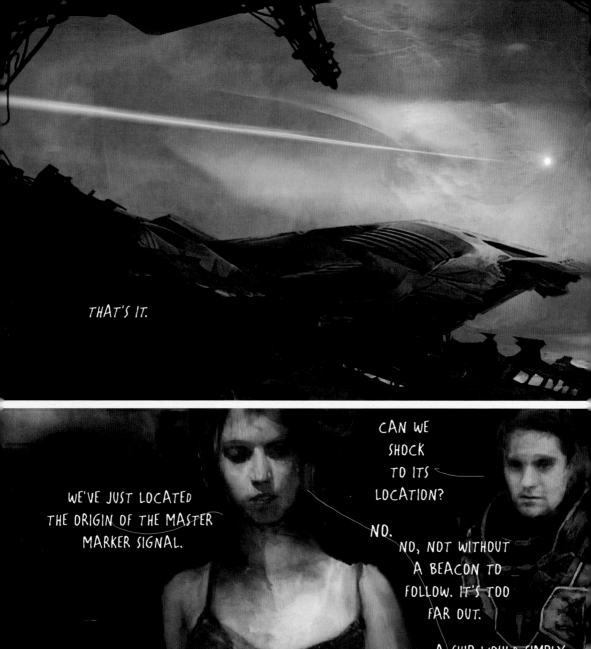

THAT'S IT.

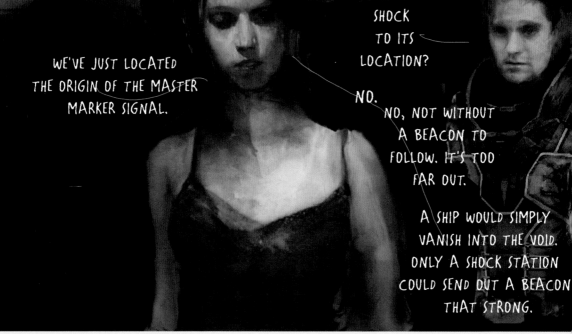

WE'VE JUST LOCATED THE ORIGIN OF THE MASTER MARKER SIGNAL.

CAN WE SHOCK TO ITS LOCATION?

NO.

NO, NOT WITHOUT A BEACON TO FOLLOW. IT'S TOO FAR OUT.

A SHIP WOULD SIMPLY VANISH INTO THE VOID. ONLY A SHOCK STATION COULD SEND OUT A BEACON THAT STRONG.

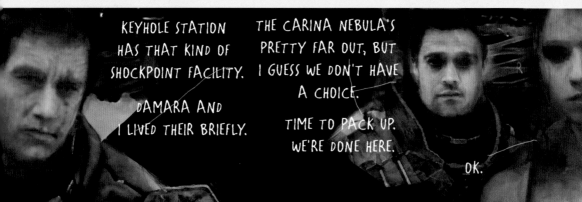

KEYHOLE STATION HAS THAT KIND OF SHOCKPOINT FACILITY.

DAMARA AND I LIVED THEIR BRIEFLY.

THE CARINA NEBULA'S PRETTY FAR OUT, BUT I GUESS WE DON'T HAVE A CHOICE.

TIME TO PACK UP. WE'RE DONE HERE.

OK.

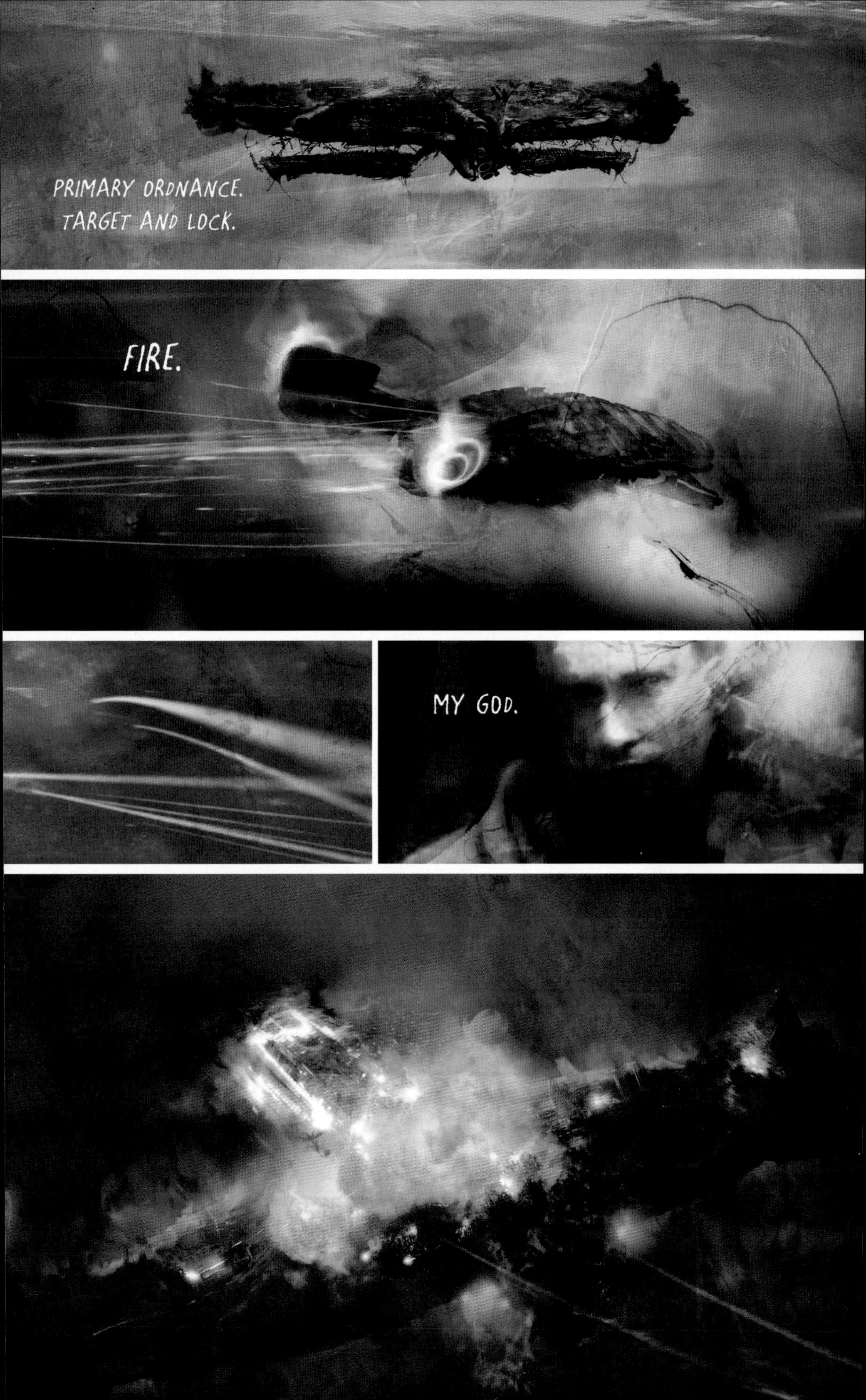
PRIMARY ORDNANCE.
TARGET AND LOCK.
FIRE.
MY GOD.

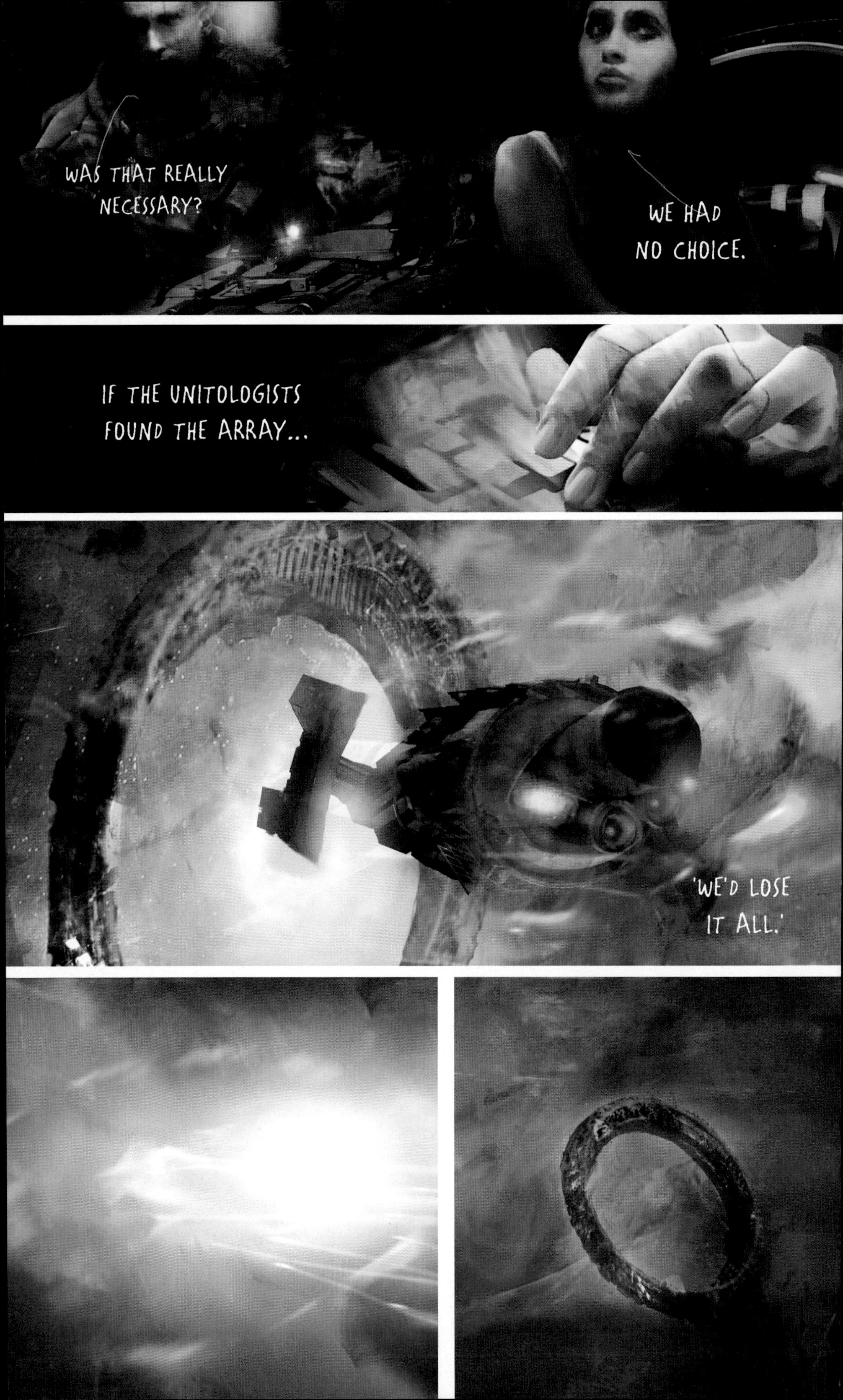
WAS THAT REALLY NECESSARY?
WE HAD NO CHOICE.
IF THE UNITOLOGISTS FOUND THE ARRAY...
'WE'D LOSE IT ALL.'

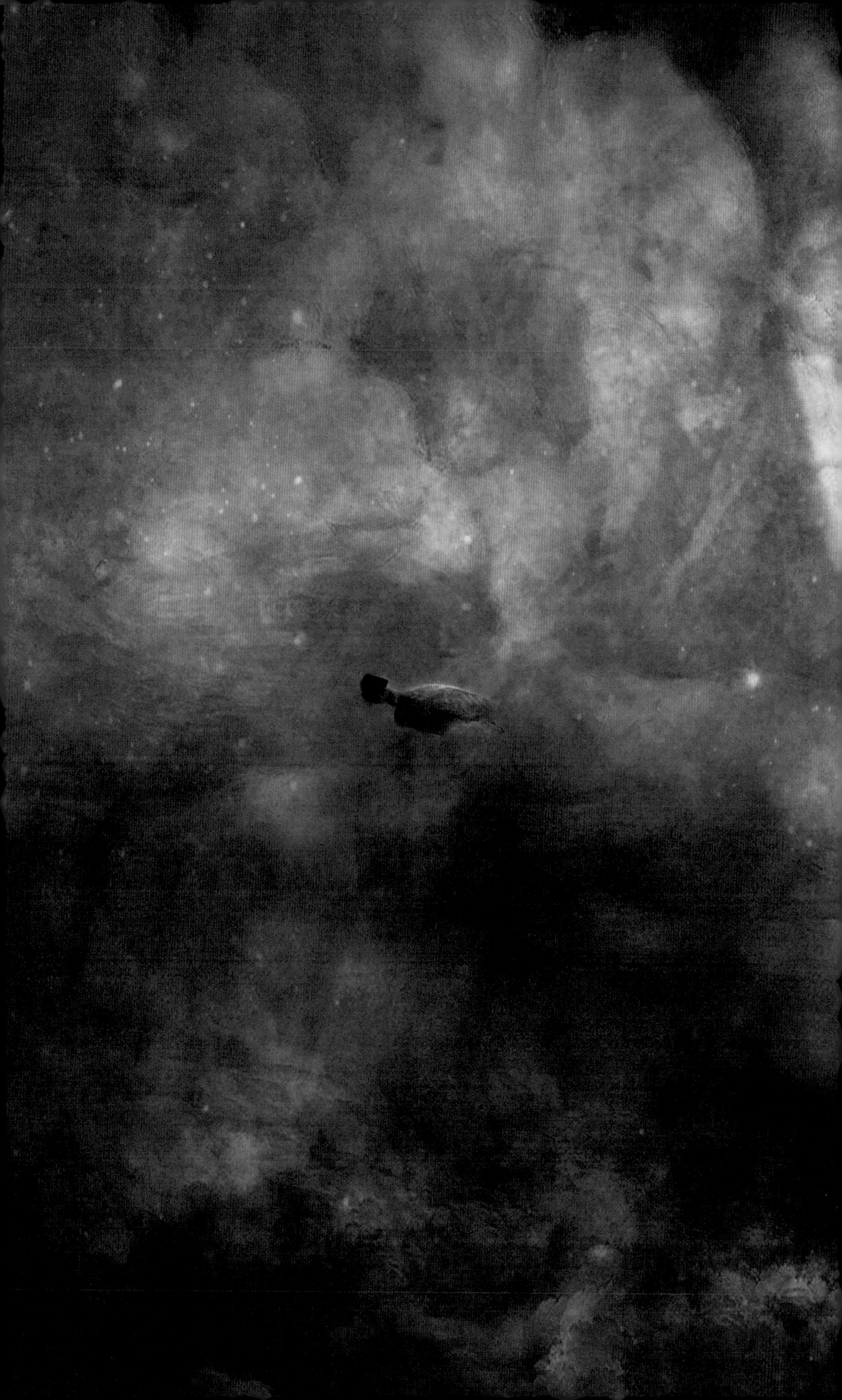

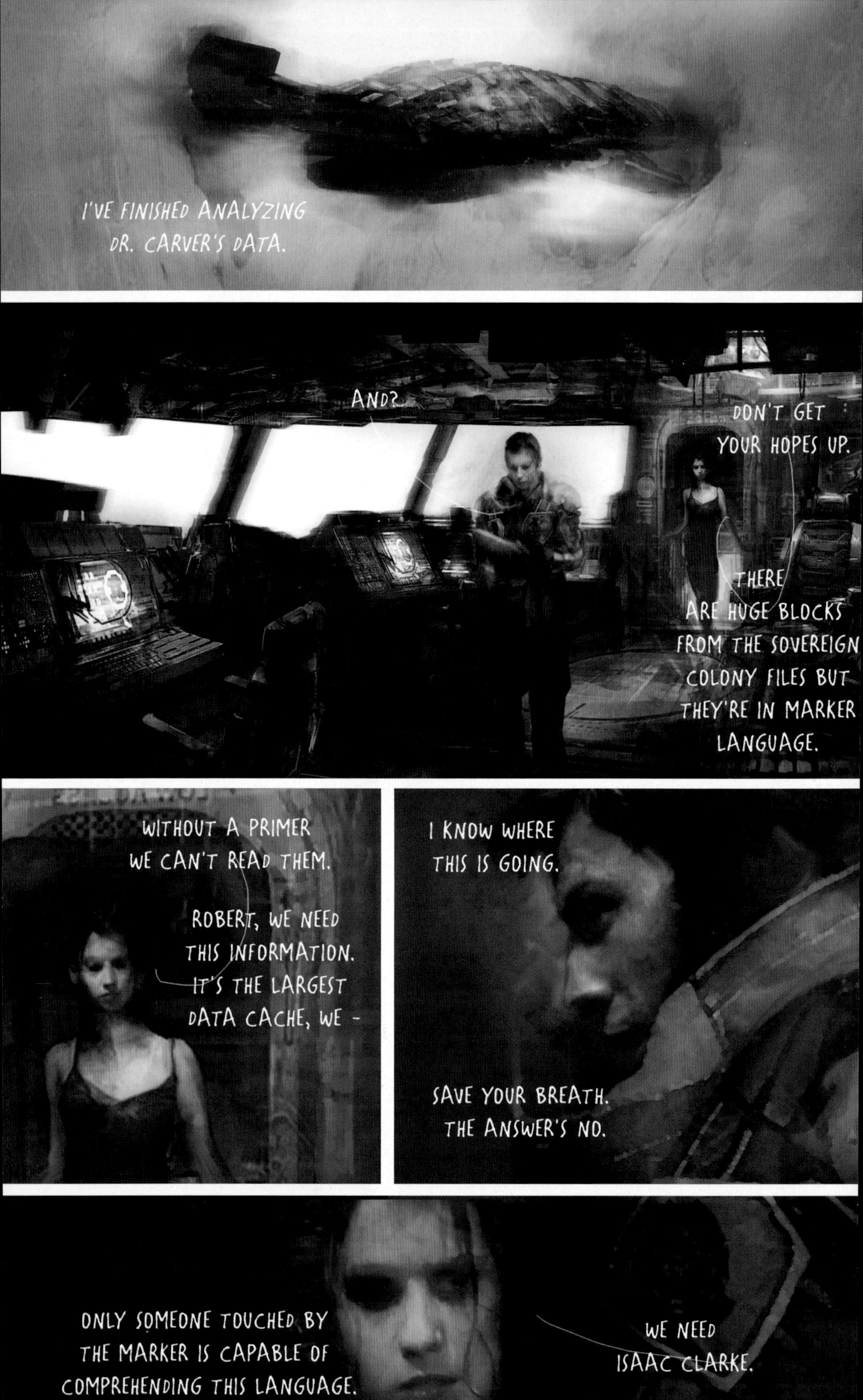
I'VE FINISHED ANALYZING DR. CARVER'S DATA.
AND?
DON'T GET YOUR HOPES UP.
THERE ARE HUGE BLOCKS FROM THE SOVEREIGN COLONY FILES BUT THEY'RE IN MARKER LANGUAGE.
WITHOUT A PRIMER WE CAN'T READ THEM.
ROBERT, WE NEED THIS INFORMATION. IT'S THE LARGEST DATA CACHE, WE -
I KNOW WHERE THIS IS GOING.
SAVE YOUR BREATH. THE ANSWER'S NO.
ONLY SOMEONE TOUCHED BY THE MARKER IS CAPABLE OF COMPREHENDING THIS LANGUAGE.
WE NEED ISAAC CLARKE.

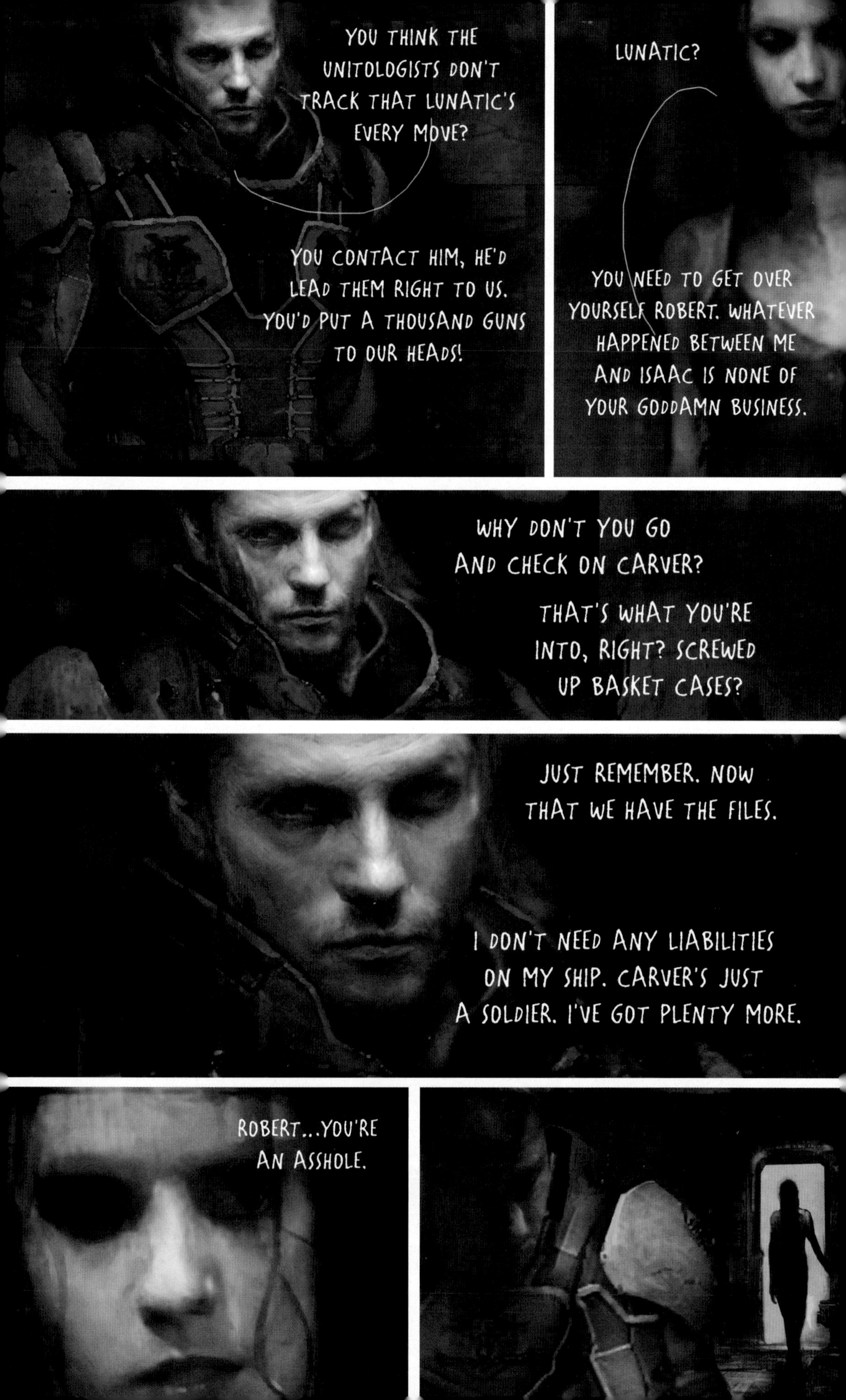
YOU THINK THE UNITOLOGISTS DON'T TRACK THAT LUNATIC'S EVERY MOVE?
YOU CONTACT HIM, HE'D LEAD THEM RIGHT TO US. YOU'D PUT A THOUSAND GUNS TO OUR HEADS!
LUNATIC?
YOU NEED TO GET OVER YOURSELF ROBERT. WHATEVER HAPPENED BETWEEN ME AND ISAAC IS NONE OF YOUR GODDAMN BUSINESS.
WHY DON'T YOU GO AND CHECK ON CARVER?
THAT'S WHAT YOU'RE INTO, RIGHT? SCREWED UP BASKET CASES?
JUST REMEMBER. NOW THAT WE HAVE THE FILES.
I DON'T NEED ANY LIABILITIES ON MY SHIP. CARVER'S JUST A SOLDIER. I'VE GOT PLENTY MORE.
ROBERT...YOU'RE AN ASSHOLE.

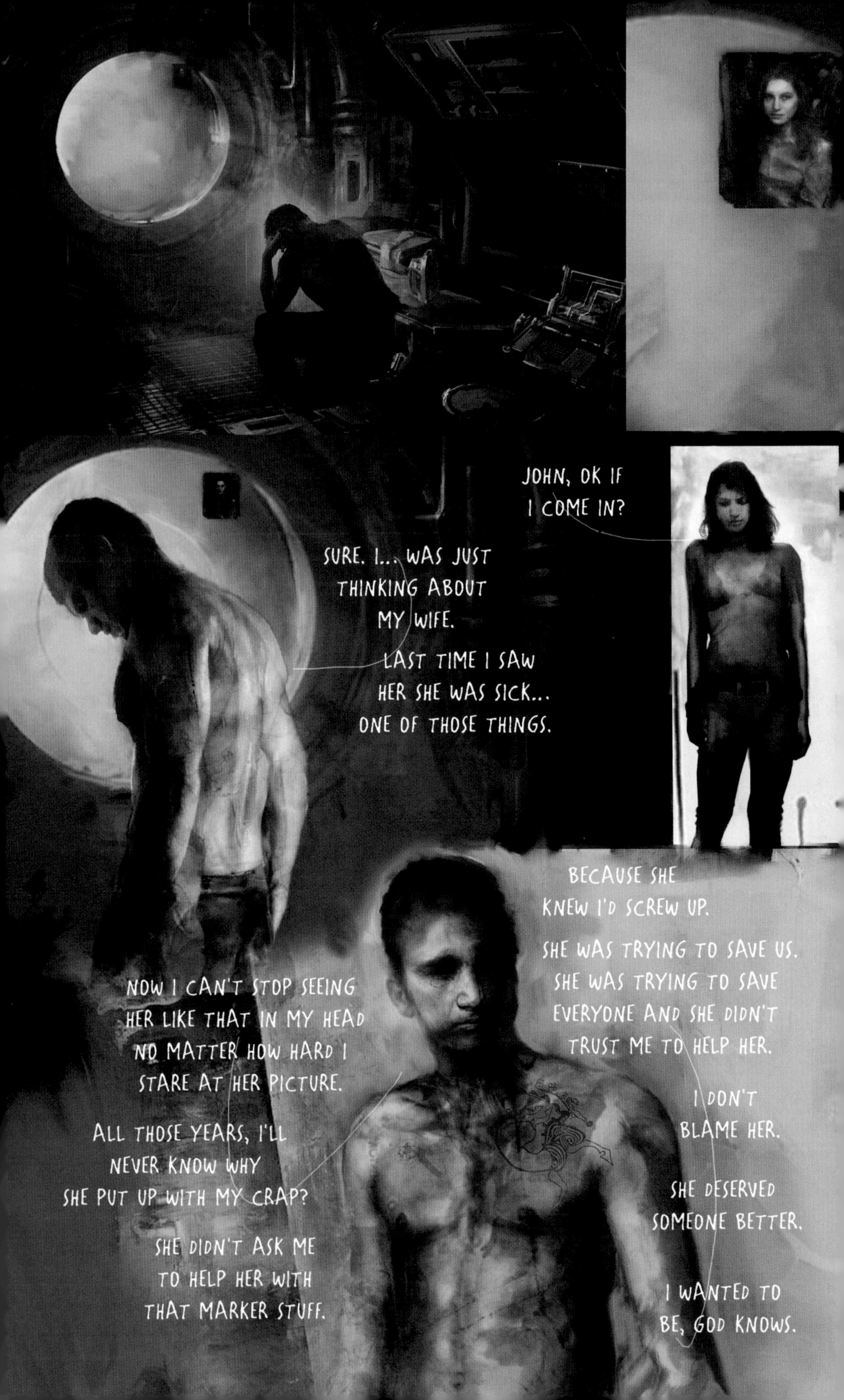
JOHN, OK IF I COME IN?
SURE. I... WAS JUST THINKING ABOUT MY WIFE.
LAST TIME I SAW HER SHE WAS SICK... ONE OF THOSE THINGS.
NOW I CAN'T STOP SEEING HER LIKE THAT IN MY HEAD NO MATTER HOW HARD I STARE AT HER PICTURE.
ALL THOSE YEARS, I'LL NEVER KNOW WHY SHE PUT UP WITH MY CRAP?
SHE DIDN'T ASK ME TO HELP HER WITH THAT MARKER STUFF.
BECAUSE SHE KNEW I'D SCREW UP.
SHE WAS TRYING TO SAVE US. SHE WAS TRYING TO SAVE EVERYONE AND SHE DIDN'T TRUST ME TO HELP HER.
I DON'T BLAME HER.
SHE DESERVED SOMEONE BETTER.
I WANTED TO BE, GOD KNOWS.

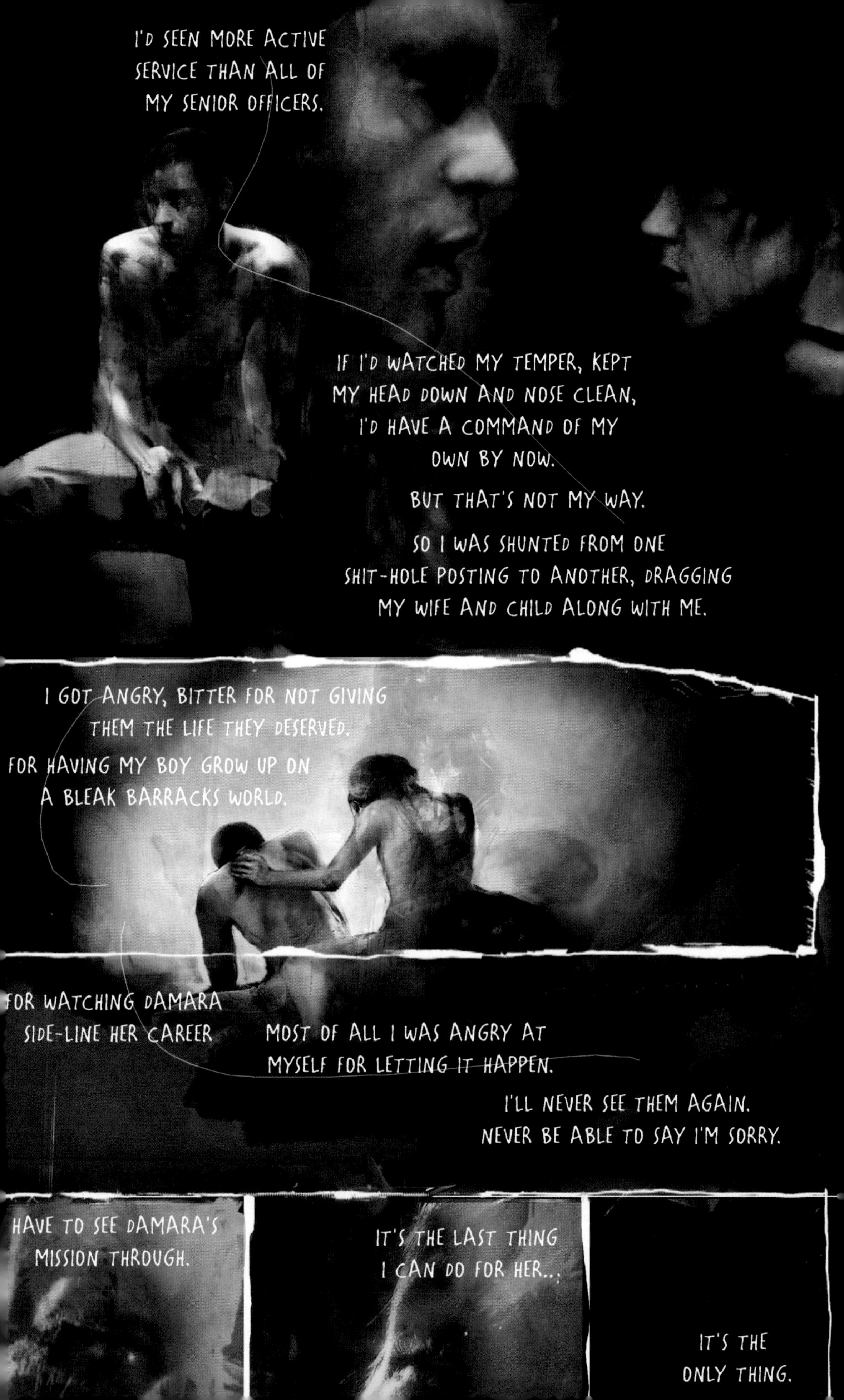
I'D SEEN MORE ACTIVE SERVICE THAN ALL OF MY SENIOR OFFICERS.
IF I'D WATCHED MY TEMPER, KEPT MY HEAD DOWN AND NOSE CLEAN, I'D HAVE A COMMAND OF MY OWN BY NOW.
BUT THAT'S NOT MY WAY.
SO I WAS SHUNTED FROM ONE SHIT-HOLE POSTING TO ANOTHER, DRAGGING MY WIFE AND CHILD ALONG WITH ME.
I GOT ANGRY, BITTER FOR NOT GIVING THEM THE LIFE THEY DESERVED.
FOR HAVING MY BOY GROW UP ON A BLEAK BARRACKS WORLD.
FOR WATCHING DAMARA SIDE-LINE HER CAREER
MOST OF ALL I WAS ANGRY AT MYSELF FOR LETTING IT HAPPEN.
I'LL NEVER SEE THEM AGAIN. NEVER BE ABLE TO SAY I'M SORRY.
HAVE TO SEE DAMARA'S MISSION THROUGH.
IT'S THE LAST THING I CAN DO FOR HER...
IT'S THE ONLY THING.

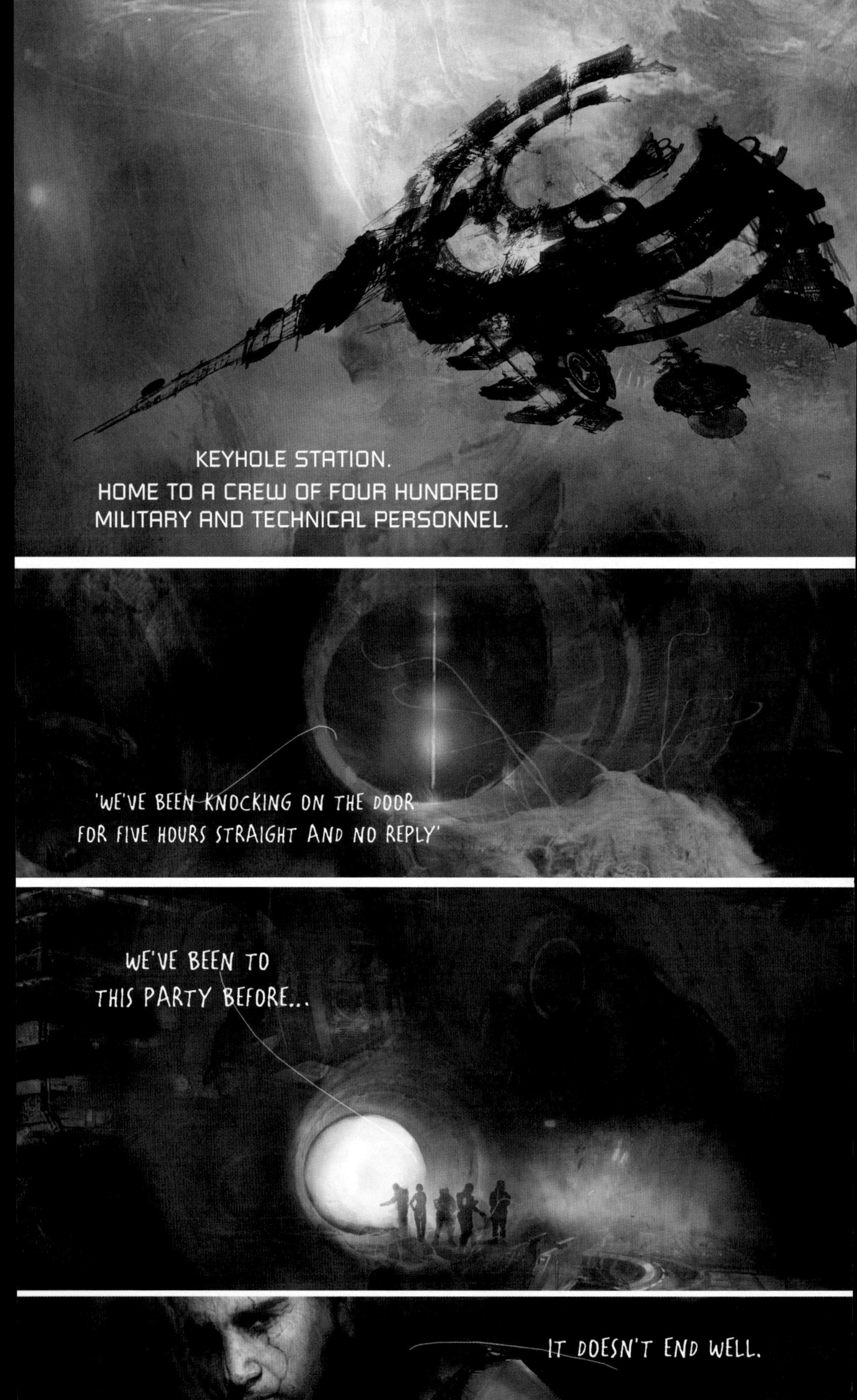
KEYHOLE STATION.
HOME TO A CREW OF FOUR HUNDRED MILITARY AND TECHNICAL PERSONNEL.
'WE'VE BEEN KNOCKING ON THE DOOR FOR FIVE HOURS STRAIGHT AND NO REPLY'
WE'VE BEEN TO THIS PARTY BEFORE...
IT DOESN'T END WELL.

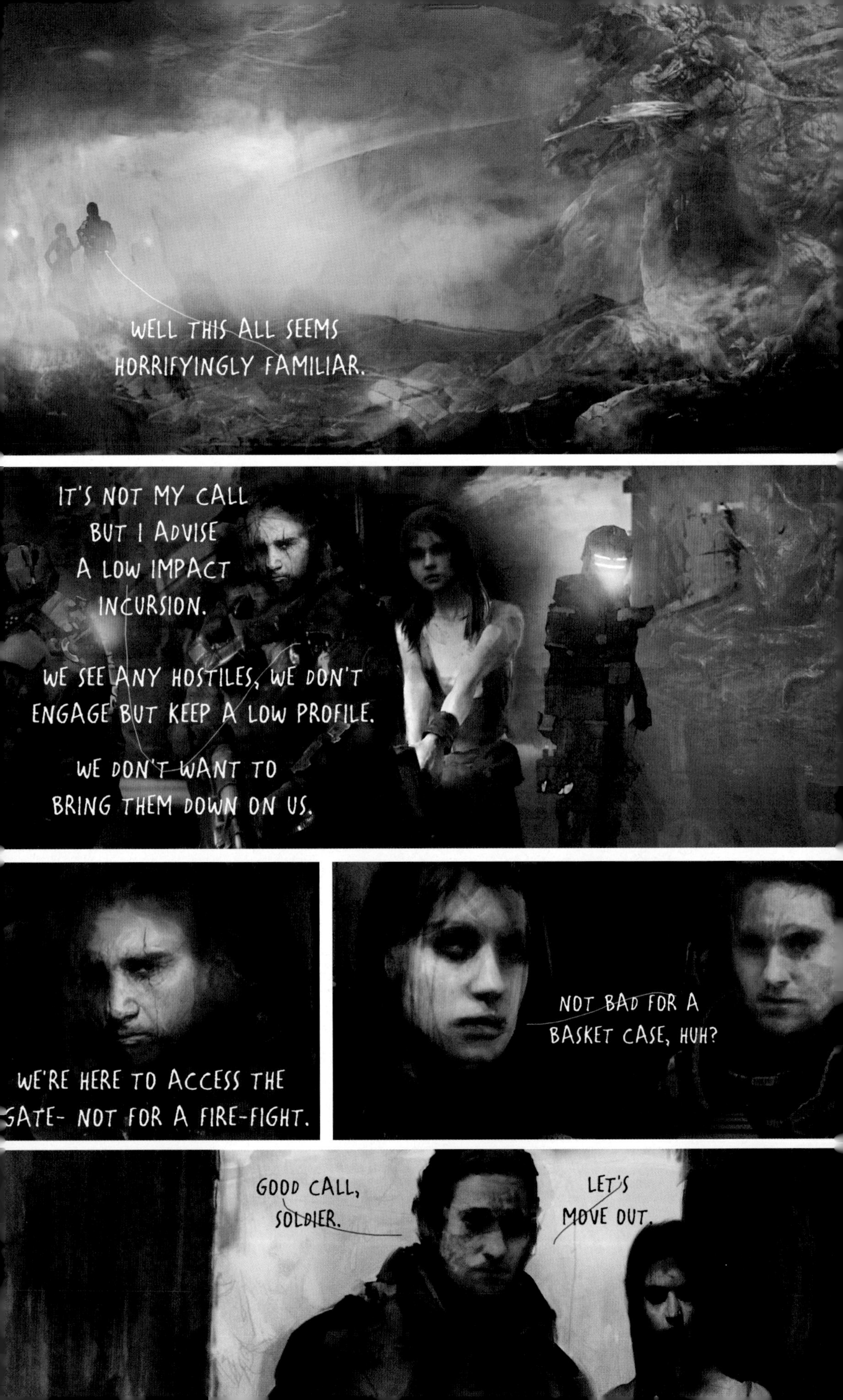
WELL THIS ALL SEEMS HORRIFYINGLY FAMILIAR.
IT'S NOT MY CALL BUT I ADVISE A LOW IMPACT INCURSION.
WE SEE ANY HOSTILES, WE DON'T ENGAGE BUT KEEP A LOW PROFILE.
WE DON'T WANT TO BRING THEM DOWN ON US.
WE'RE HERE TO ACCESS THE GATE- NOT FOR A FIRE-FIGHT.
NOT BAD FOR A BASKET CASE, HUH?
GOOD CALL, SOLDIER.
LET'S MOVE OUT.

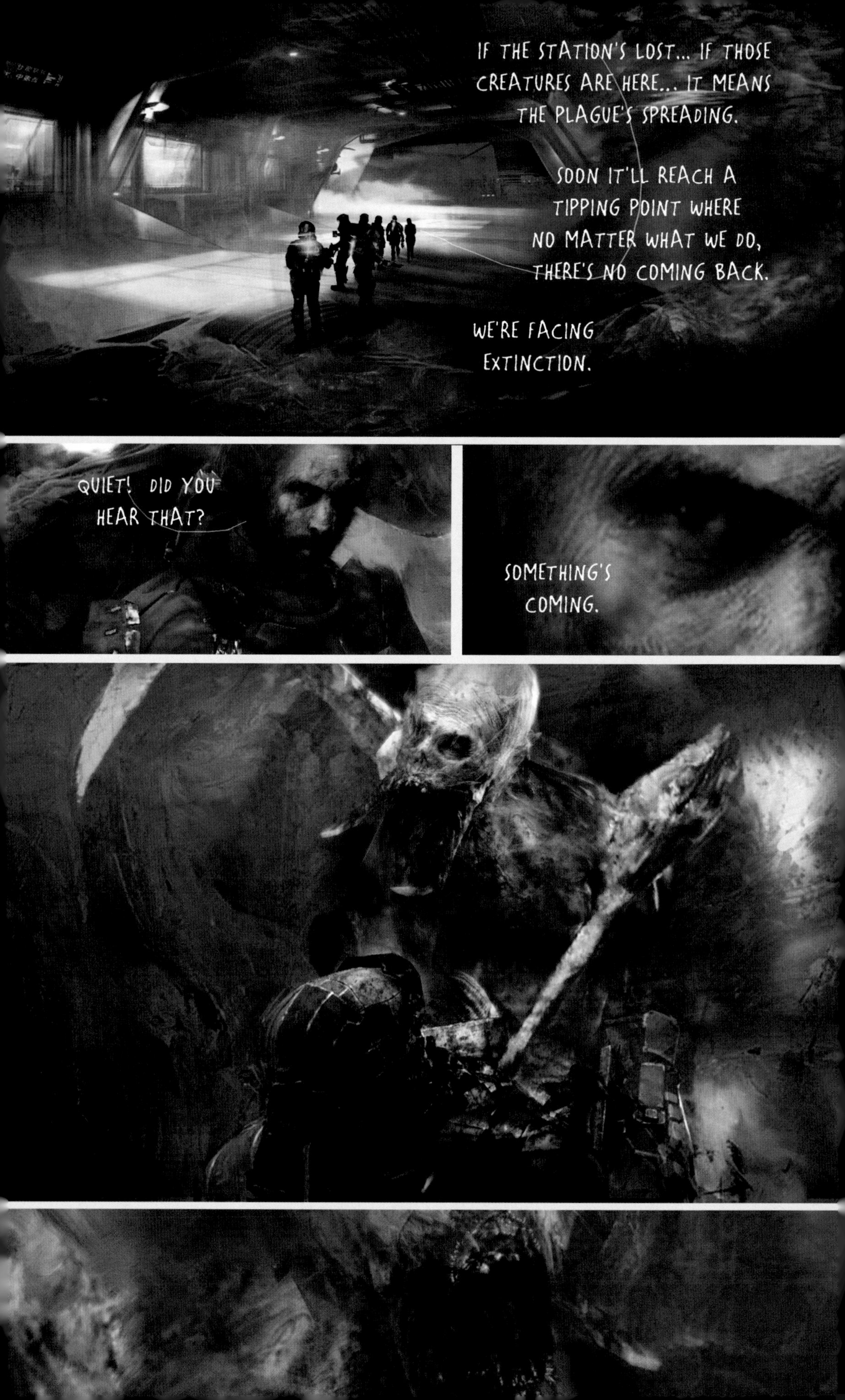
IF THE STATION'S LOST... IF THOSE CREATURES ARE HERE... IT MEANS THE PLAGUE'S SPREADING.
SOON IT'LL REACH A TIPPING POINT WHERE NO MATTER WHAT WE DO, THERE'S NO COMING BACK.
WE'RE FACING EXTINCTION.
QUIET! DID YOU HEAR THAT?
SOMETHING'S COMING.

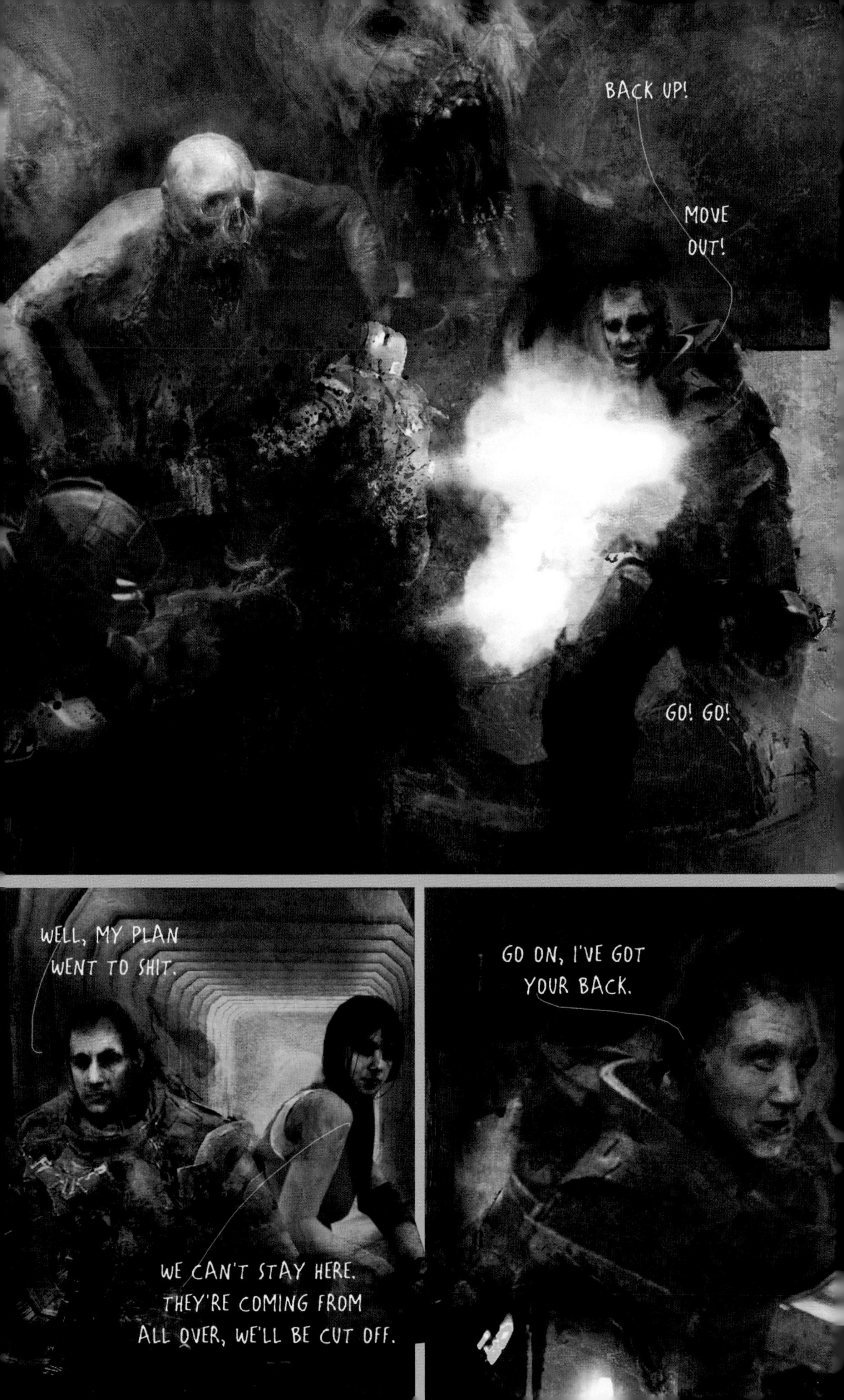
BACK UP!
MOVE OUT!
GO! GO!
WELL, MY PLAN WENT TO SHIT.
WE CAN'T STAY HERE. THEY'RE COMING FROM ALL OVER, WE'LL BE CUT OFF.
GO ON, I'VE GOT YOUR BACK.

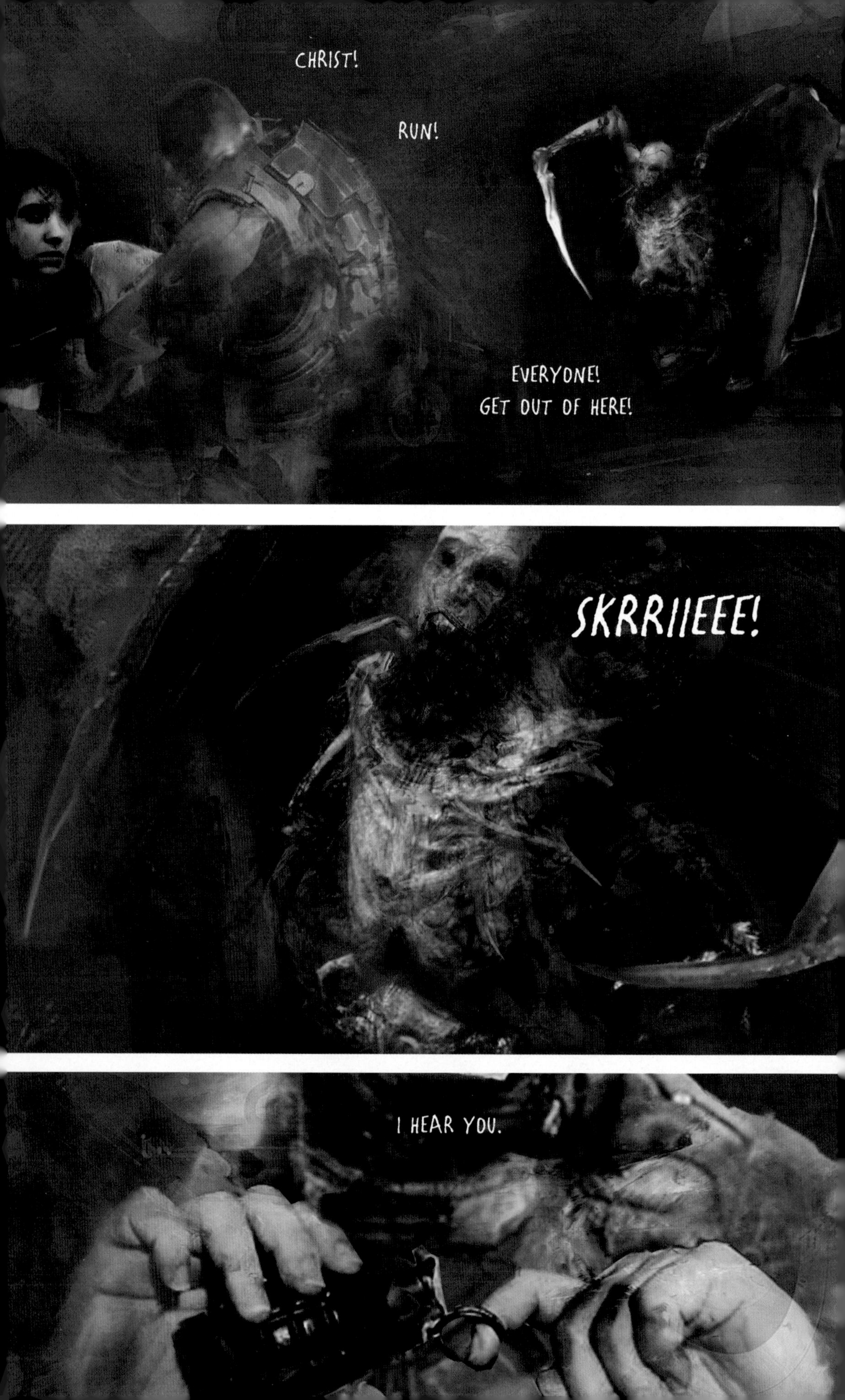
CHRIST!
RUN!
EVERYONE! GET OUT OF HERE!
SKRRIIEEE!
I HEAR YOU.

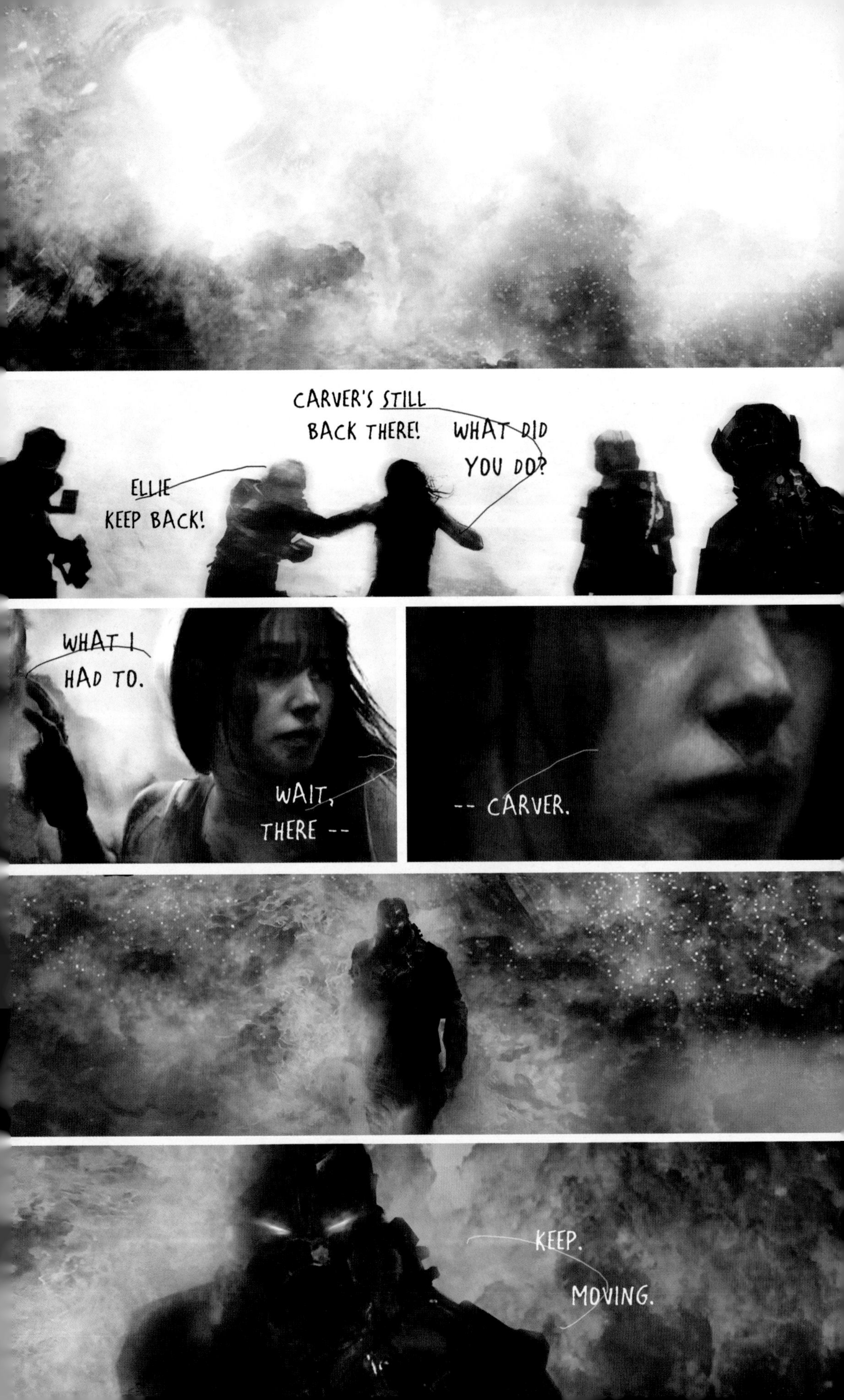
CARVER'S STILL BACK THERE!
ELLIE KEEP BACK!
WHAT DID YOU DO?
WHAT I HAD TO.
WAIT, THERE --
-- CARVER.
KEEP.
MOVING.

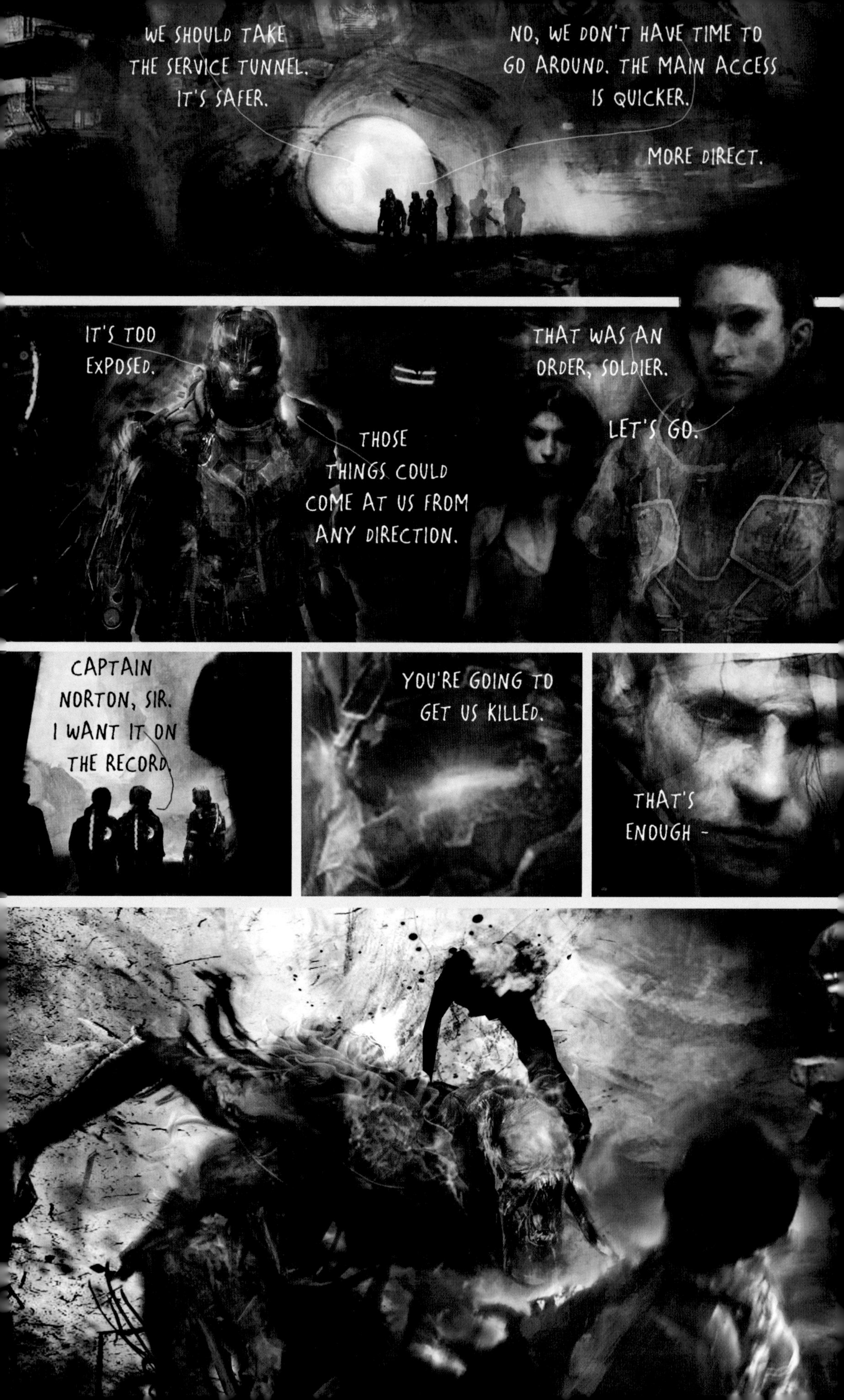
WE SHOULD TAKE THE SERVICE TUNNEL. IT'S SAFER.
NO, WE DON'T HAVE TIME TO GO AROUND. THE MAIN ACCESS IS QUICKER.
MORE DIRECT.
IT'S TOO EXPOSED.
THOSE THINGS COULD COME AT US FROM ANY DIRECTION.
THAT WAS AN ORDER, SOLDIER.
LET'S GO.
CAPTAIN NORTON, SIR. I WANT IT ON THE RECORD.
YOU'RE GOING TO GET US KILLED.
THAT'S ENOUGH -

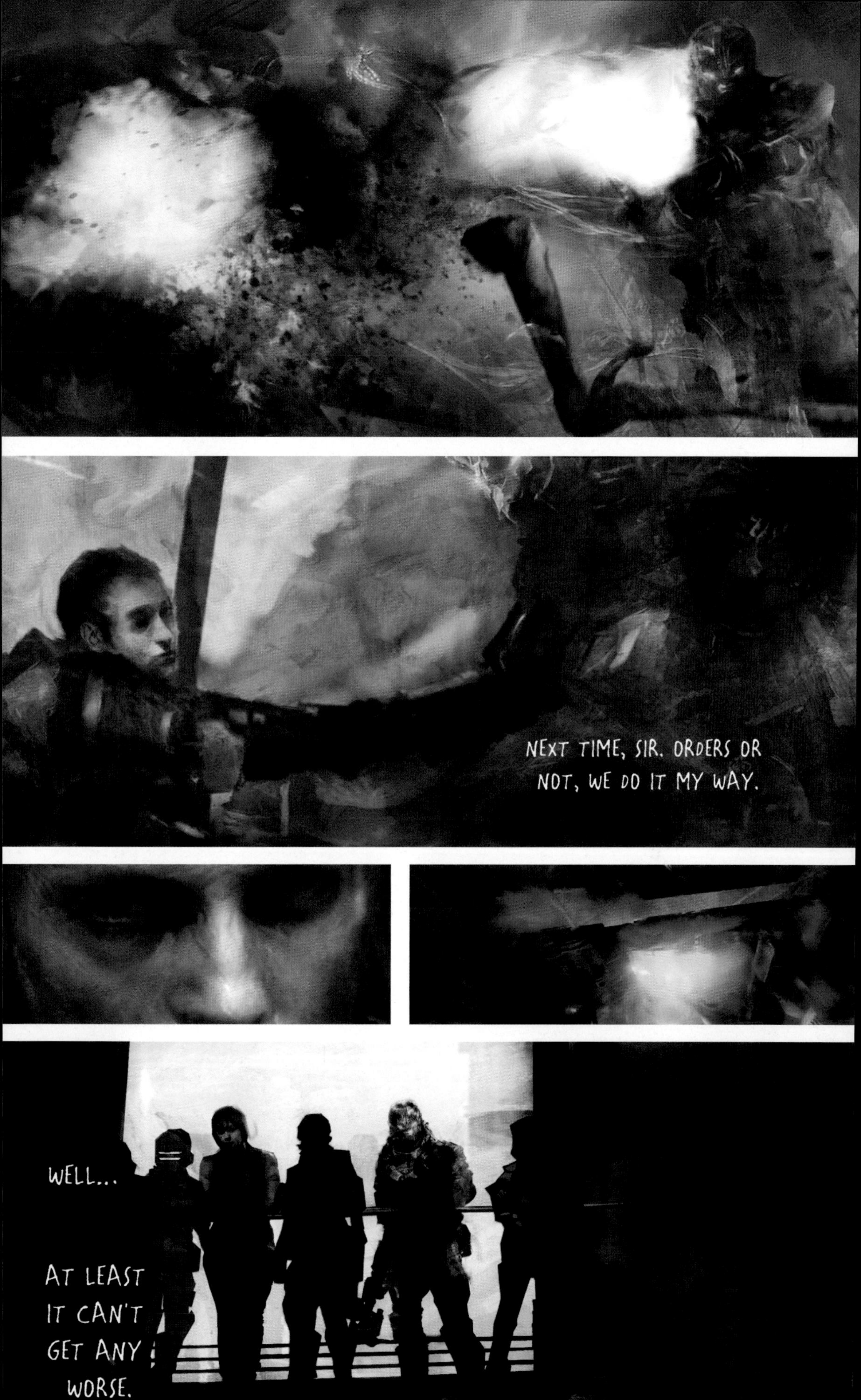
NEXT TIME, SIR. ORDERS OR NOT, WE DO IT MY WAY.
WELL...
AT LEAST IT CAN'T GET ANY WORSE.

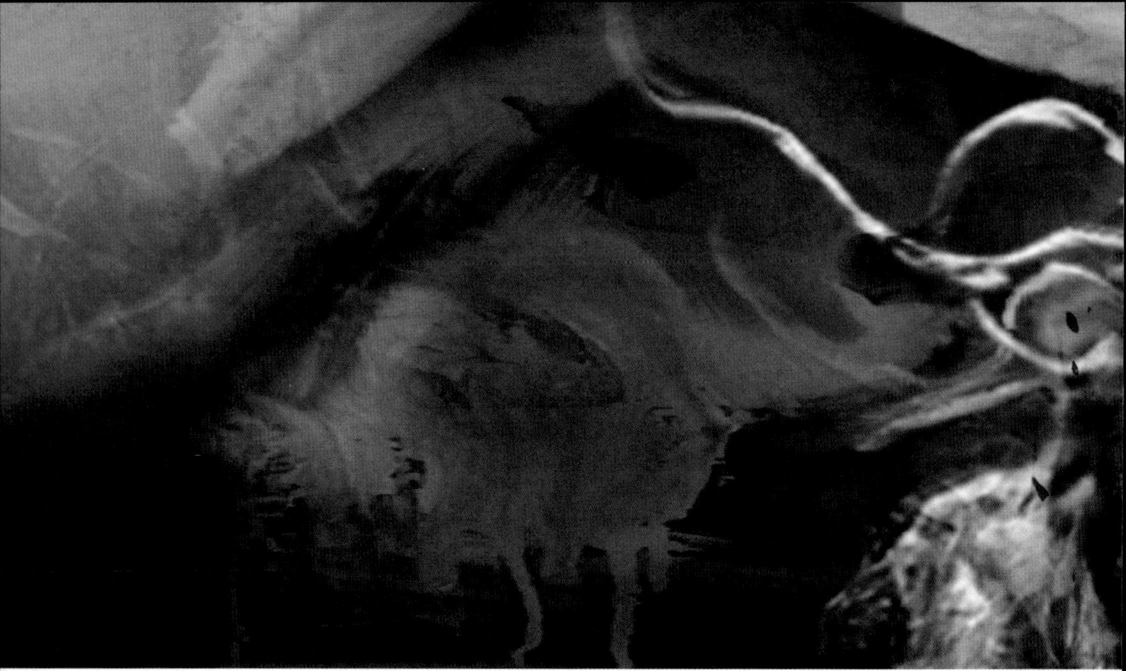

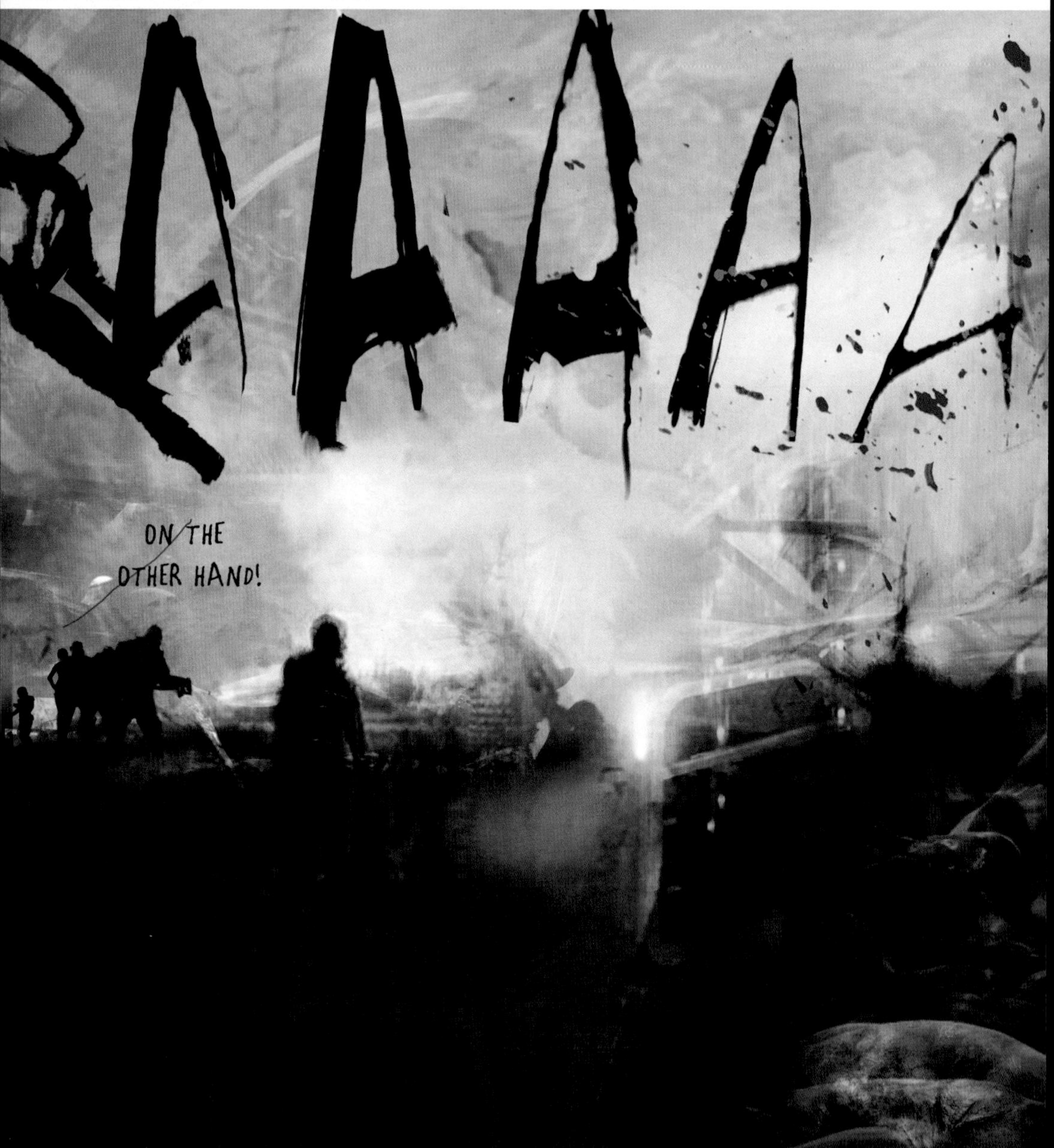
RAAAAA
ON THE OTHER HAND!

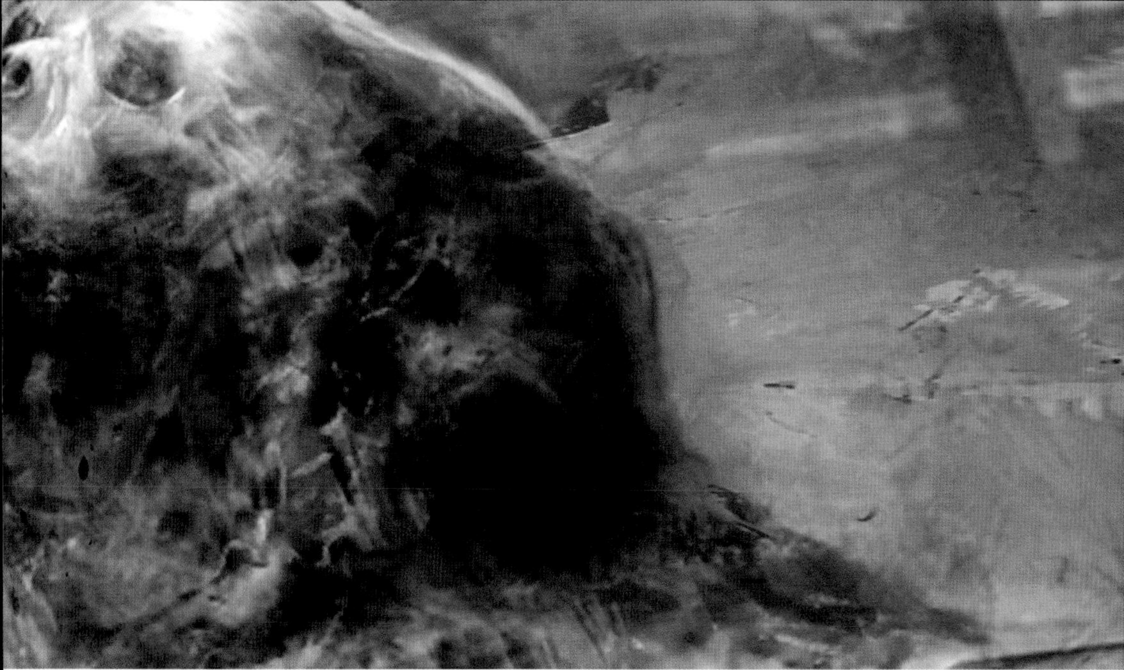

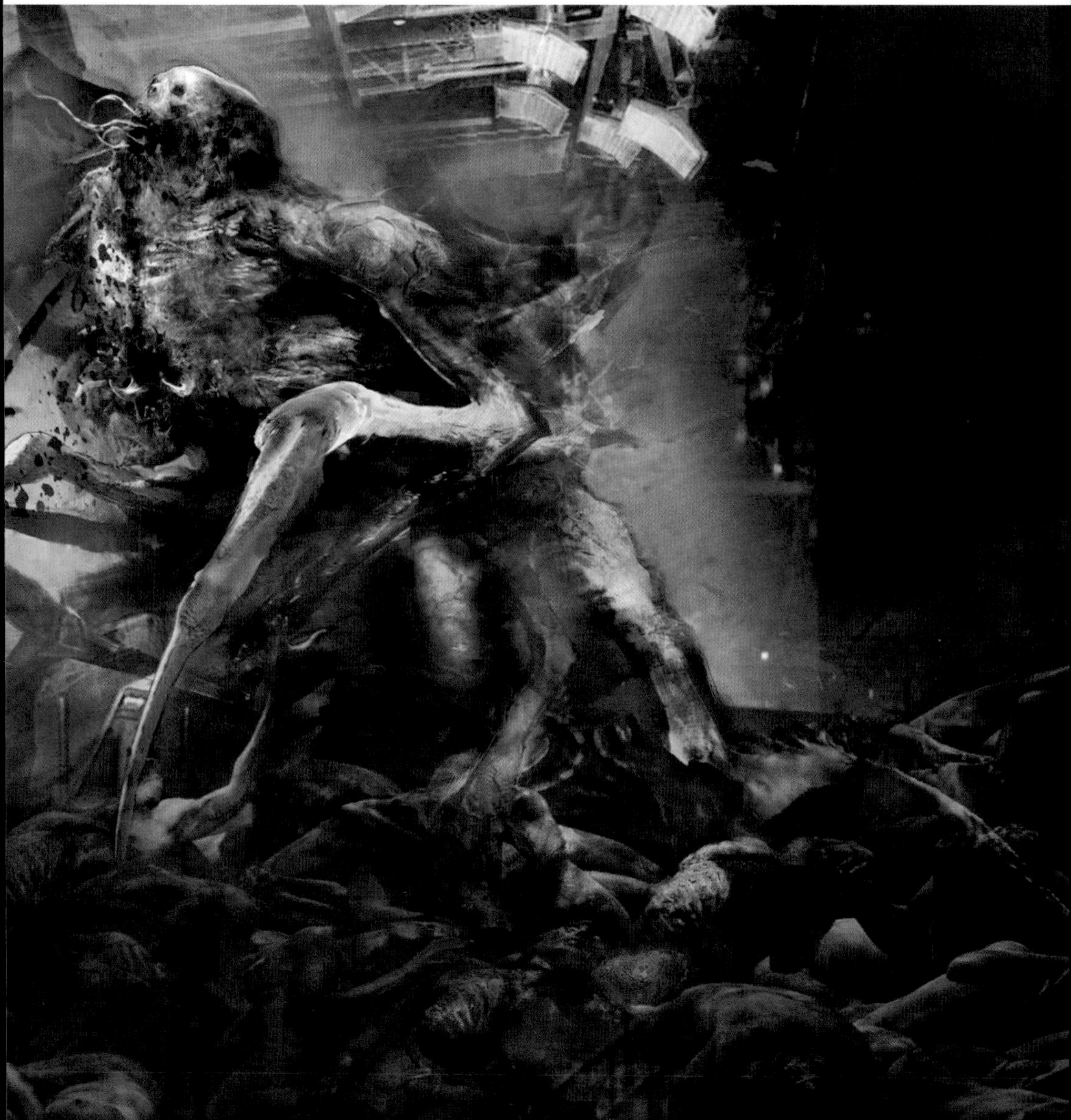

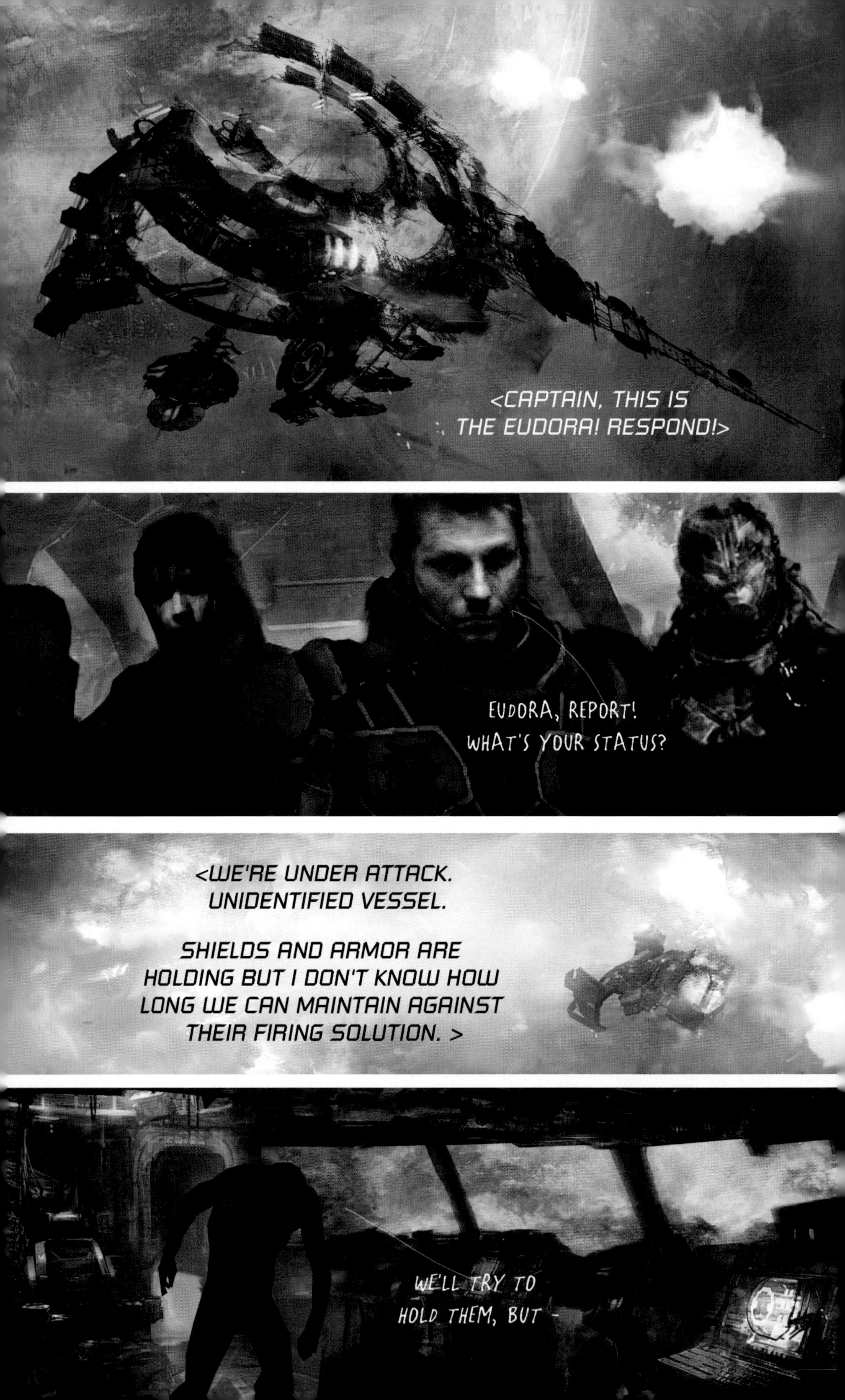
<CAPTAIN, THIS IS THE EUDORA! RESPOND!>
EUDORA, REPORT! WHAT'S YOUR STATUS?
<WE'RE UNDER ATTACK. UNIDENTIFIED VESSEL.
SHIELDS AND ARMOR ARE HOLDING BUT I DON'T KNOW HOW LONG WE CAN MAINTAIN AGAINST THEIR FIRING SOLUTION. >
WE'LL TRY TO HOLD THEM, BUT -

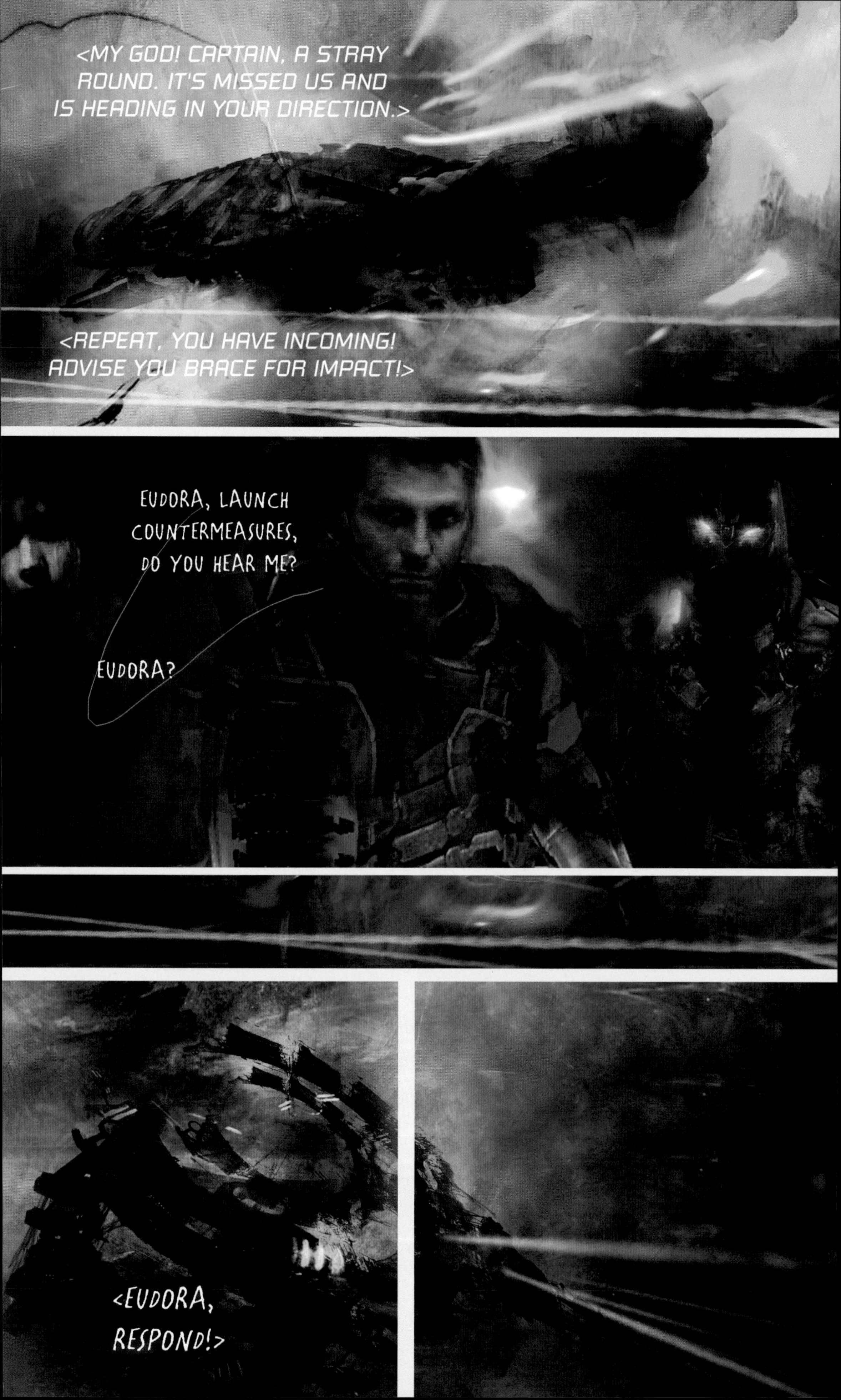
<MY GOD! CAPTAIN, A STRAY ROUND. IT'S MISSED US AND IS HEADING IN YOUR DIRECTION.>
<REPEAT, YOU HAVE INCOMING! ADVISE YOU BRACE FOR IMPACT!>
EUDORA, LAUNCH COUNTERMEASURES, DO YOU HEAR ME?
EUDORA?
<EUDORA, RESPOND!>

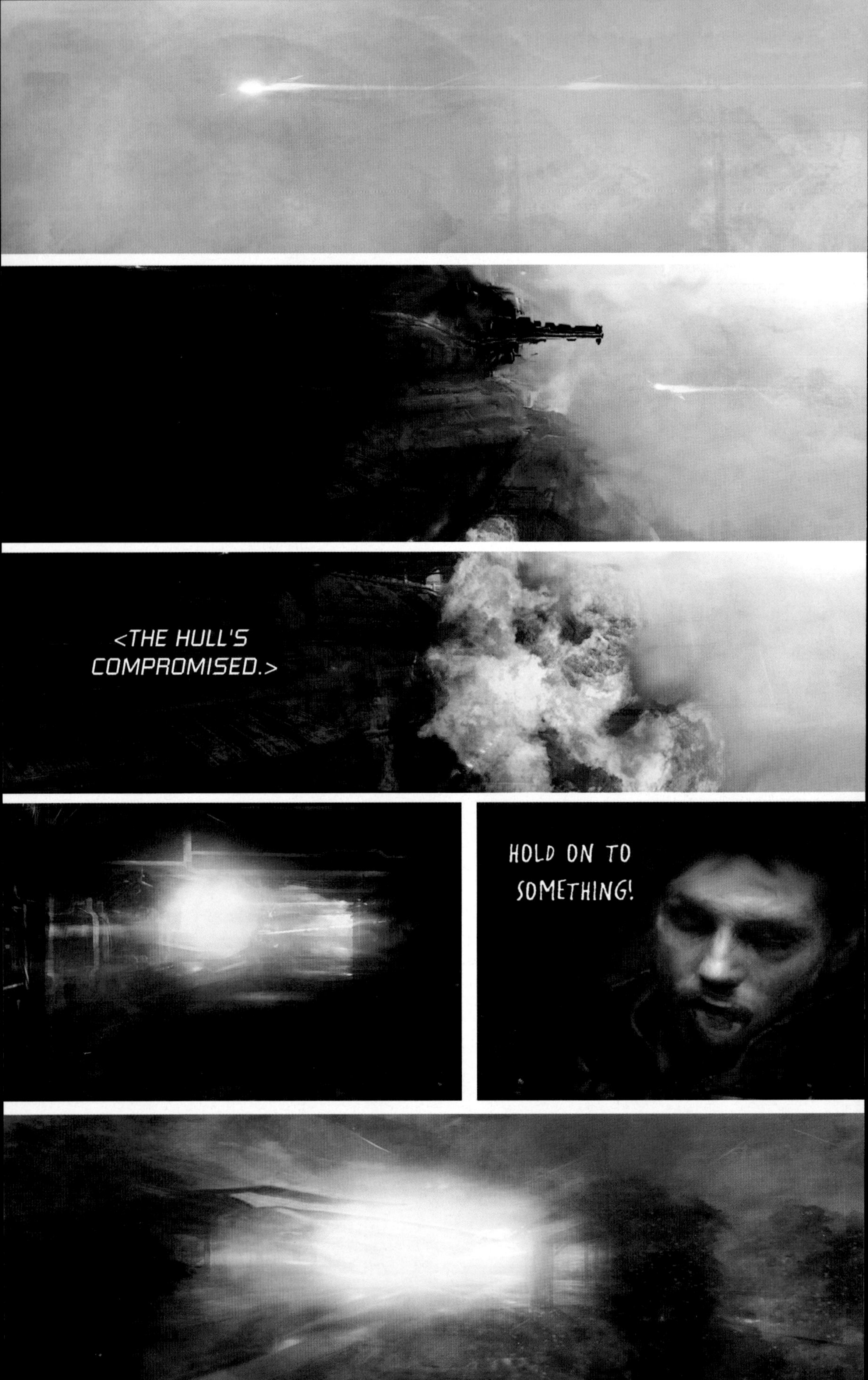
<THE HULL'S COMPROMISED.>
HOLD ON TO SOMETHING!

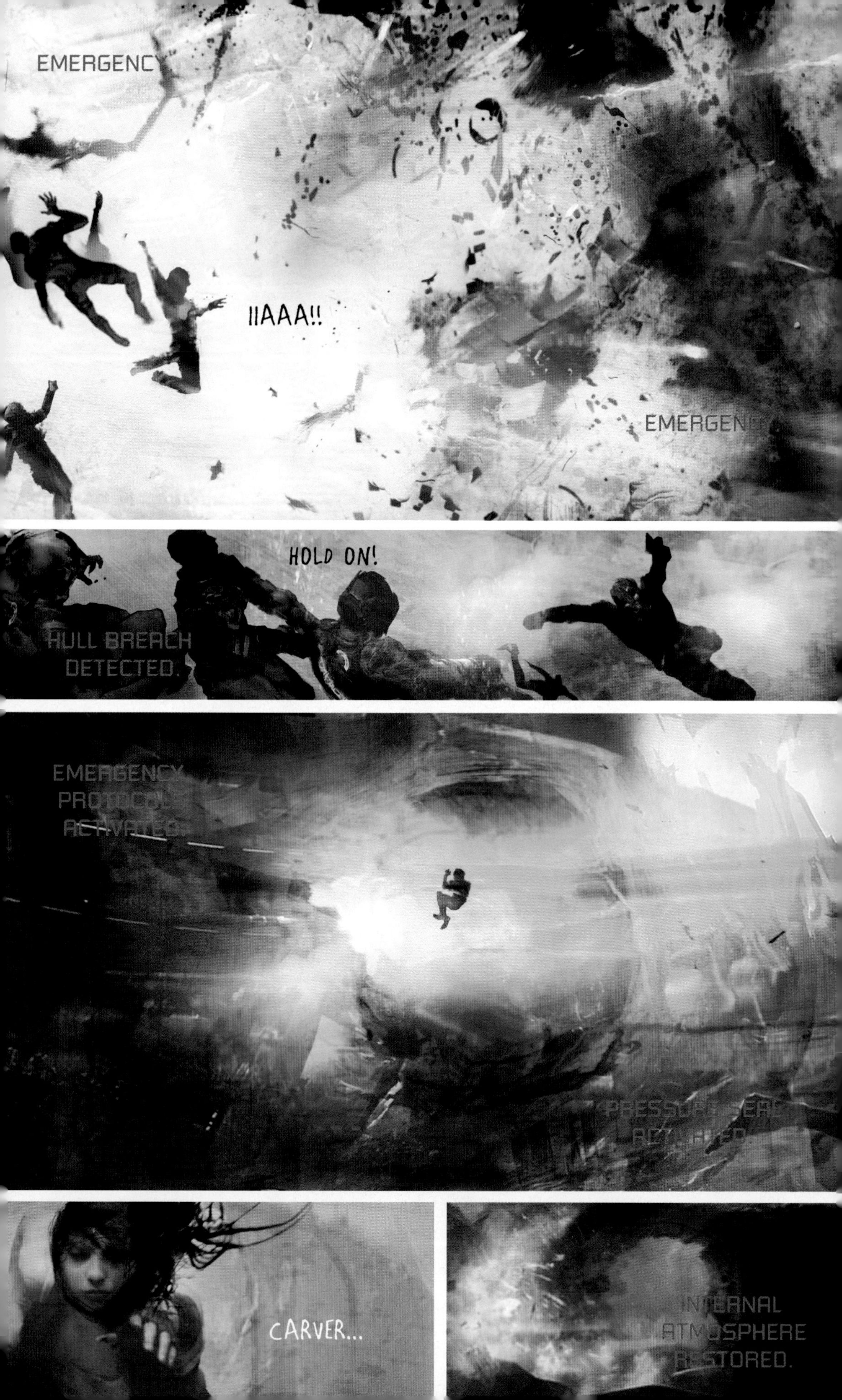
EMERGENCY
IIAAA!!
EMERGENCY
HOLD ON!
HULL BREACH DETECTED.
EMERGENCY PROTOCOLS ACTIVATED.
PRESSURE SEAL ACTIVATED.
CARVER...
INTERNAL ATMOSPHERE RESTORED.

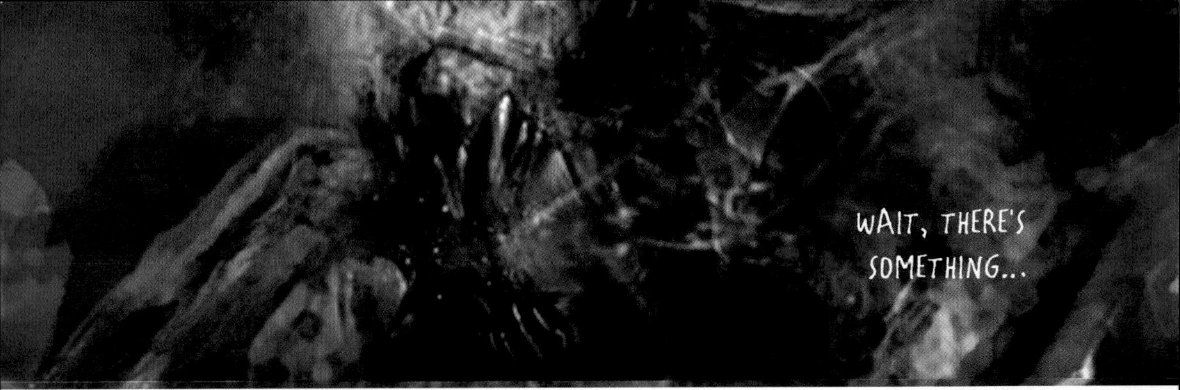
WAIT, THERE'S SOMETHING...
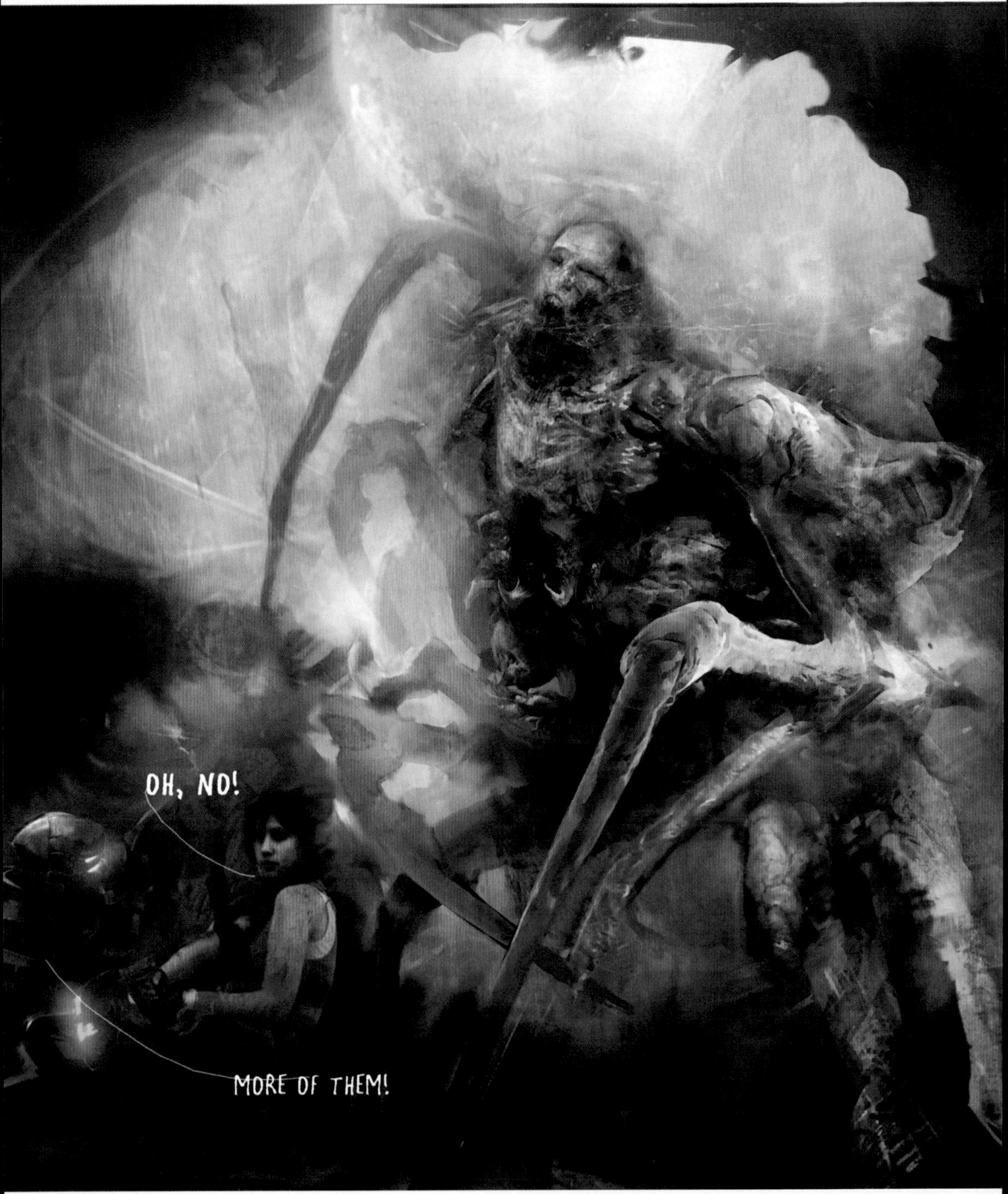
OH, NO!
MORE OF THEM!
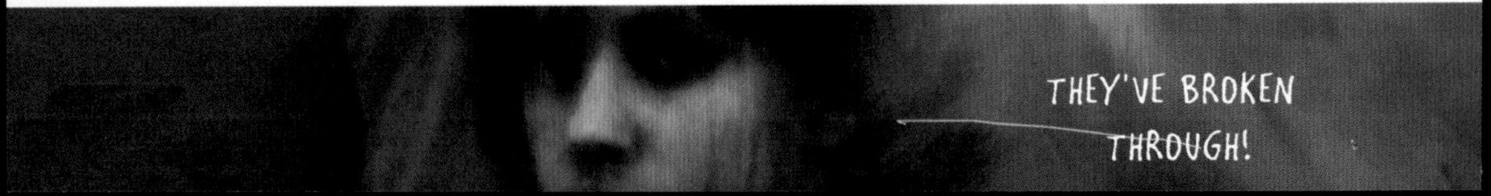
THEY'VE BROKEN THROUGH!

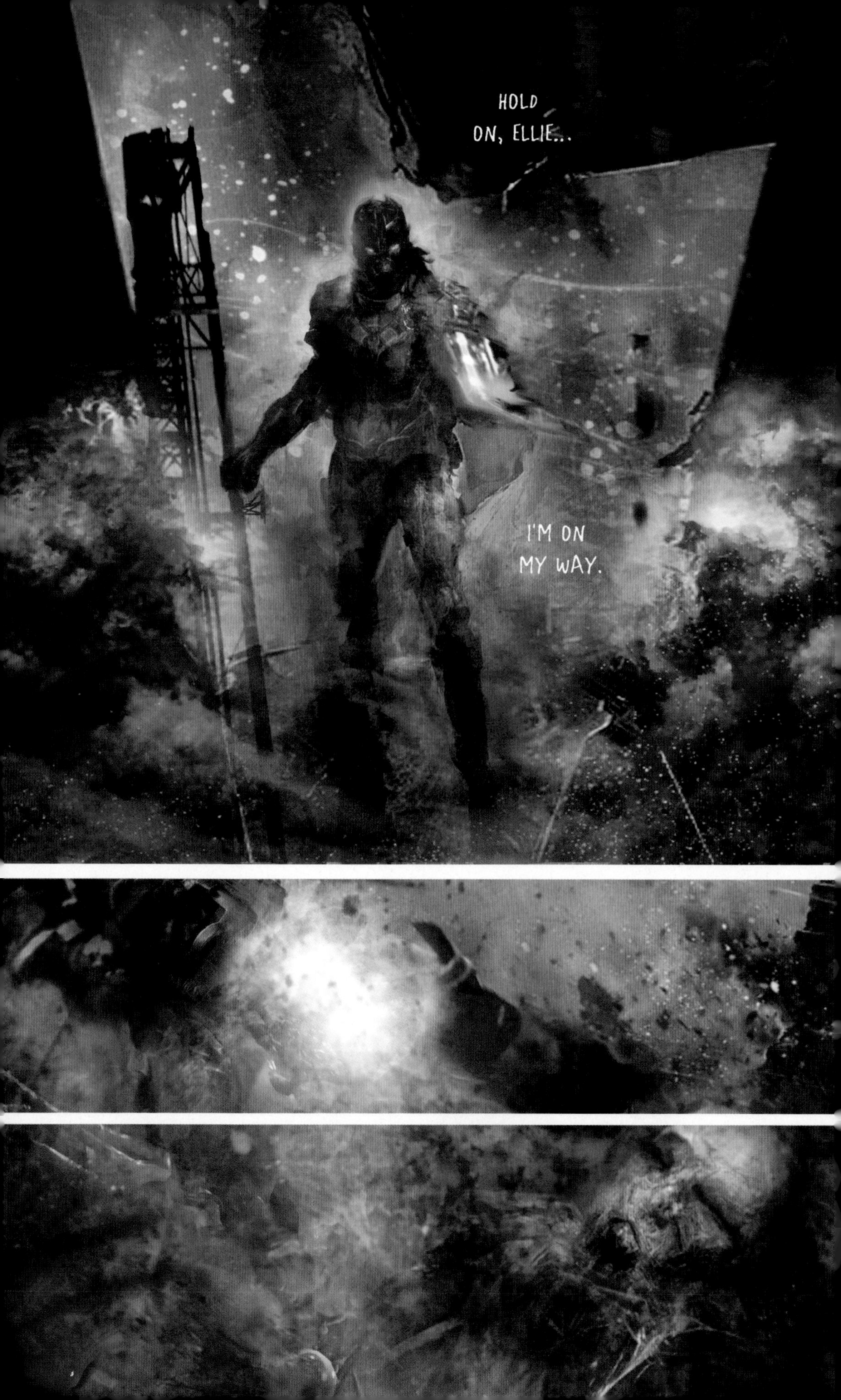
HOLD ON, ELLIE...
I'M ON MY WAY.

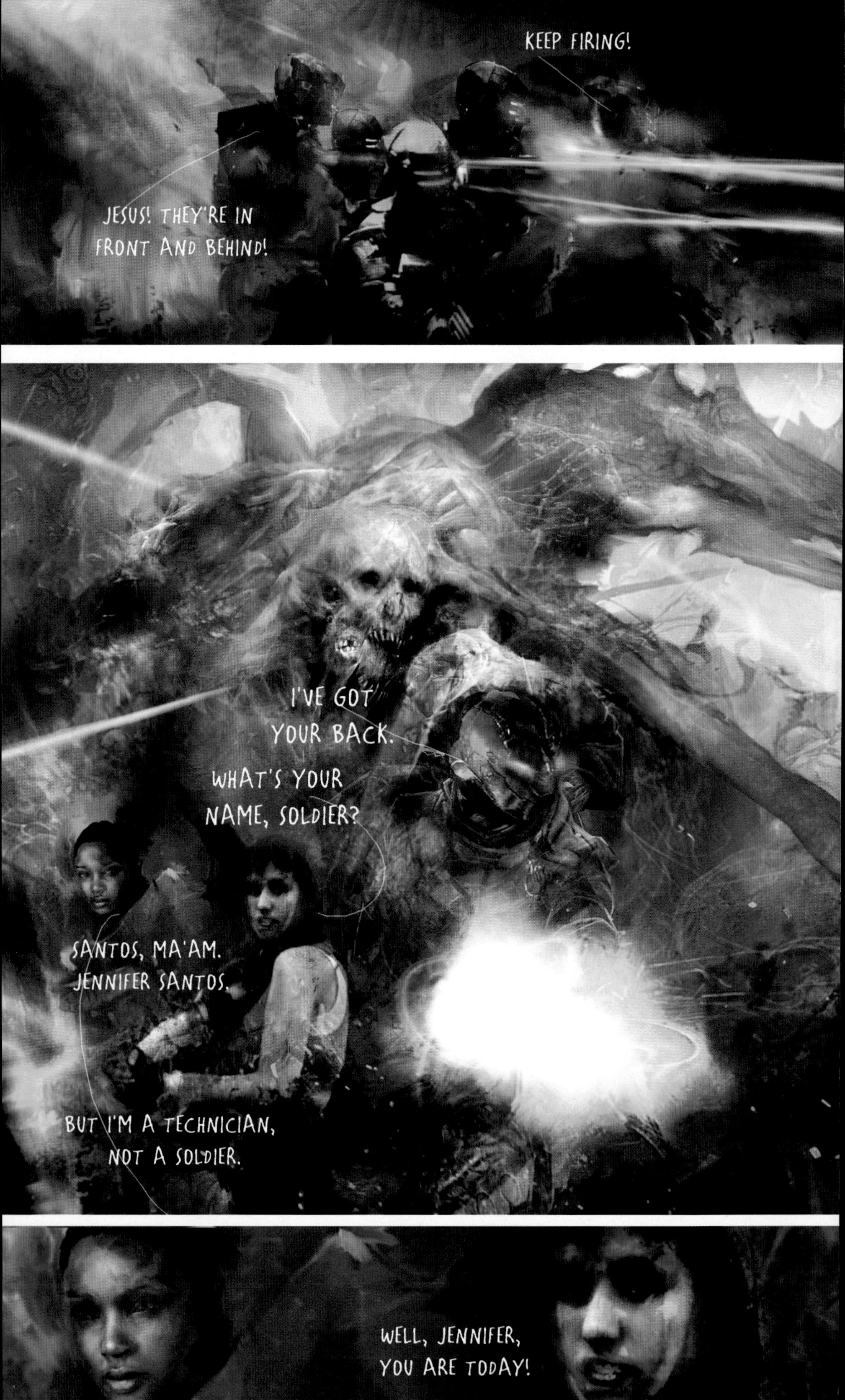
KEEP FIRING!
JESUS! THEY'RE IN FRONT AND BEHIND!
I'VE GOT YOUR BACK.
WHAT'S YOUR NAME, SOLDIER?
SANTOS, MA'AM. JENNIFER SANTOS.
BUT I'M A TECHNICIAN, NOT A SOLDIER.
WELL, JENNIFER, YOU ARE TODAY!

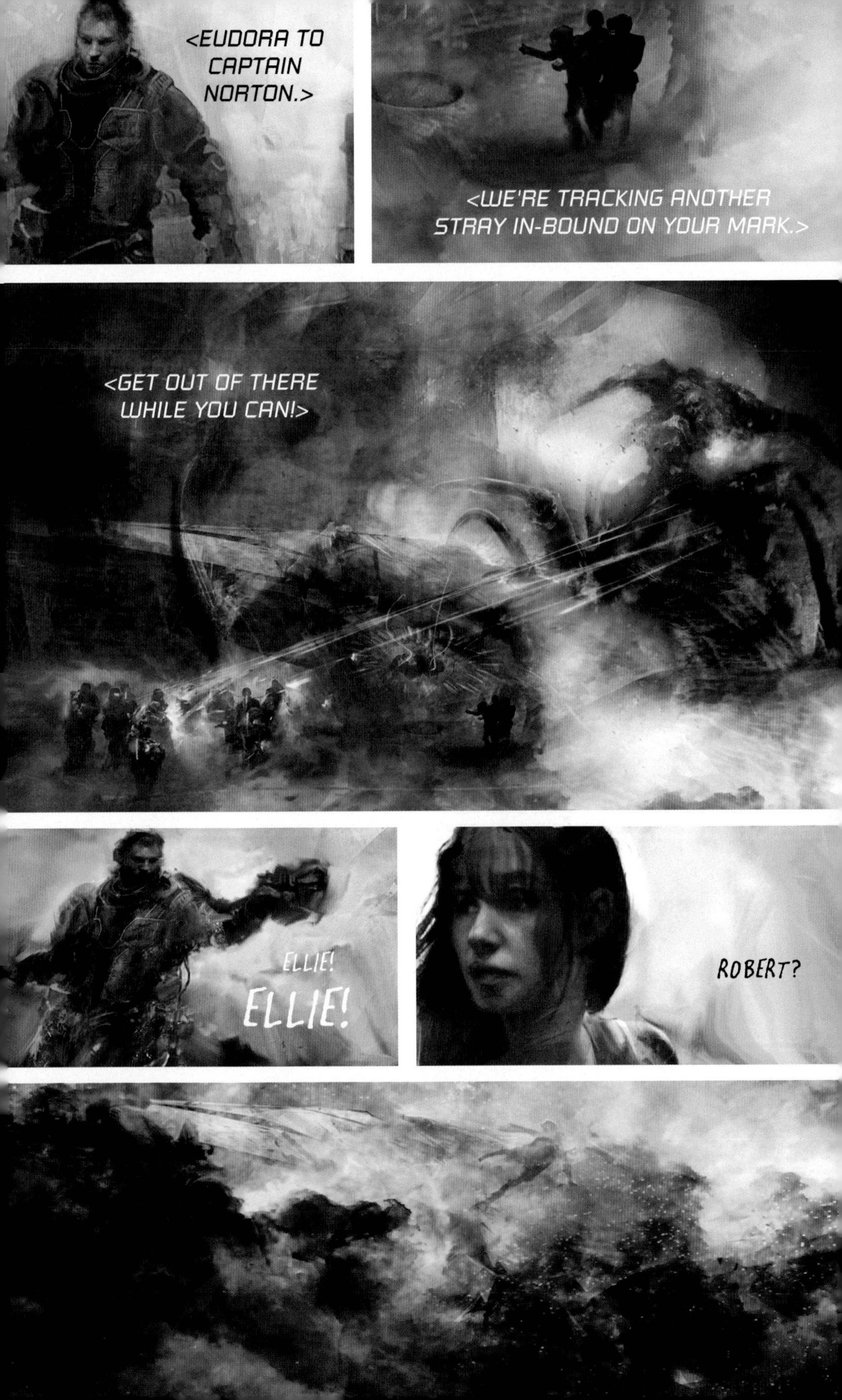
<EUDORA TO CAPTAIN NORTON.>
<WE'RE TRACKING ANOTHER STRAY IN-BOUND ON YOUR MARK.>
<GET OUT OF THERE WHILE YOU CAN!>
ELLIE!
ELLIE!
ROBERT?

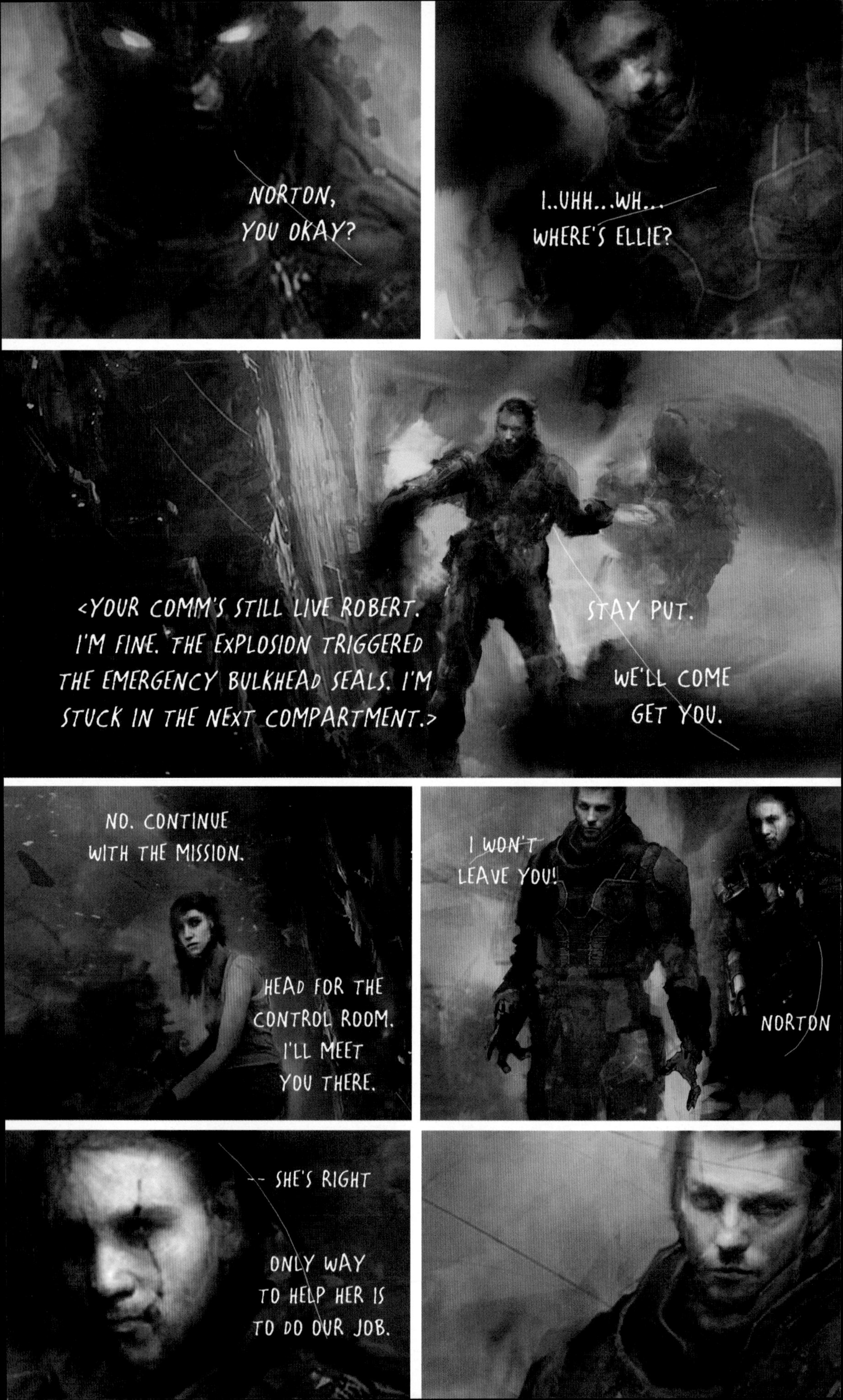
NORTON,
YOU OKAY?
I..UHH...WH...
WHERE'S ELLIE?
<YOUR COMM'S STILL LIVE ROBERT.
STAY PUT.
WE'LL COME GET YOU.
I'M FINE. THE EXPLOSION TRIGGERED THE EMERGENCY BULKHEAD SEALS. I'M STUCK IN THE NEXT COMPARTMENT.>
NO. CONTINUE WITH THE MISSION.
HEAD FOR THE CONTROL ROOM. I'LL MEET YOU THERE.
I WON'T LEAVE YOU!
NORTON
-- SHE'S RIGHT
ONLY WAY TO HELP HER IS TO DO OUR JOB.

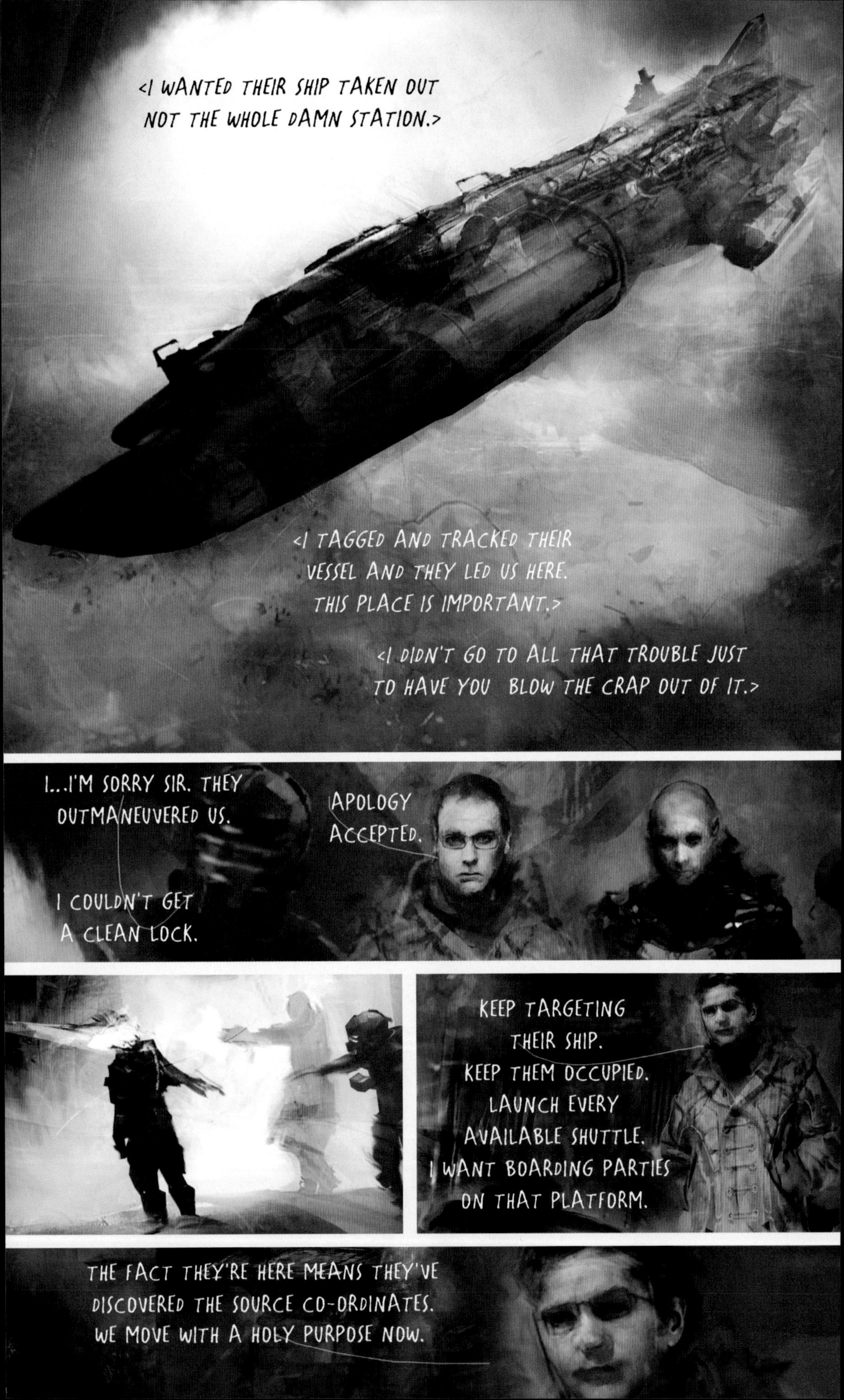

<I WANTED THEIR SHIP TAKEN OUT NOT THE WHOLE DAMN STATION.>
<I TAGGED AND TRACKED THEIR VESSEL AND THEY LED US HERE. THIS PLACE IS IMPORTANT.>
<I DIDN'T GO TO ALL THAT TROUBLE JUST TO HAVE YOU BLOW THE CRAP OUT OF IT.>
I...I'M SORRY SIR. THEY OUTMANEUVERED US.
I COULDN'T GET A CLEAN LOCK.
APOLOGY ACCEPTED.
KEEP TARGETING THEIR SHIP. KEEP THEM OCCUPIED. LAUNCH EVERY AVAILABLE SHUTTLE. I WANT BOARDING PARTIES ON THAT PLATFORM.
THE FACT THEY'RE HERE MEANS THEY'VE DISCOVERED THE SOURCE CO-ORDINATES. WE MOVE WITH A HOLY PURPOSE NOW.

CARVER, I...UH, I OWE YOU AN APOLOGY.

SIR?

YOU WERE STATIONED HERE.

YOU KNOW THE TERRITORY. I SHOULD'VE LISTENED TO YOU.

NO SHIT, TELL THAT TO THE MEN WHO DIED BACK THERE!

WITH RESPECT, SIR. I KILLED MY WIFE AND KID TODAY.

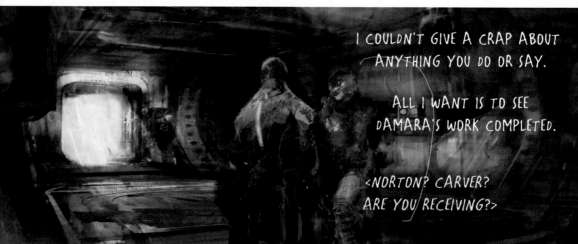

I COULDN'T GIVE A CRAP ABOUT ANYTHING YOU DO OR SAY.

ALL I WANT IS TO SEE DAMARA'S WORK COMPLETED.

<NORTON? CARVER? ARE YOU RECEIVING?>

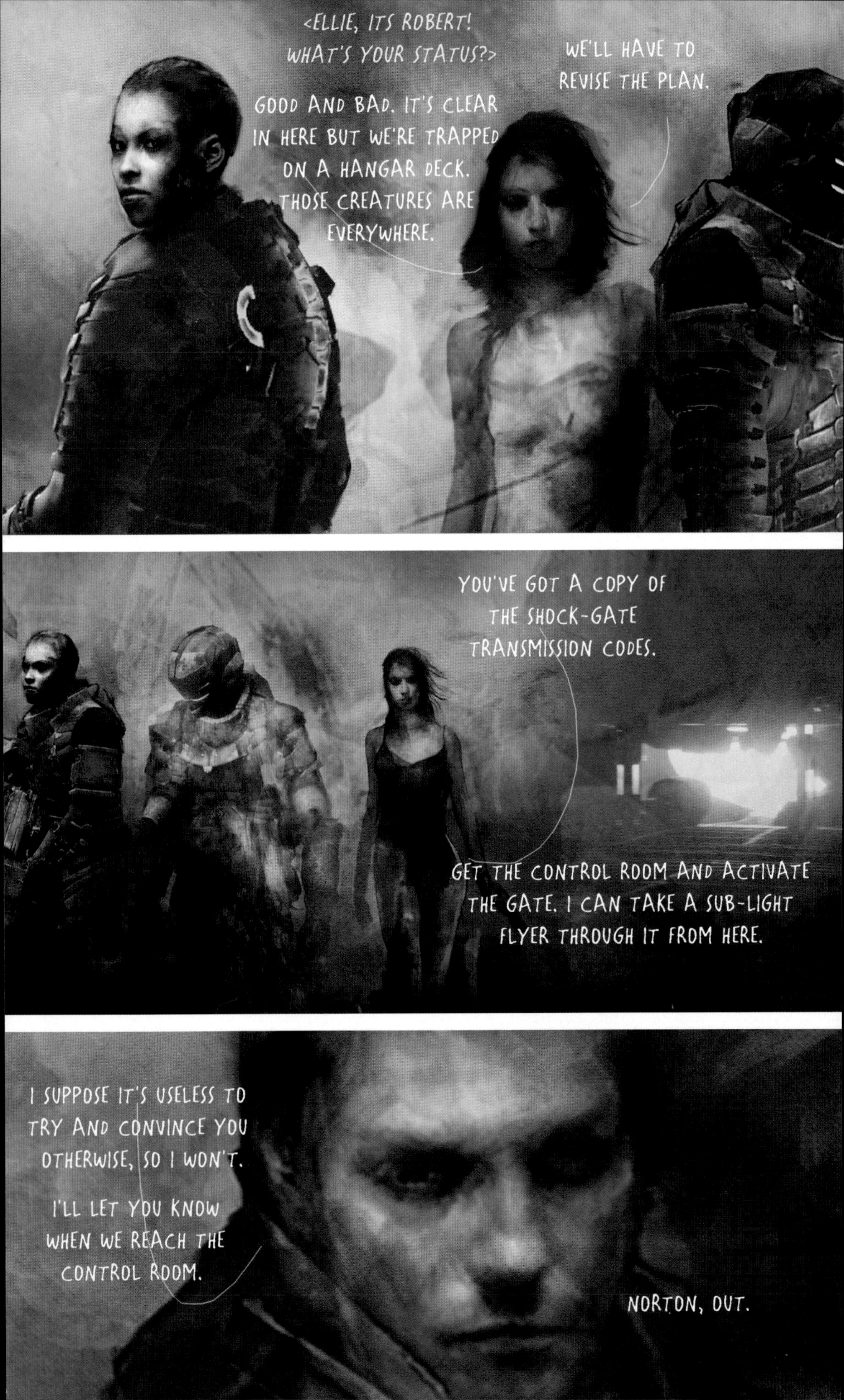

<ELLIE, ITS ROBERT! WHAT'S YOUR STATUS?>
GOOD AND BAD. IT'S CLEAR IN HERE BUT WE'RE TRAPPED ON A HANGAR DECK. THOSE CREATURES ARE EVERYWHERE.
WE'LL HAVE TO REVISE THE PLAN.
YOU'VE GOT A COPY OF THE SHOCK-GATE TRANSMISSION CODES.
GET THE CONTROL ROOM AND ACTIVATE THE GATE. I CAN TAKE A SUB-LIGHT FLYER THROUGH IT FROM HERE.
I SUPPOSE IT'S USELESS TO TRY AND CONVINCE YOU OTHERWISE, SO I WON'T.
I'LL LET YOU KNOW WHEN WE REACH THE CONTROL ROOM.
NORTON, OUT.

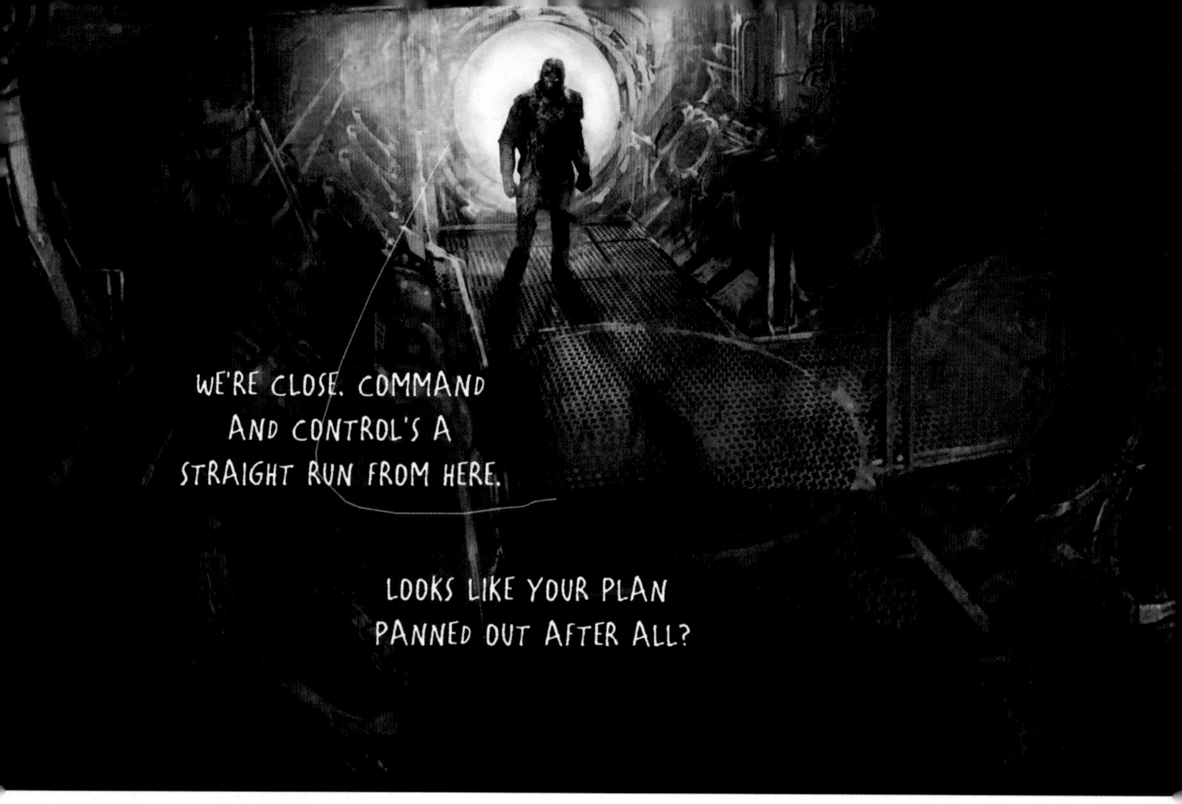
WE'RE CLOSE. COMMAND AND CONTROL'S A STRAIGHT RUN FROM HERE.
LOOKS LIKE YOUR PLAN PANNED OUT AFTER ALL?

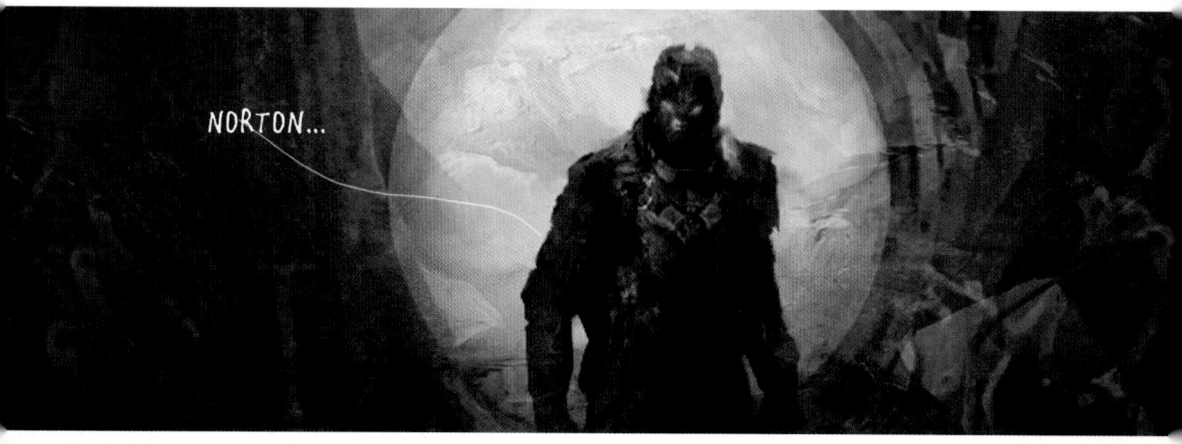
NORTON...

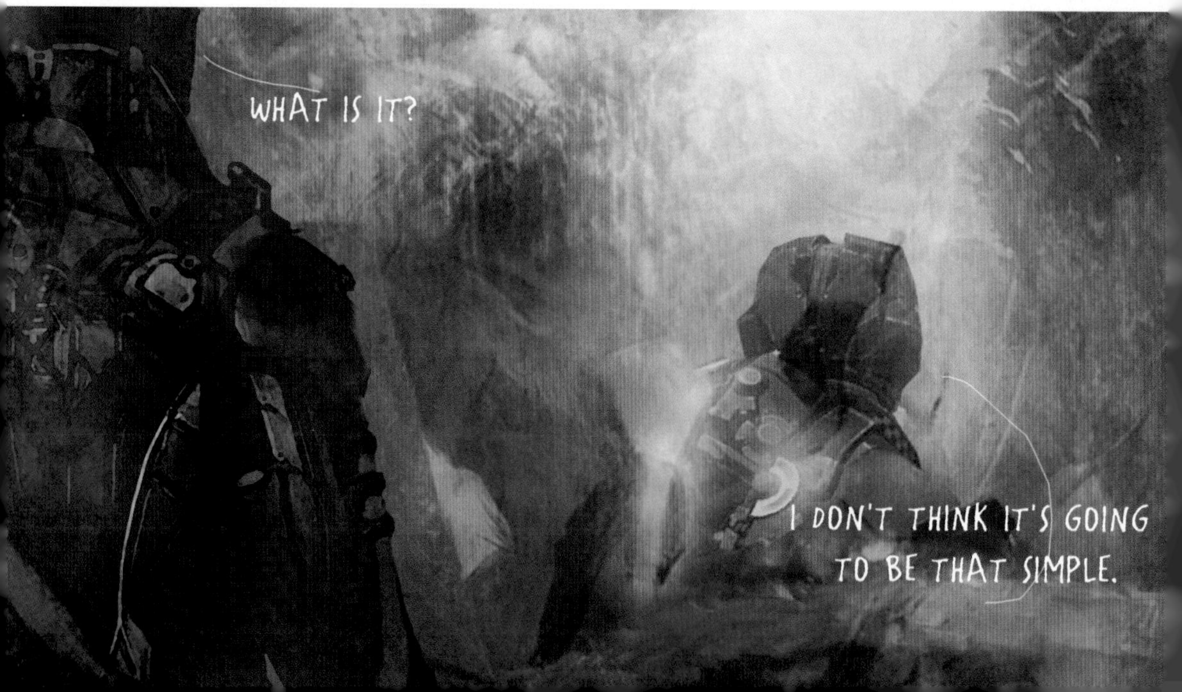
WHAT IS IT?
I DON'T THINK IT'S GOING TO BE THAT SIMPLE.

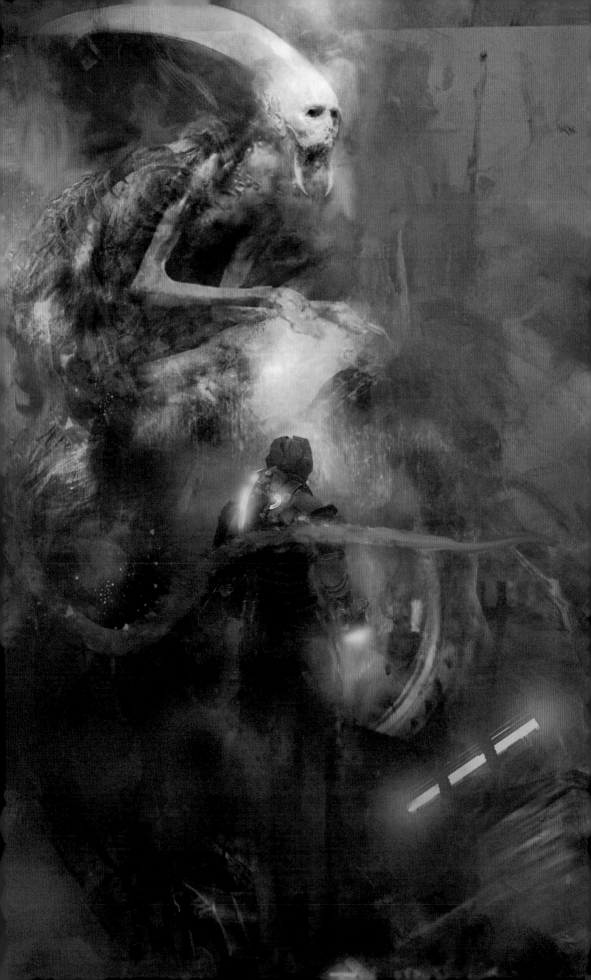

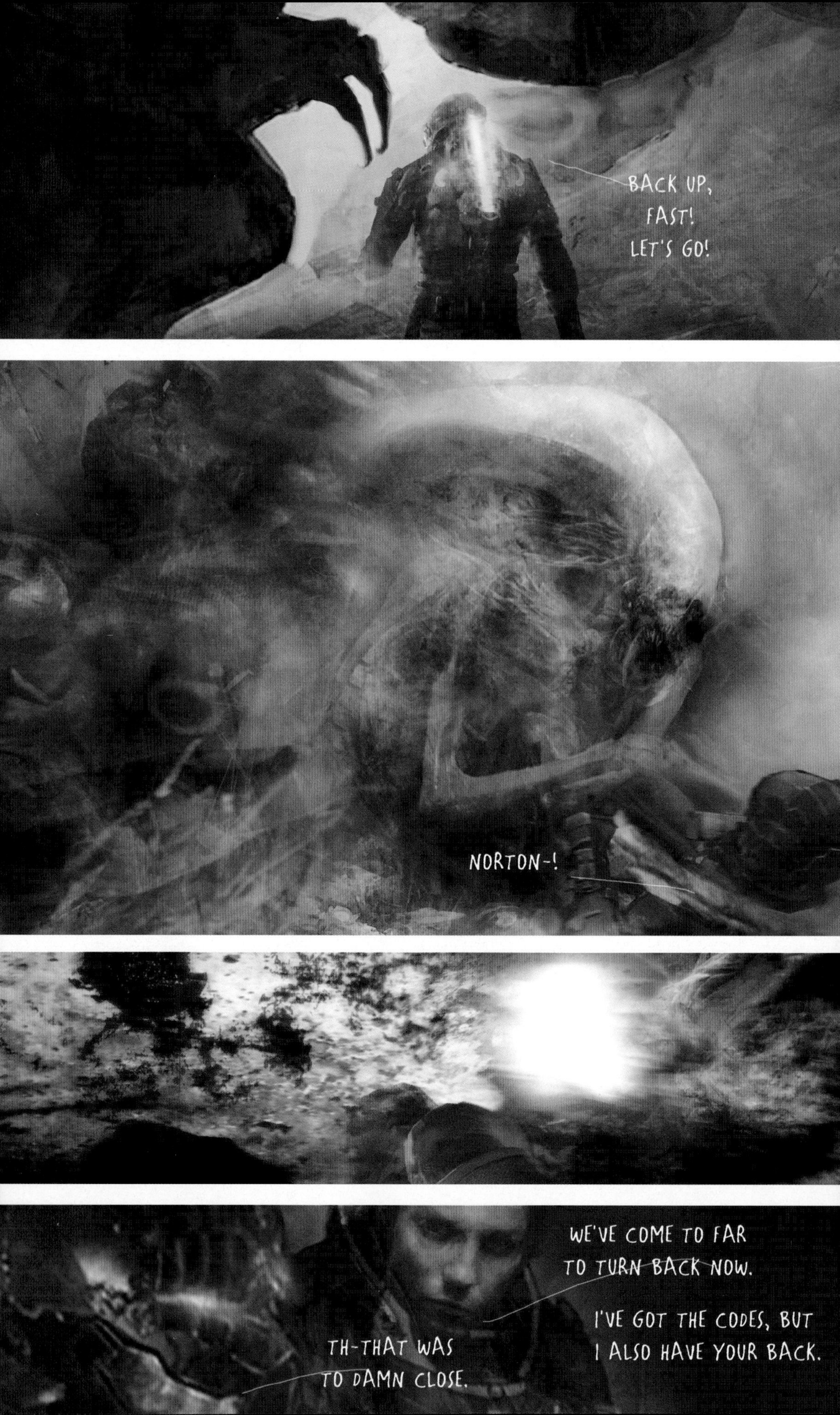
BACK UP, FAST! LET'S GO!
NORTON-!
WE'VE COME TO FAR TO TURN BACK NOW.
I'VE GOT THE CODES, BUT I ALSO HAVE YOUR BACK.
TH-THAT WAS TO DAMN CLOSE.

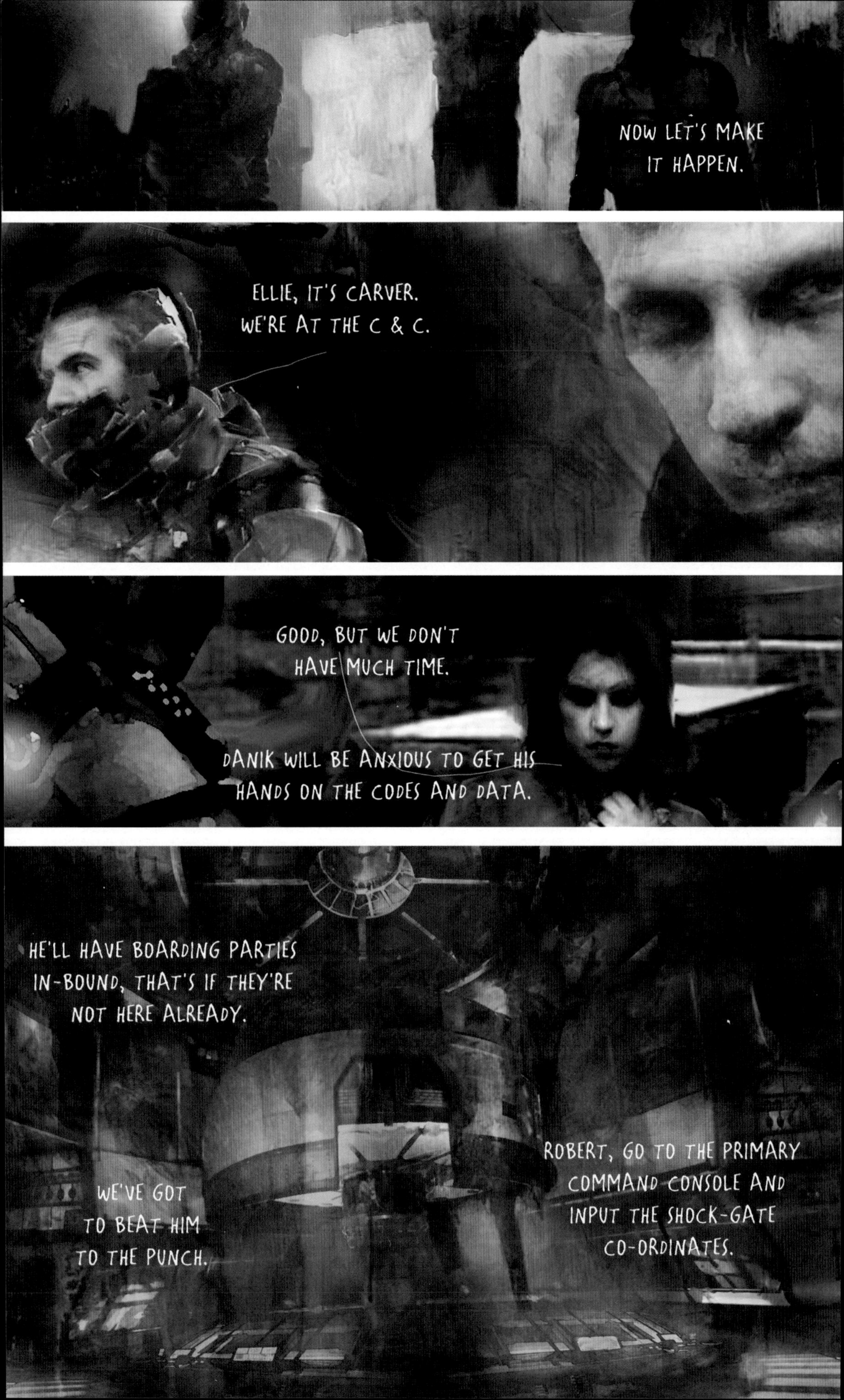
NOW LET'S MAKE IT HAPPEN.
ELLIE, IT'S CARVER. WE'RE AT THE C & C.
GOOD, BUT WE DON'T HAVE MUCH TIME.
DANIK WILL BE ANXIOUS TO GET HIS HANDS ON THE CODES AND DATA.
HE'LL HAVE BOARDING PARTIES IN-BOUND, THAT'S IF THEY'RE NOT HERE ALREADY.
WE'VE GOT TO BEAT HIM TO THE PUNCH.
ROBERT, GO TO THE PRIMARY COMMAND CONSOLE AND INPUT THE SHOCK-GATE CO-ORDINATES.

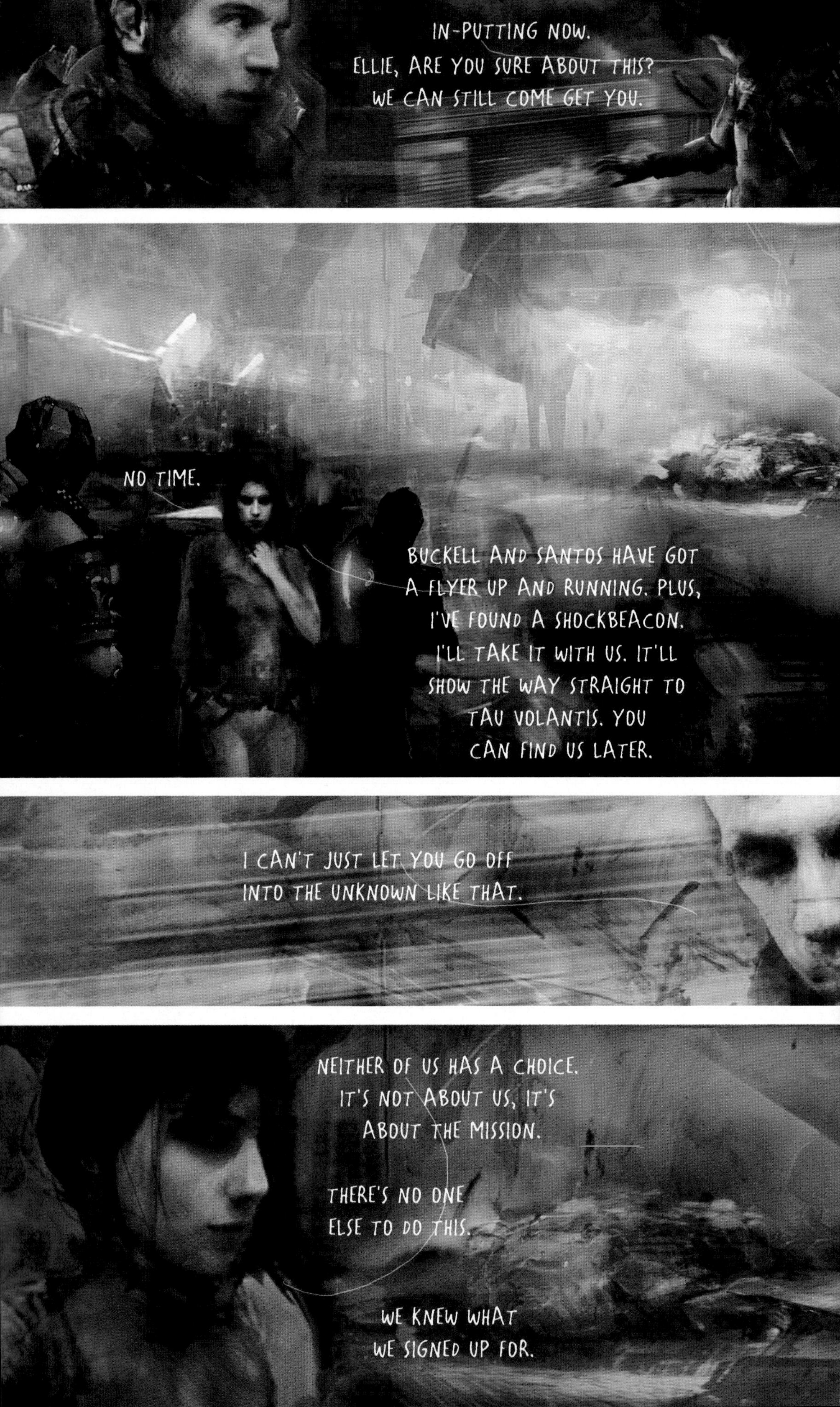

IN-PUTTING NOW.
ELLIE, ARE YOU SURE ABOUT THIS? WE CAN STILL COME GET YOU.
NO TIME.
BUCKELL AND SANTOS HAVE GOT A FLYER UP AND RUNNING. PLUS, I'VE FOUND A SHOCKBEACON. I'LL TAKE IT WITH US. IT'LL SHOW THE WAY STRAIGHT TO TAU VOLANTIS. YOU CAN FIND US LATER.
I CAN'T JUST LET YOU GO OFF INTO THE UNKNOWN LIKE THAT.
NEITHER OF US HAS A CHOICE. IT'S NOT ABOUT US, IT'S ABOUT THE MISSION.
THERE'S NO ONE ELSE TO DO THIS.
WE KNEW WHAT WE SIGNED UP FOR.

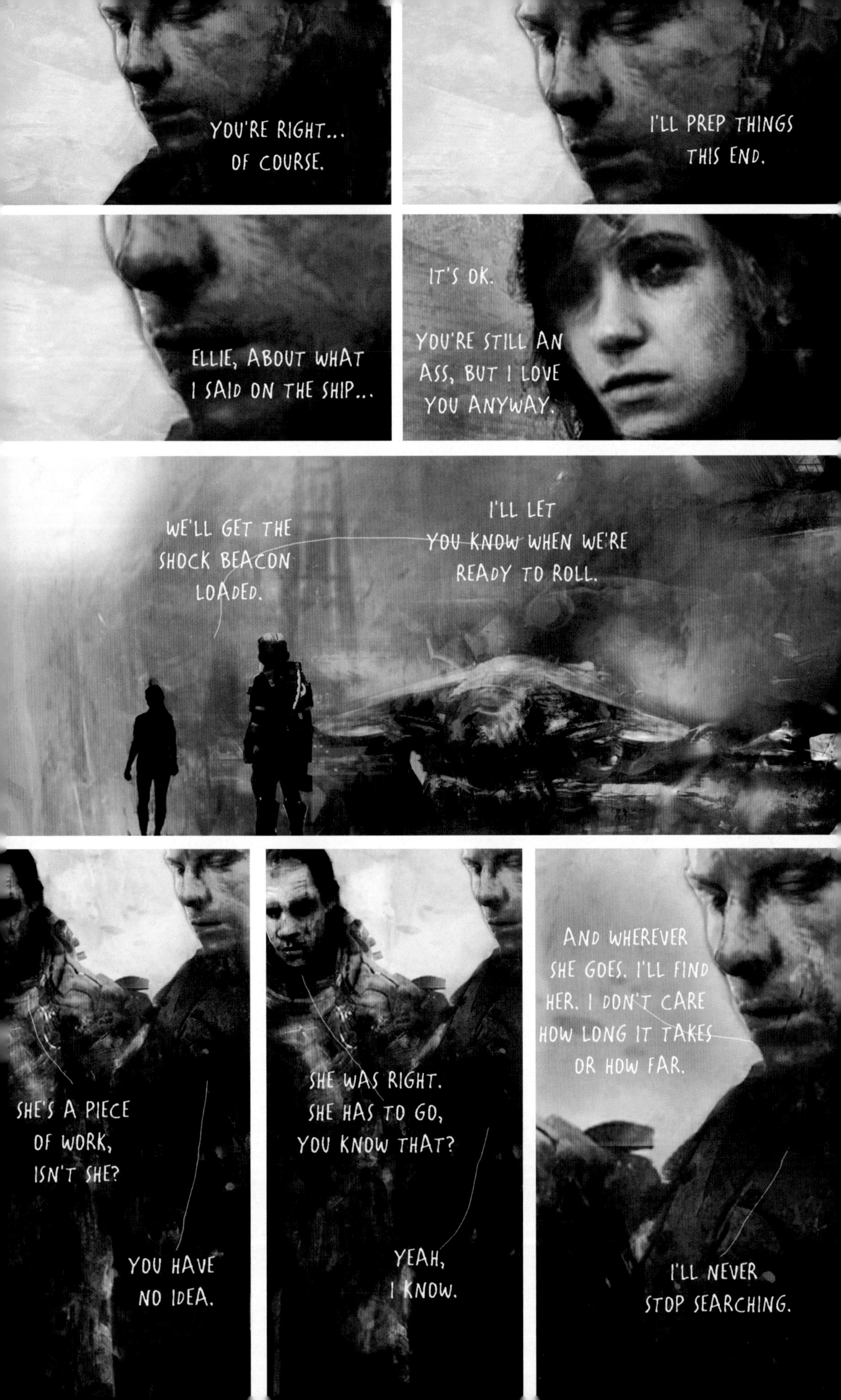
YOU'RE RIGHT... OF COURSE.
I'LL PREP THINGS THIS END.
ELLIE, ABOUT WHAT I SAID ON THE SHIP...
IT'S OK.
YOU'RE STILL AN ASS, BUT I LOVE YOU ANYWAY.
WE'LL GET THE SHOCK BEACON LOADED.
I'LL LET YOU KNOW WHEN WE'RE READY TO ROLL.
SHE'S A PIECE OF WORK, ISN'T SHE?
YOU HAVE NO IDEA.
SHE WAS RIGHT. SHE HAS TO GO, YOU KNOW THAT?
YEAH, I KNOW.
AND WHEREVER SHE GOES. I'LL FIND HER. I DON'T CARE HOW LONG IT TAKES OR HOW FAR.
I'LL NEVER STOP SEARCHING.

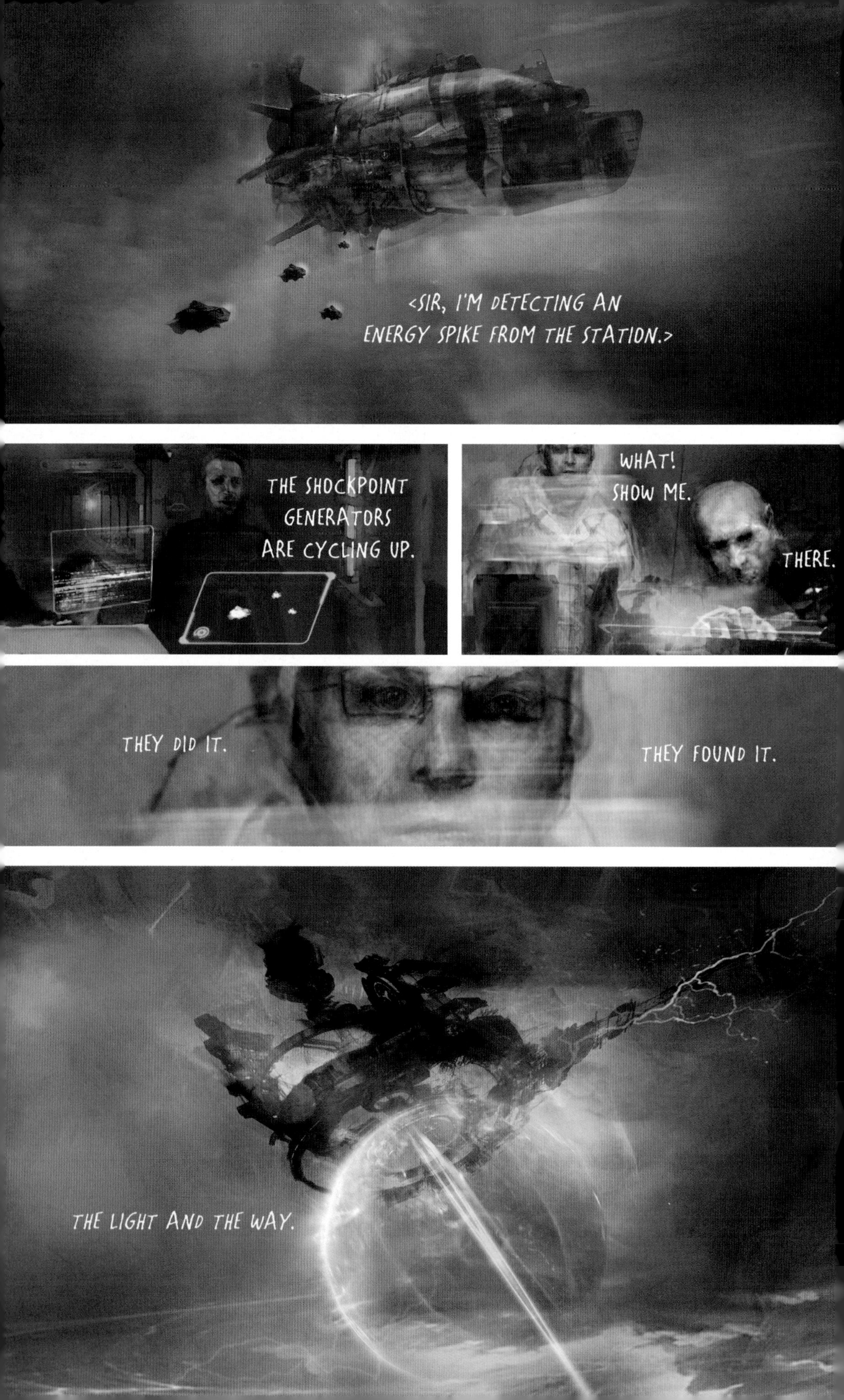
<SIR, I'M DETECTING AN ENERGY SPIKE FROM THE STATION.>
THE SHOCKPOINT GENERATORS ARE CYCLING UP.
WHAT! SHOW ME.
THERE.
THEY DID IT.
THEY FOUND IT.
THE LIGHT AND THE WAY.

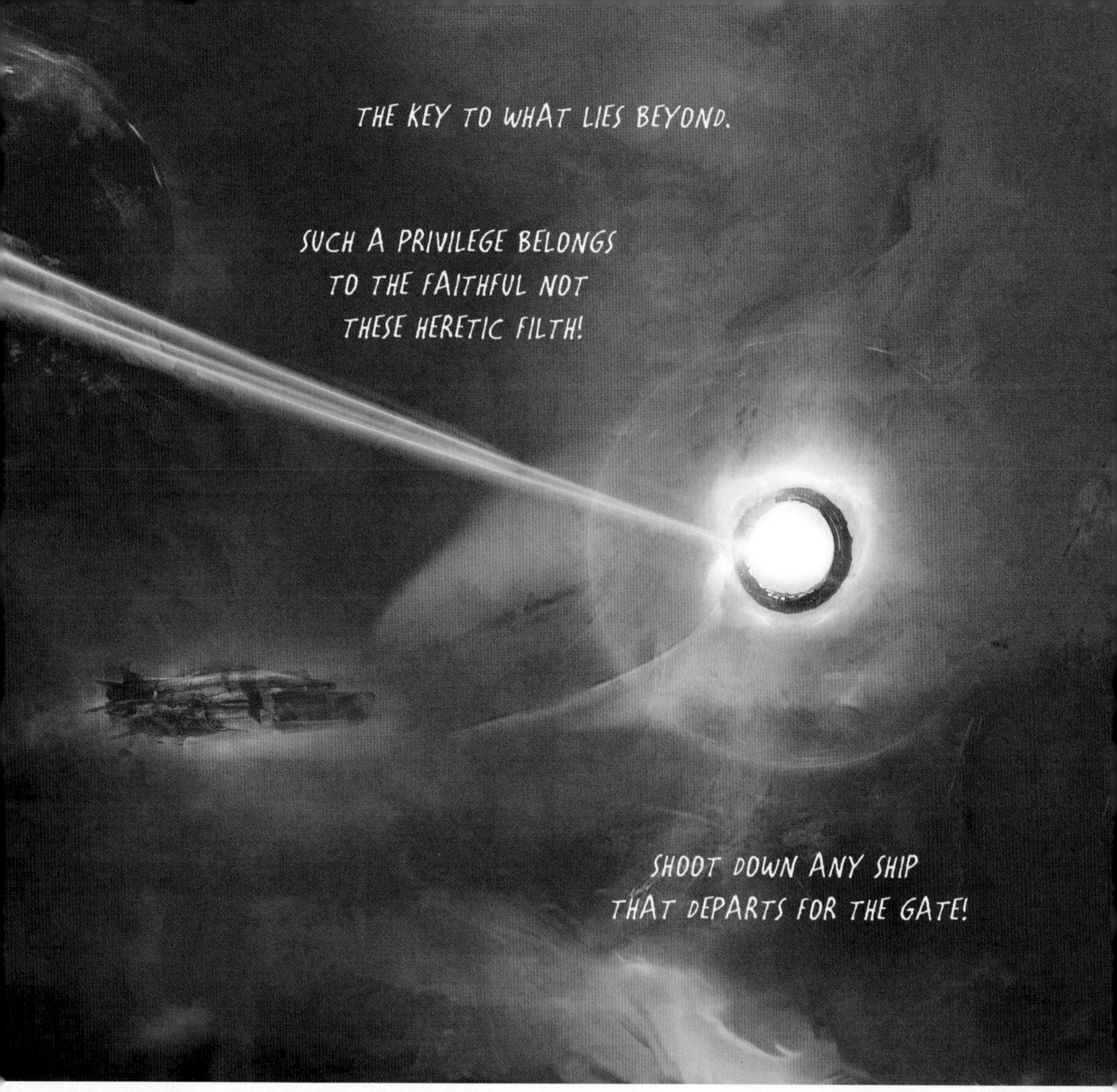
THE KEY TO WHAT LIES BEYOND.
SUCH A PRIVILEGE BELONGS TO THE FAITHFUL NOT THESE HERETIC FILTH!
SHOOT DOWN ANY SHIP THAT DEPARTS FOR THE GATE!
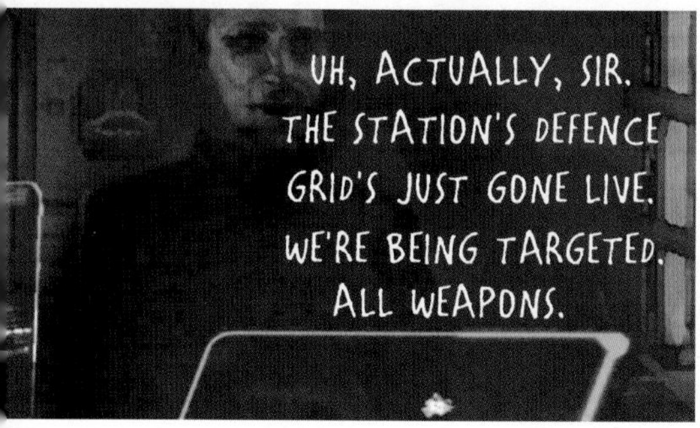
UH, ACTUALLY, SIR. THE STATION'S DEFENCE GRID'S JUST GONE LIVE. WE'RE BEING TARGETED. ALL WEAPONS.
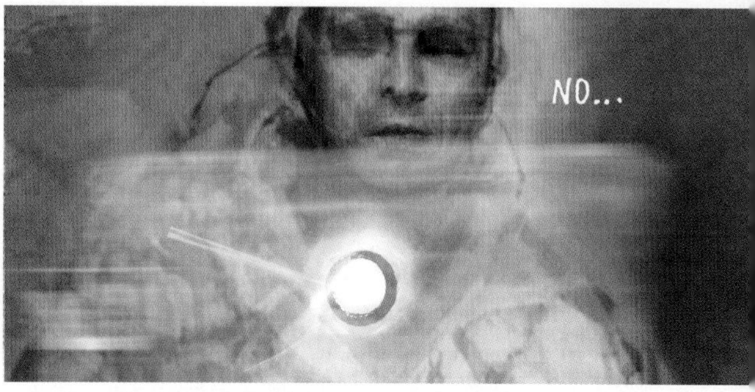
NO...
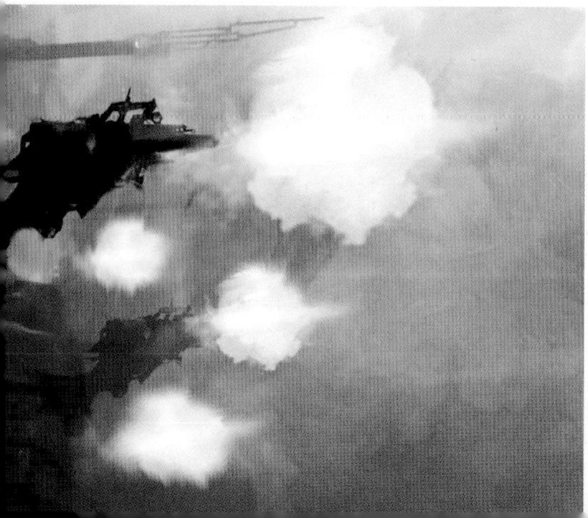
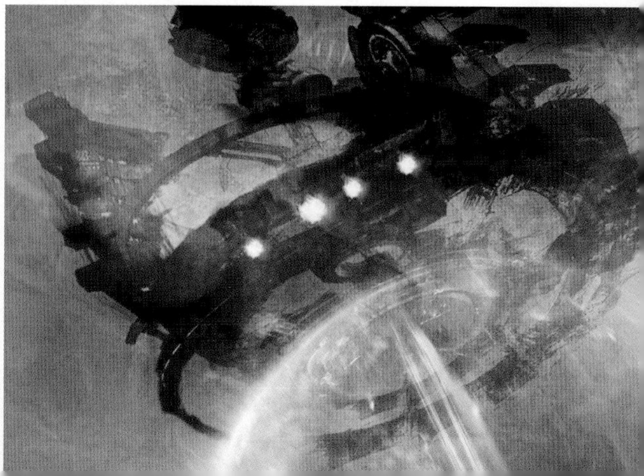

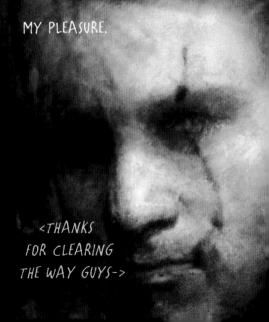

NICE WORK.

MY PLEASURE.

<THANKS
FOR CLEARING
THE WAY GUYS->

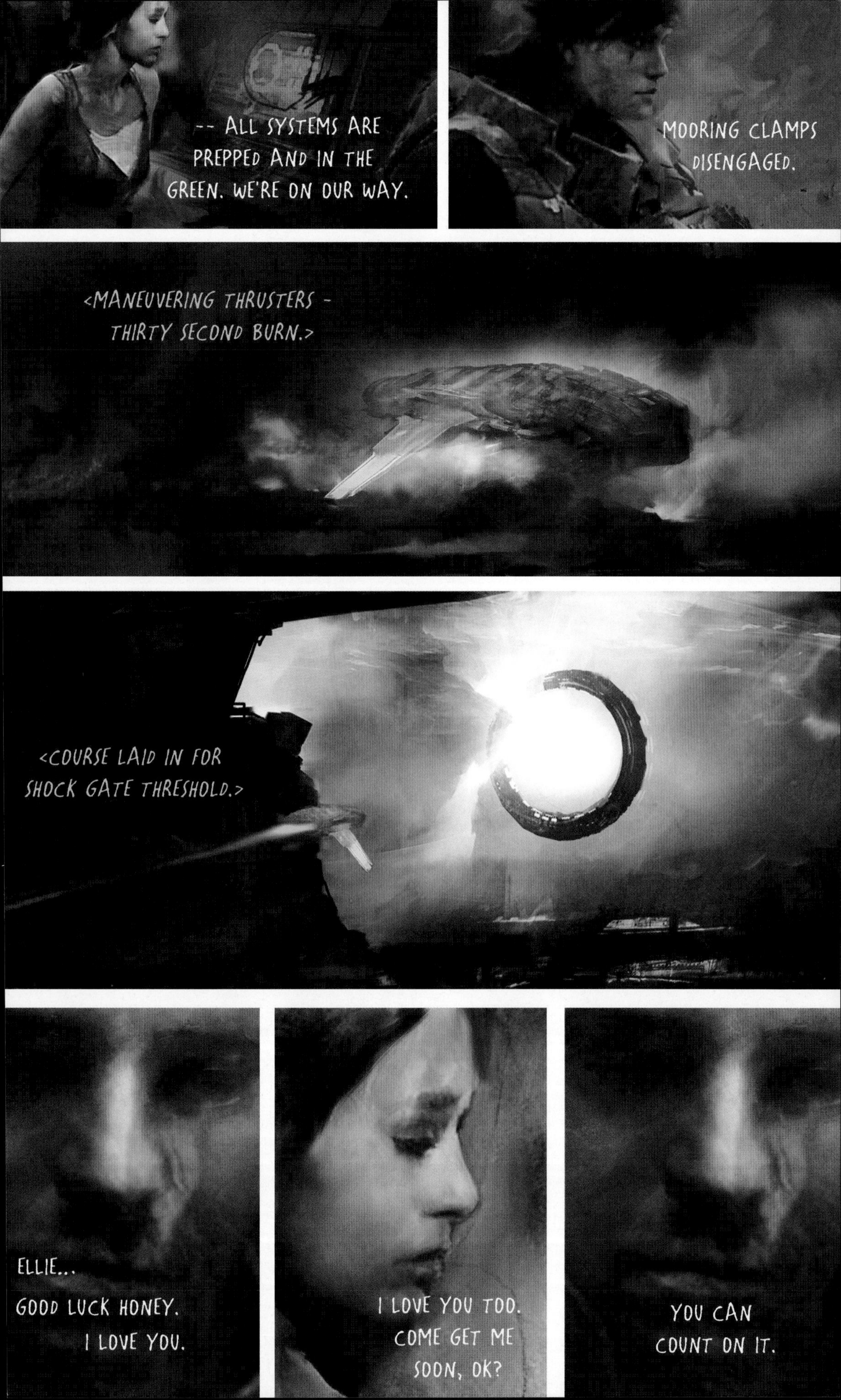
-- ALL SYSTEMS ARE PREPPED AND IN THE GREEN. WE'RE ON OUR WAY.
MOORING CLAMPS DISENGAGED.
<MANEUVERING THRUSTERS - THIRTY SECOND BURN.>
<COURSE LAID IN FOR SHOCK GATE THRESHOLD.>
ELLIE...
GOOD LUCK HONEY.
I LOVE YOU.
I LOVE YOU TOO.
COME GET ME SOON, OK?
YOU CAN COUNT ON IT.

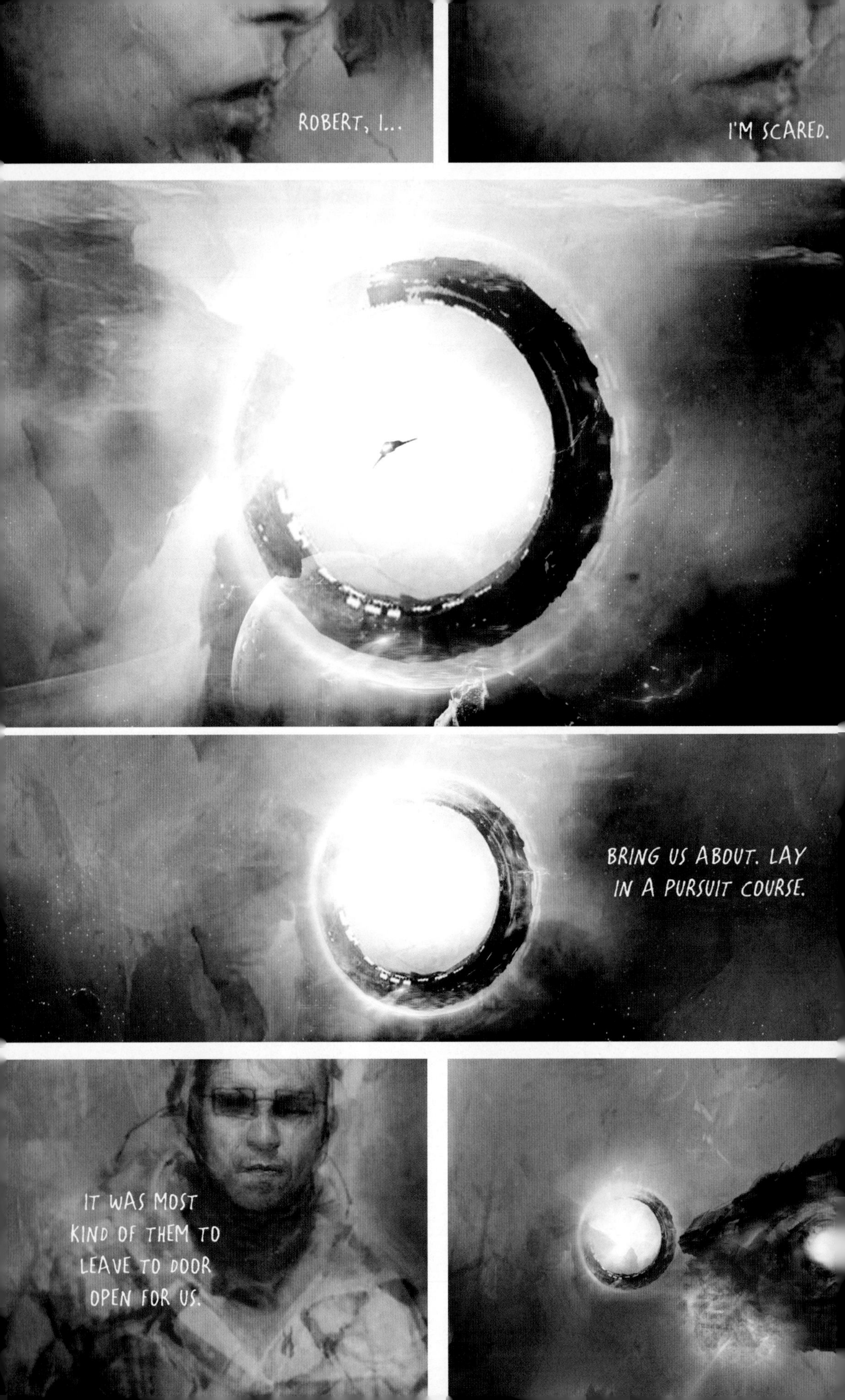

ROBERT, I...
I'M SCARED.
BRING US ABOUT. LAY IN A PURSUIT COURSE.
IT WAS MOST KIND OF THEM TO LEAVE TO DOOR OPEN FOR US.

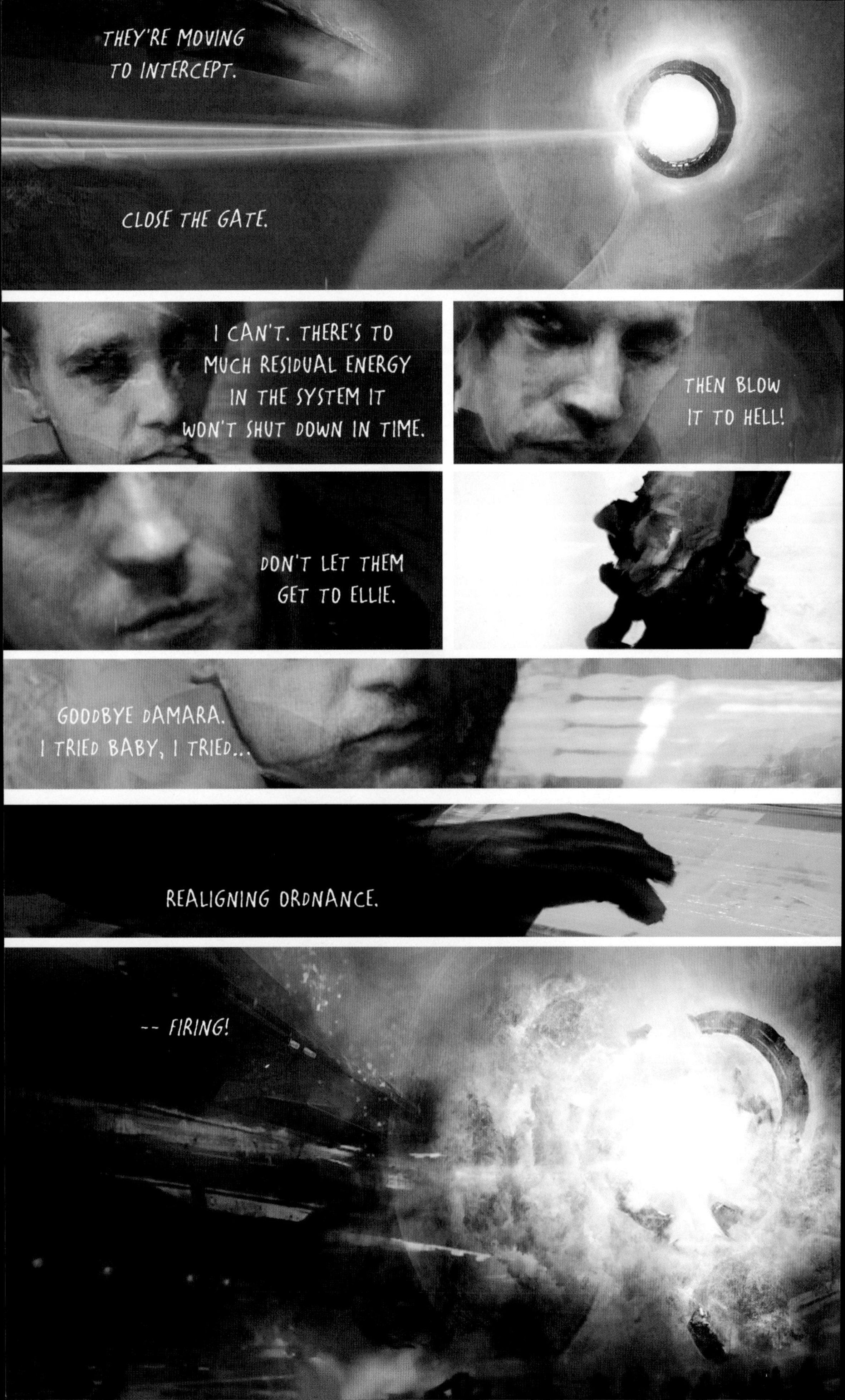
THEY'RE MOVING TO INTERCEPT.
CLOSE THE GATE.
I CAN'T. THERE'S TO MUCH RESIDUAL ENERGY IN THE SYSTEM IT WON'T SHUT DOWN IN TIME.
THEN BLOW IT TO HELL!
DON'T LET THEM GET TO ELLIE.
GOODBYE DAMARA. I TRIED BABY, I TRIED...
REALIGNING ORDNANCE.
-- FIRING!

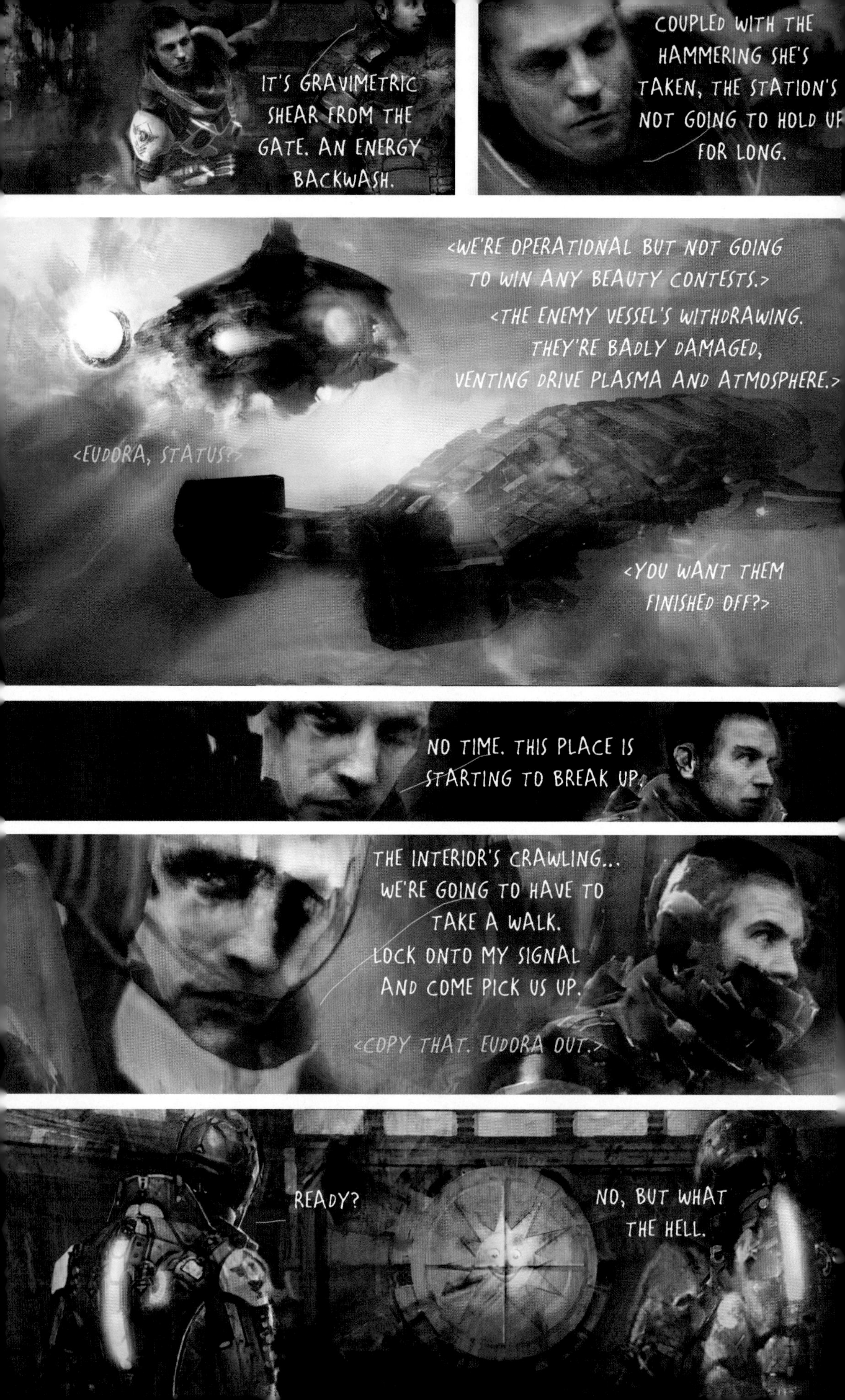

IT'S GRAVIMETRIC SHEAR FROM THE GATE. AN ENERGY BACKWASH.
COUPLED WITH THE HAMMERING SHE'S TAKEN, THE STATION'S NOT GOING TO HOLD UP FOR LONG.
<EUDORA, STATUS?>
<WE'RE OPERATIONAL BUT NOT GOING TO WIN ANY BEAUTY CONTESTS.>
<THE ENEMY VESSEL'S WITHDRAWING. THEY'RE BADLY DAMAGED, VENTING DRIVE PLASMA AND ATMOSPHERE.>
<YOU WANT THEM FINISHED OFF?>
NO TIME. THIS PLACE IS STARTING TO BREAK UP.
THE INTERIOR'S CRAWLING... WE'RE GOING TO HAVE TO TAKE A WALK. LOCK ONTO MY SIGNAL AND COME PICK US UP.
<COPY THAT. EUDORA OUT.>
READY?
NO, BUT WHAT THE HELL.

ACTIVATE YOUR MAGNETIC GRAPPLES!
CARVER, YOU OK?
YEAH. JUST TRYING TO HOLD ONTO MY LUNCH.
I FORGOT WHY I HATED ZERO-G COMBAT TRAINING SO MUCH.
NORTON TO EUDORA, WE'RE OUT!

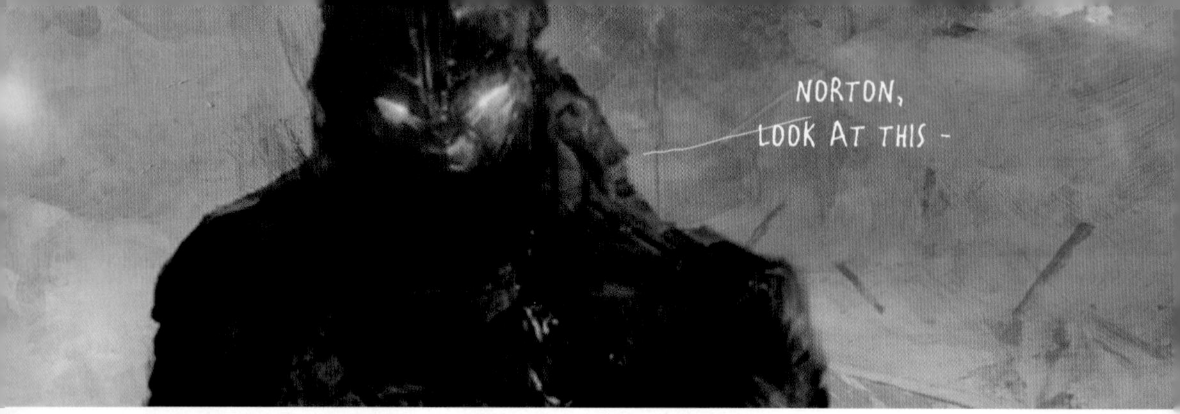
NORTON,
LOOK AT THIS -

BETWEEN US AND THE ENERGY WAKE FROM THE GATE, I GUESS WE BROKE THEM!
MY GOD! THE UNITOLOGIST'S SHIP!
TOO BAD, I WAS LOOKING FORWARD TO PERSONALLY EMPTYING A CLIP INTO DANI

THAT SAID, I DON'T THINK THIS PLACE IS GOING TO STAY IN ONE PIECE MUCH LONGER.

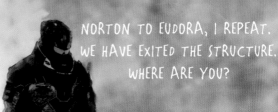

NORTON TO EUDORA, I REPEAT. WE HAVE EXITED THE STRUCTURE. WHERE ARE YOU?

<WE'RE IN-BOUND ON YOUR MARK, SIR.>

<BUT THE GRAVIMETRIC DISTORTION'S MAKING IT HARD TO MANEUVER THIS CLOSE TO THE STRUCTURE.>

<SKRRKKK>

<THE STATION'S BREAKING UP.>

TELL US SOMETHING WE DON'T KNOW.

<SKRRKKK>

<EUDORA TO NORTON. WE HAVE YOU ON VISUAL. STAND-BY.>

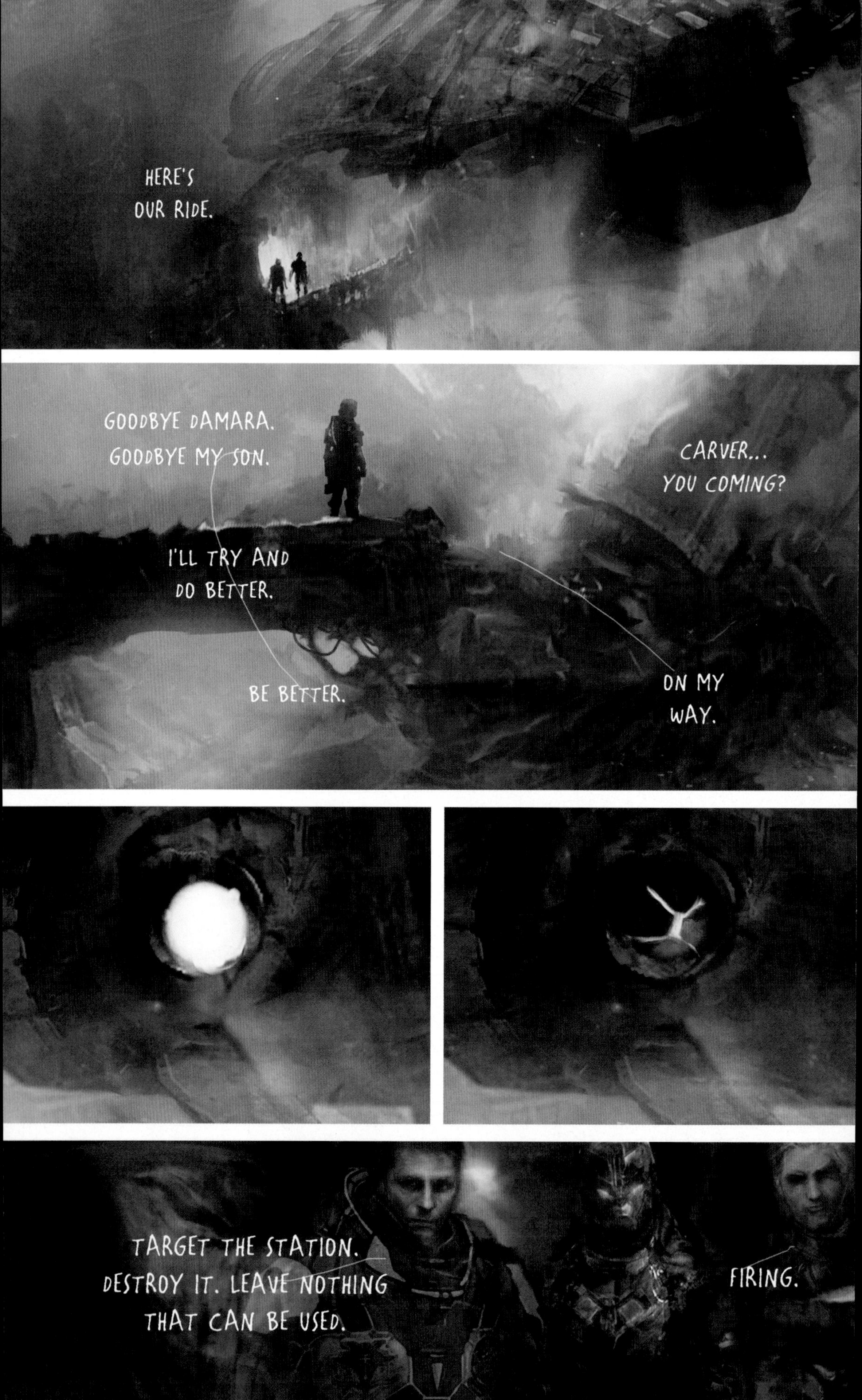
HERE'S OUR RIDE.
GOODBYE DAMARA. GOODBYE MY SON.
I'LL TRY AND DO BETTER.
BE BETTER.
CARVER... YOU COMING?
ON MY WAY.
TARGET THE STATION. DESTROY IT. LEAVE NOTHING THAT CAN BE USED.
FIRING.

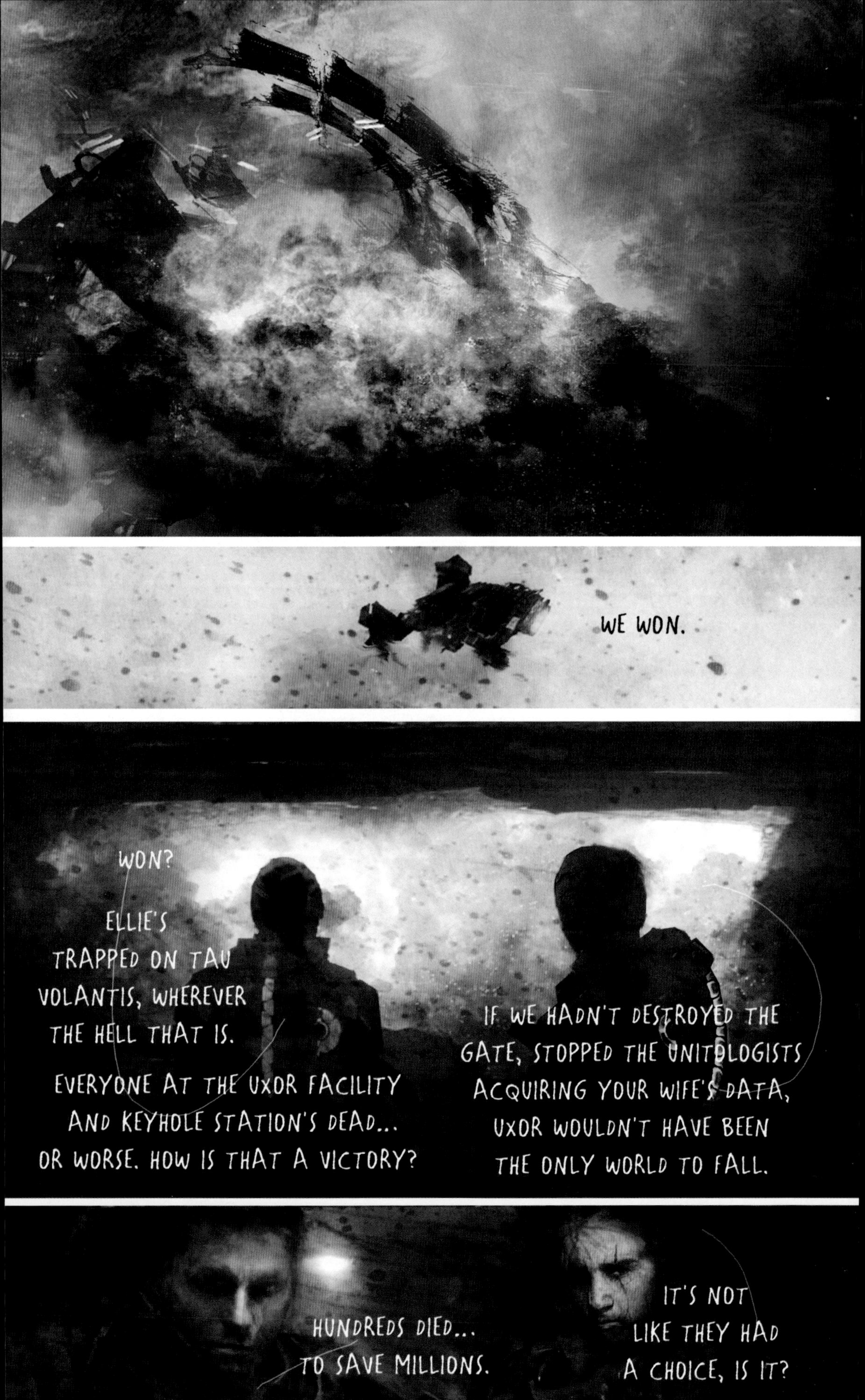
WE WON.
WON?
ELLIE'S TRAPPED ON TAU VOLANTIS, WHEREVER THE HELL THAT IS.
EVERYONE AT THE UXOR FACILITY AND KEYHOLE STATION'S DEAD... OR WORSE. HOW IS THAT A VICTORY?
IF WE HADN'T DESTROYED THE GATE, STOPPED THE UNITOLOGISTS ACQUIRING YOUR WIFE'S DATA, UXOR WOULDN'T HAVE BEEN THE ONLY WORLD TO FALL.
HUNDREDS DIED... TO SAVE MILLIONS.
IT'S NOT LIKE THEY HAD A CHOICE, IS IT?

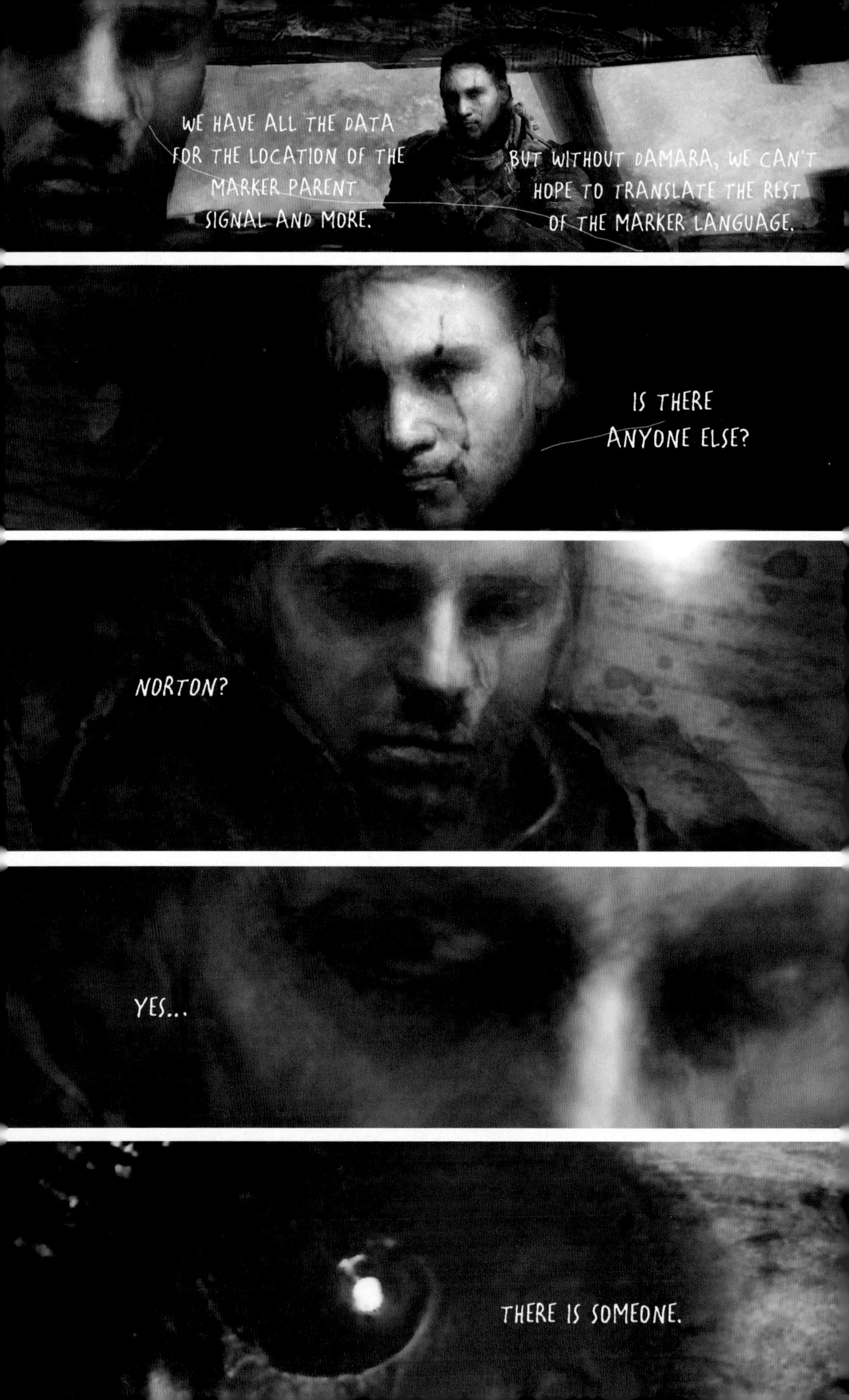
WE HAVE ALL THE DATA FOR THE LOCATION OF THE MARKER PARENT SIGNAL AND MORE.
BUT WITHOUT DAMARA, WE CAN'T HOPE TO TRANSLATE THE REST OF THE MARKER LANGUAGE.
IS THERE ANYONE ELSE?
NORTON?
YES...
THERE IS SOMEONE.

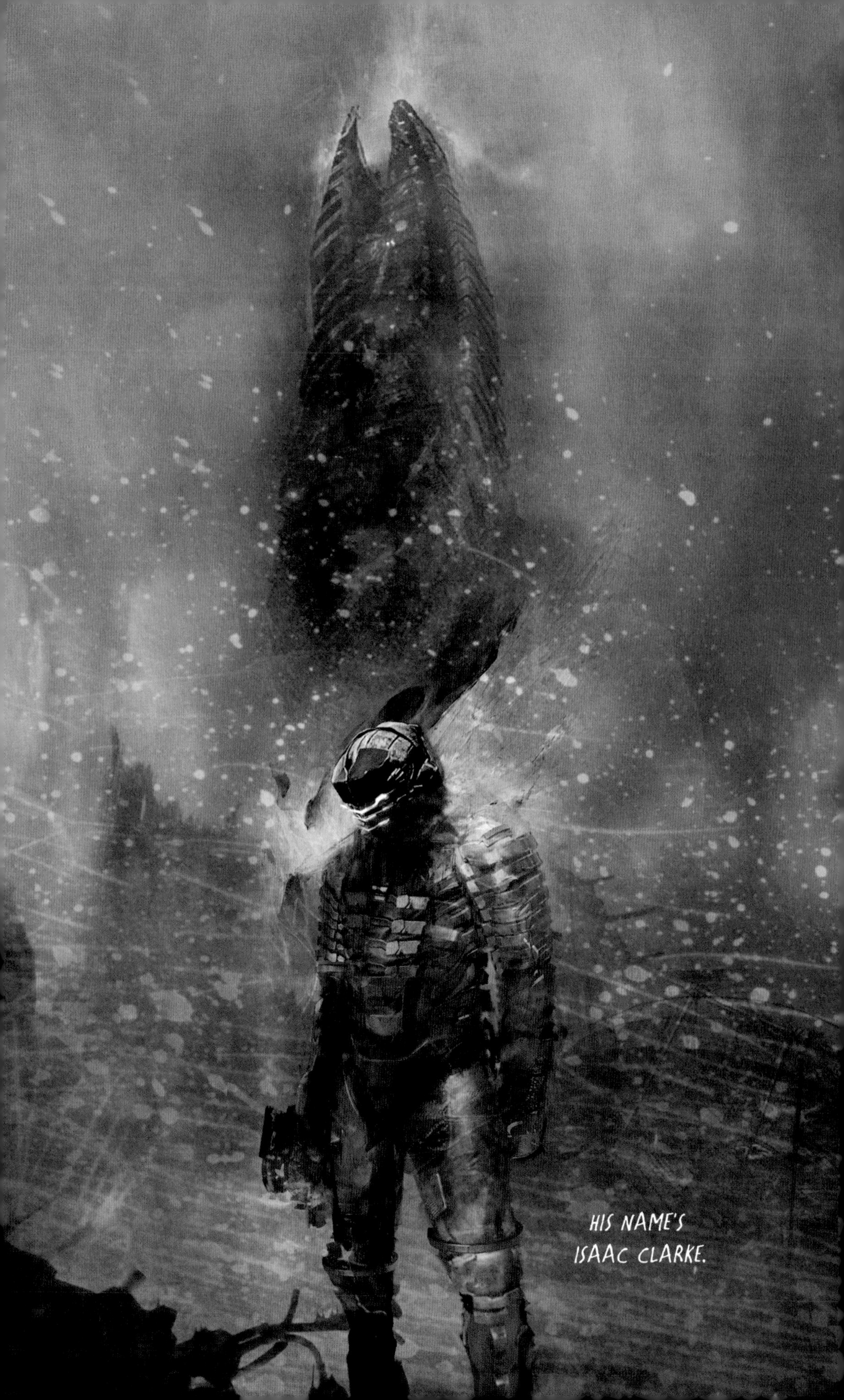
HIS NAME'S
ISAAC CLARKE.

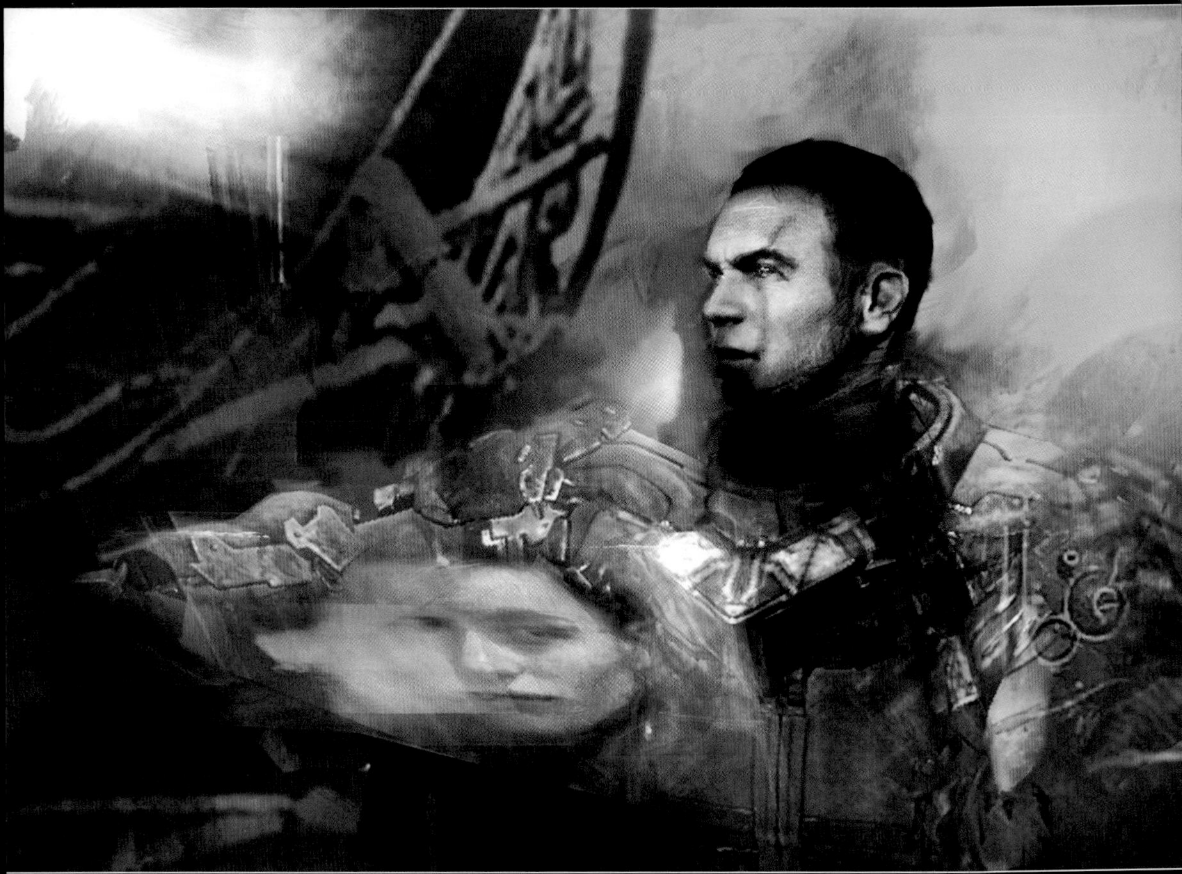

DEAD SPACE LIBERATION GALLERY

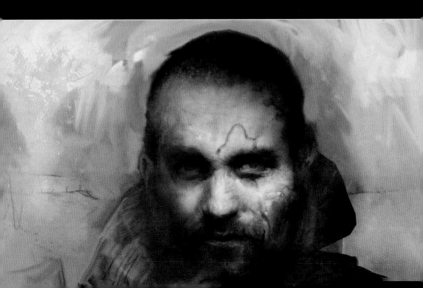

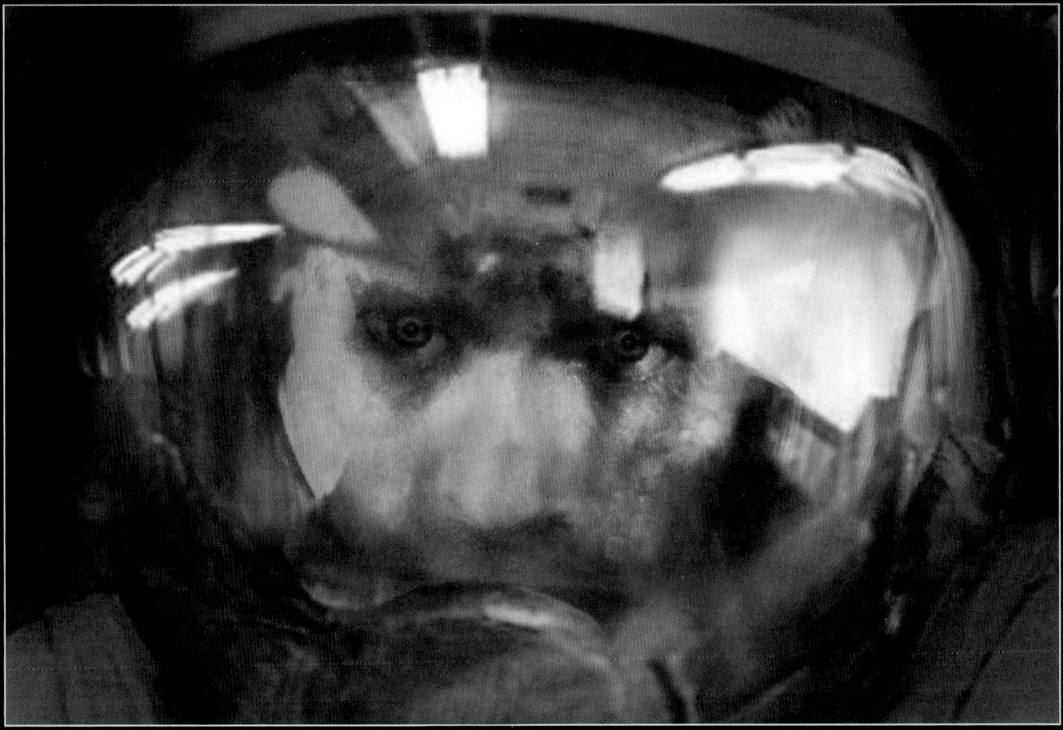

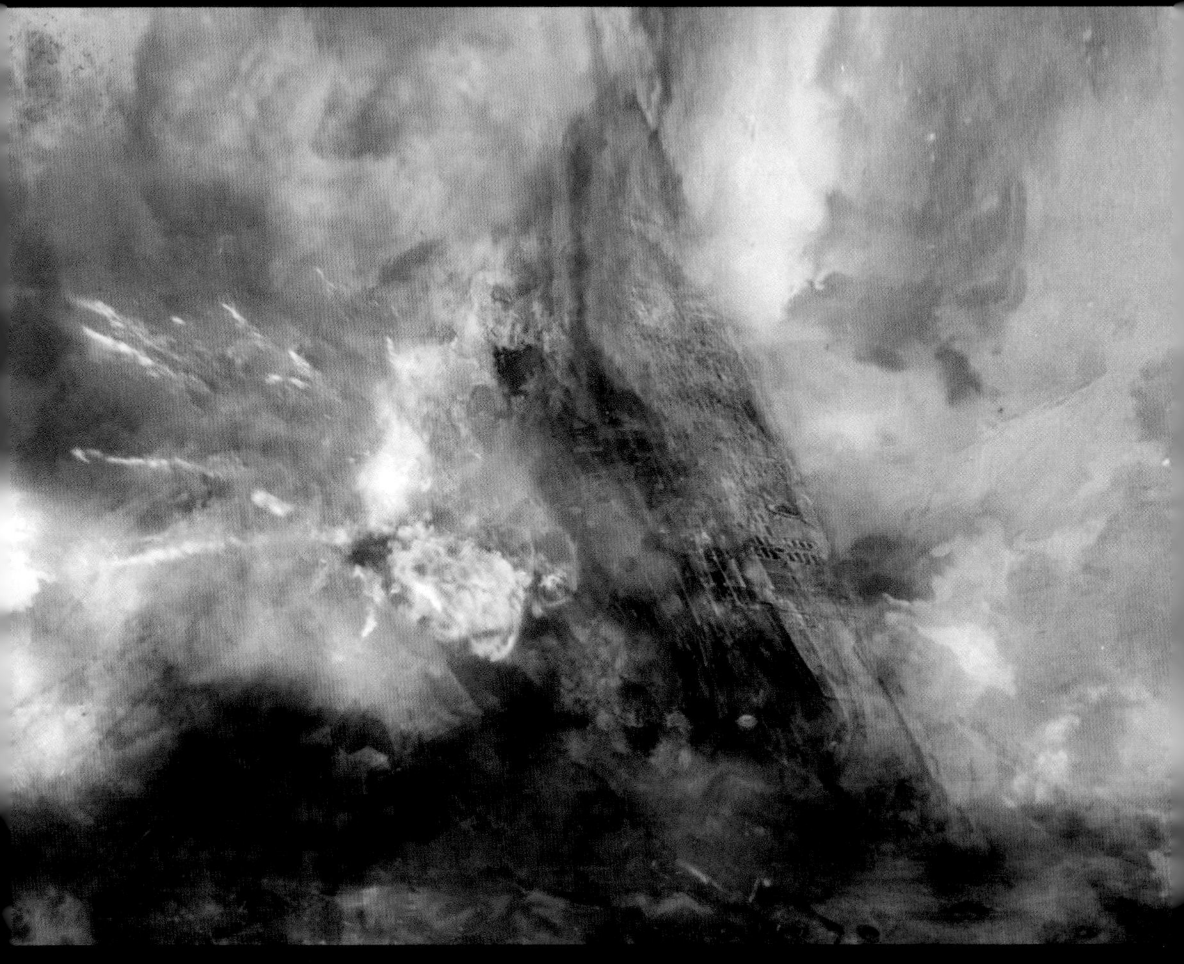

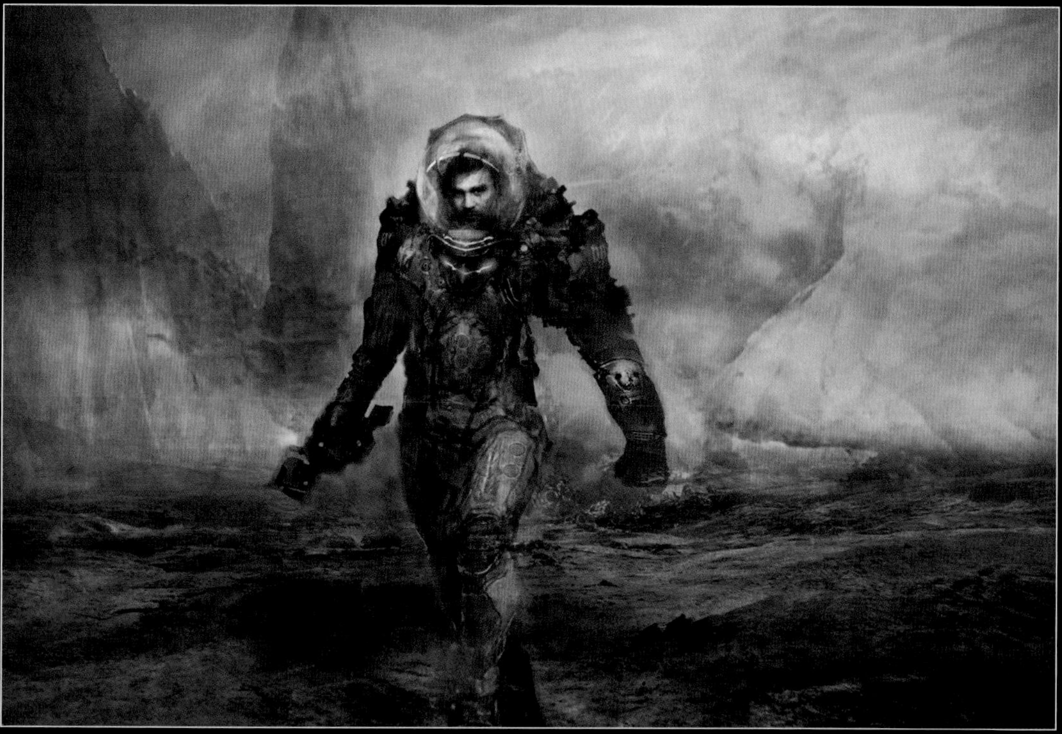

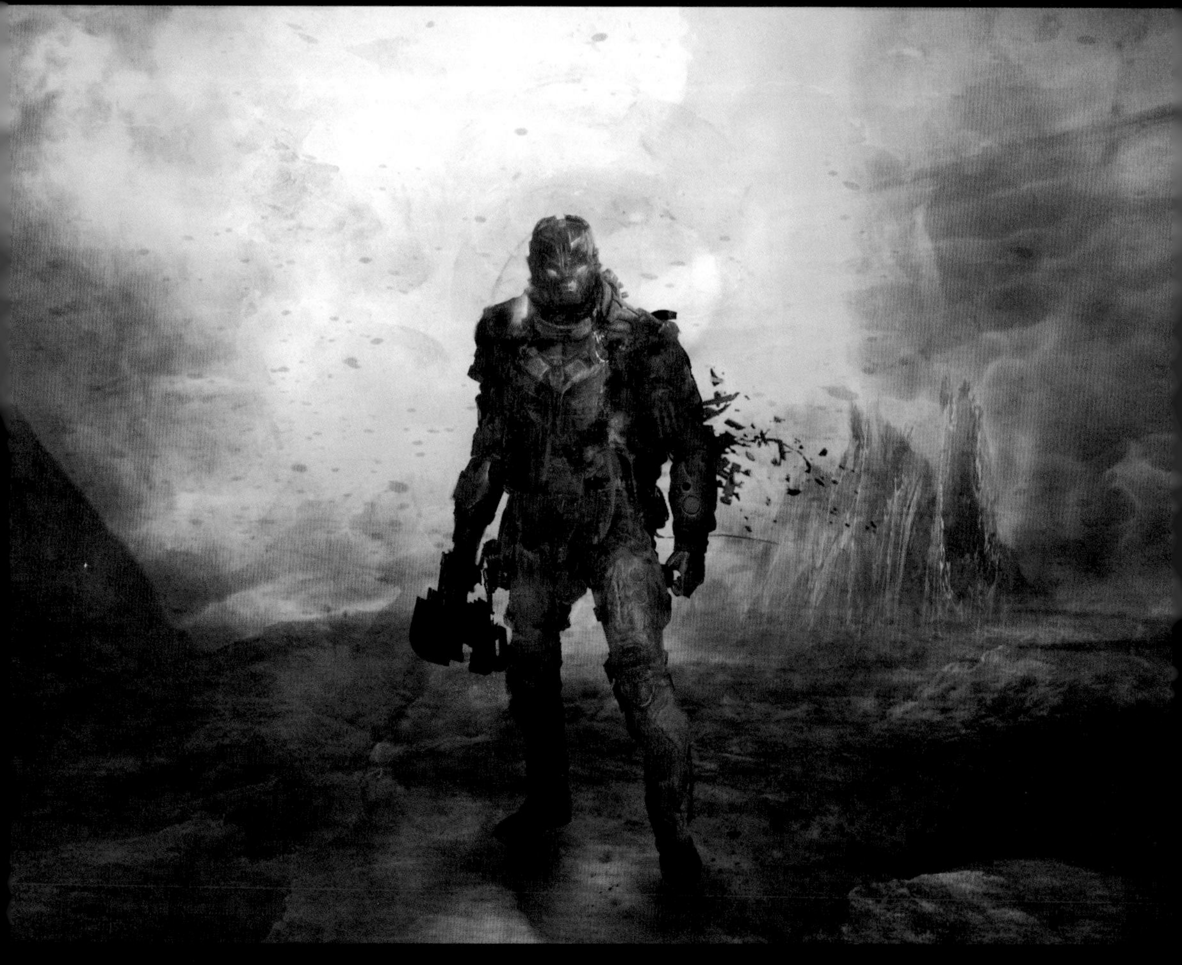

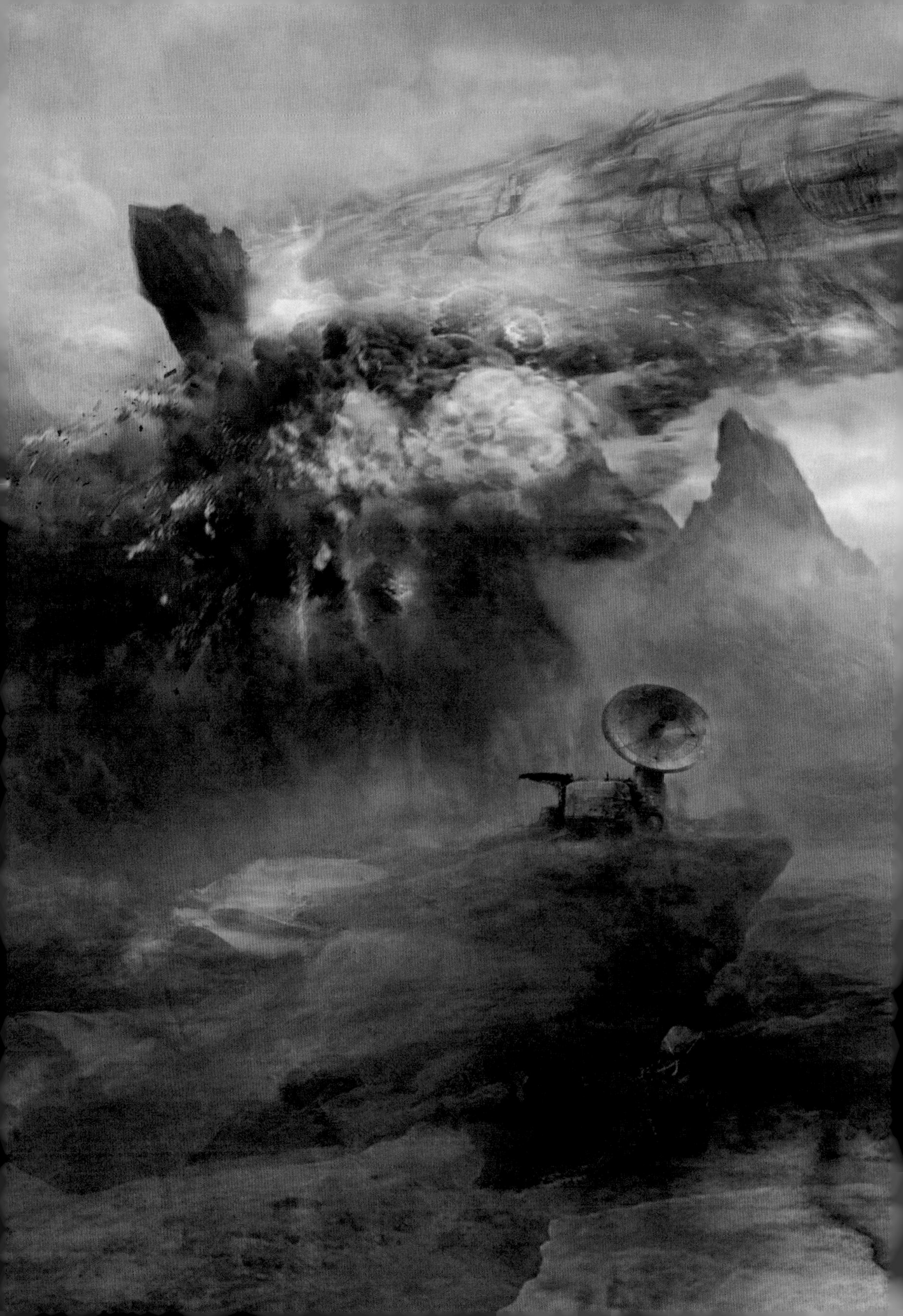

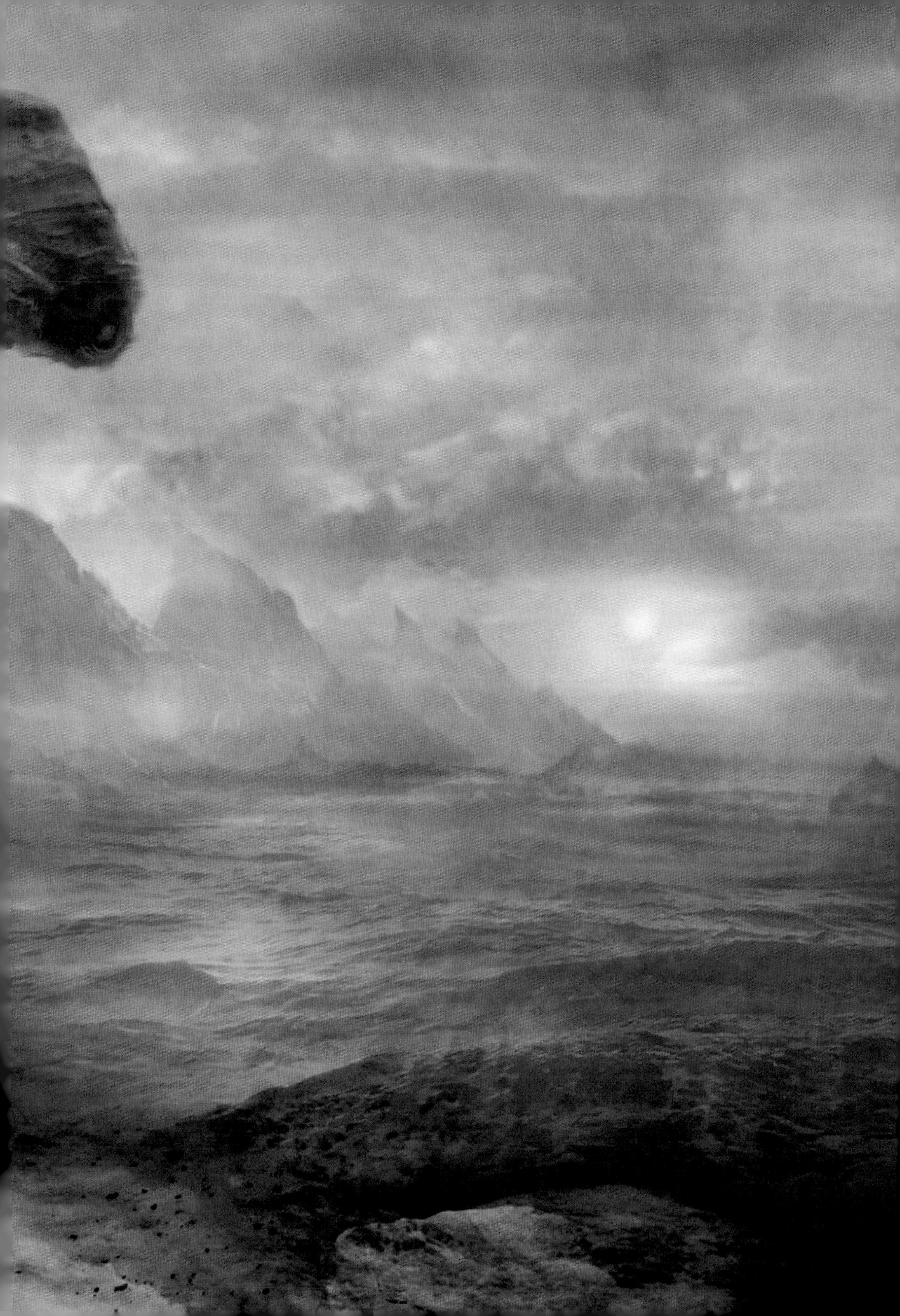

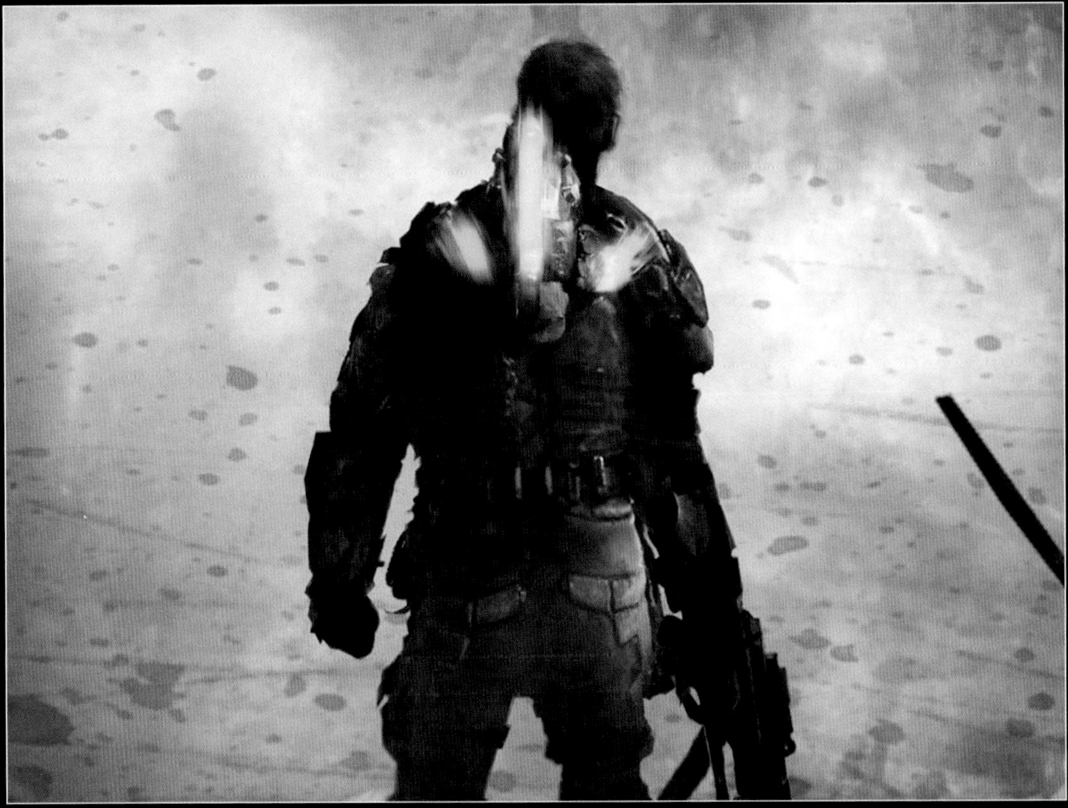

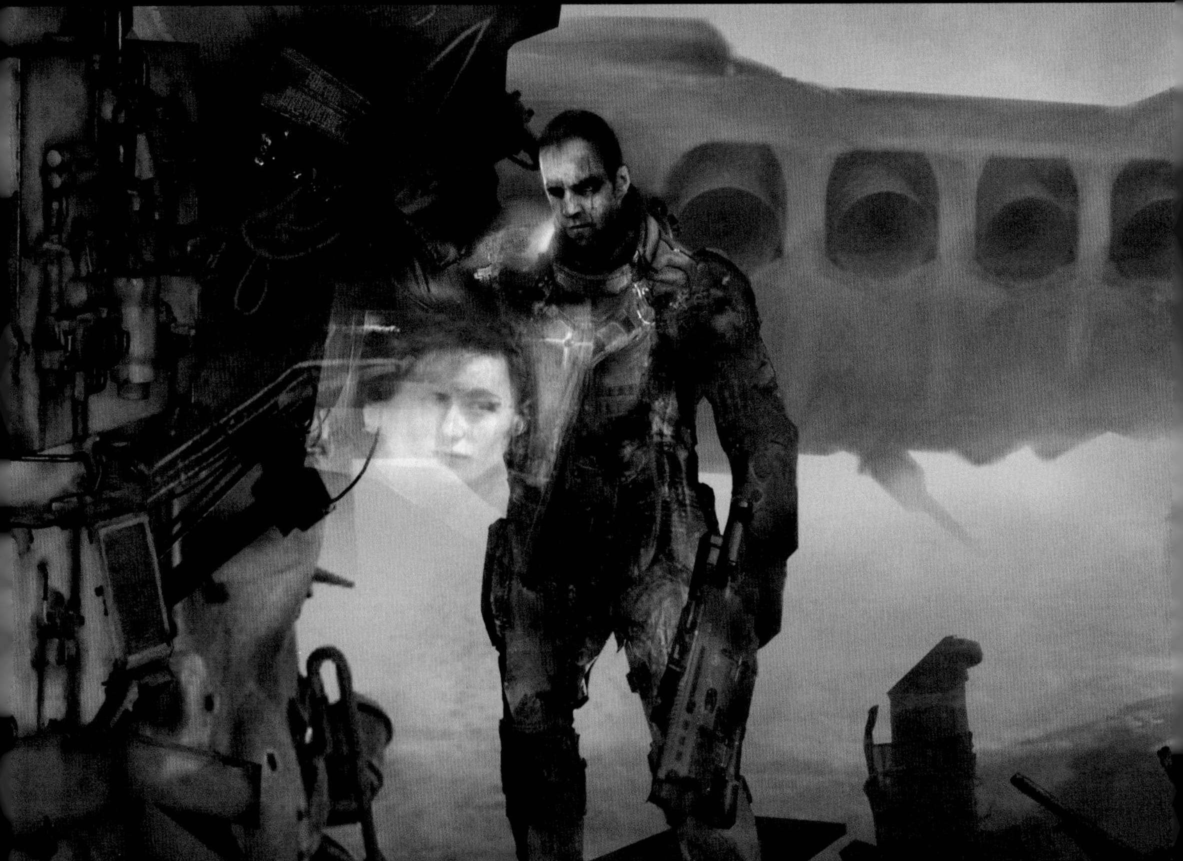

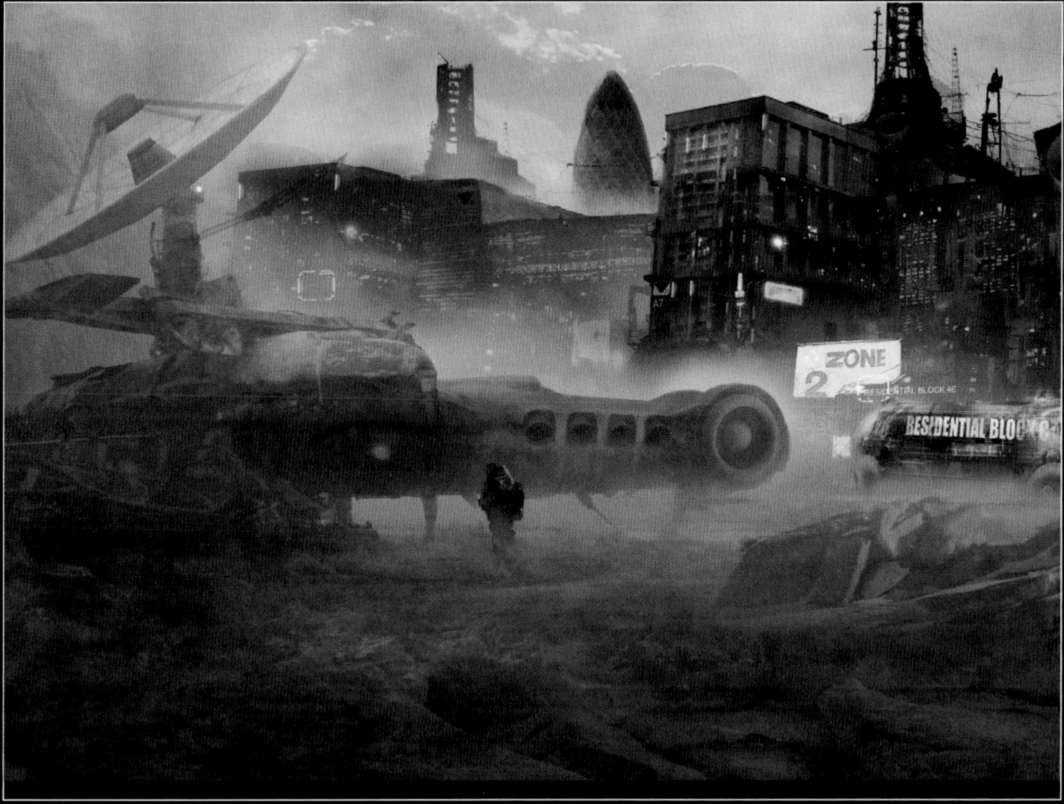
A7
ZONE
2
RESIDENTIAL BLOCK 4E

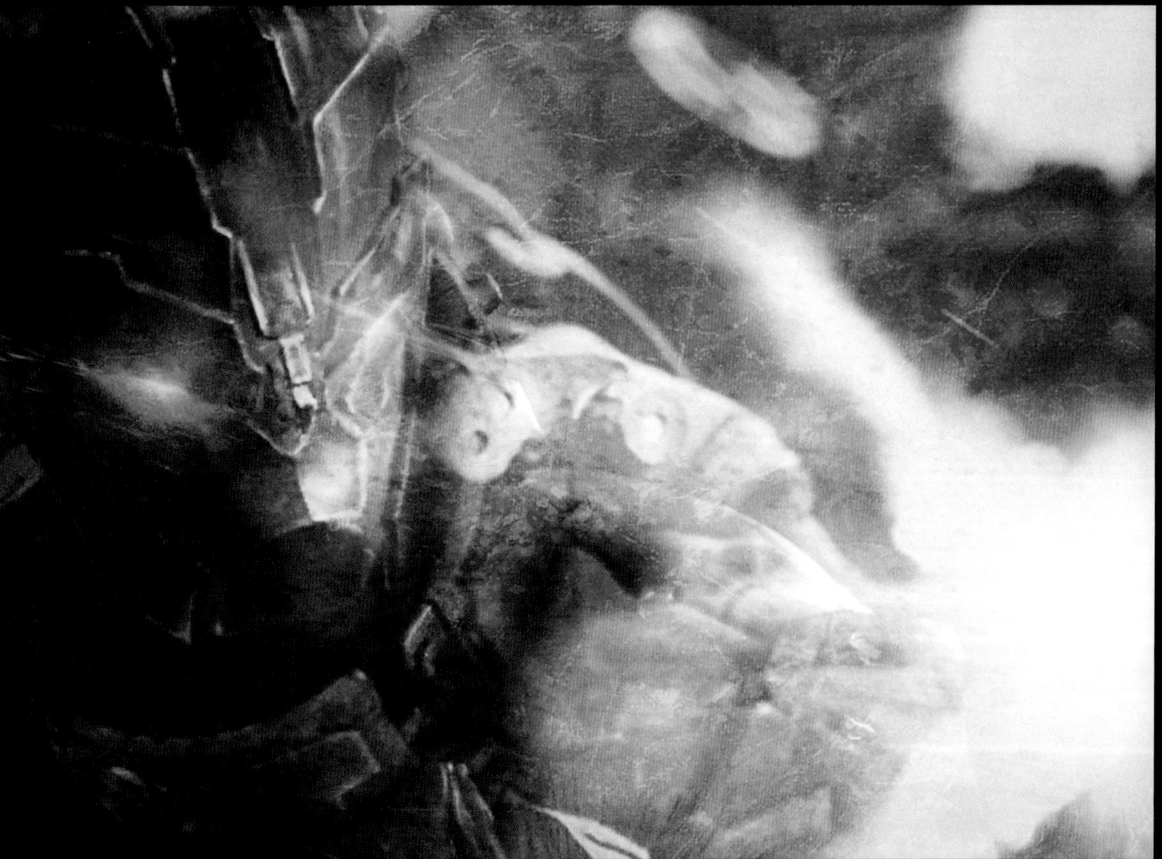

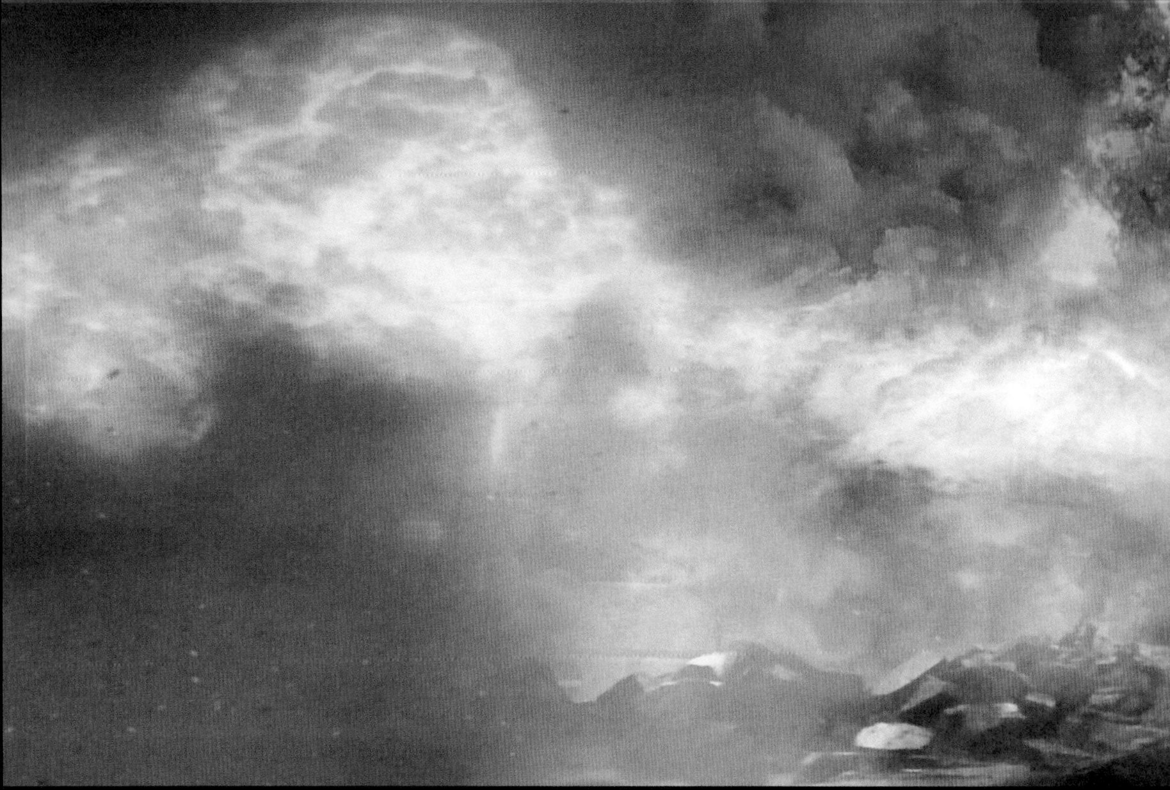

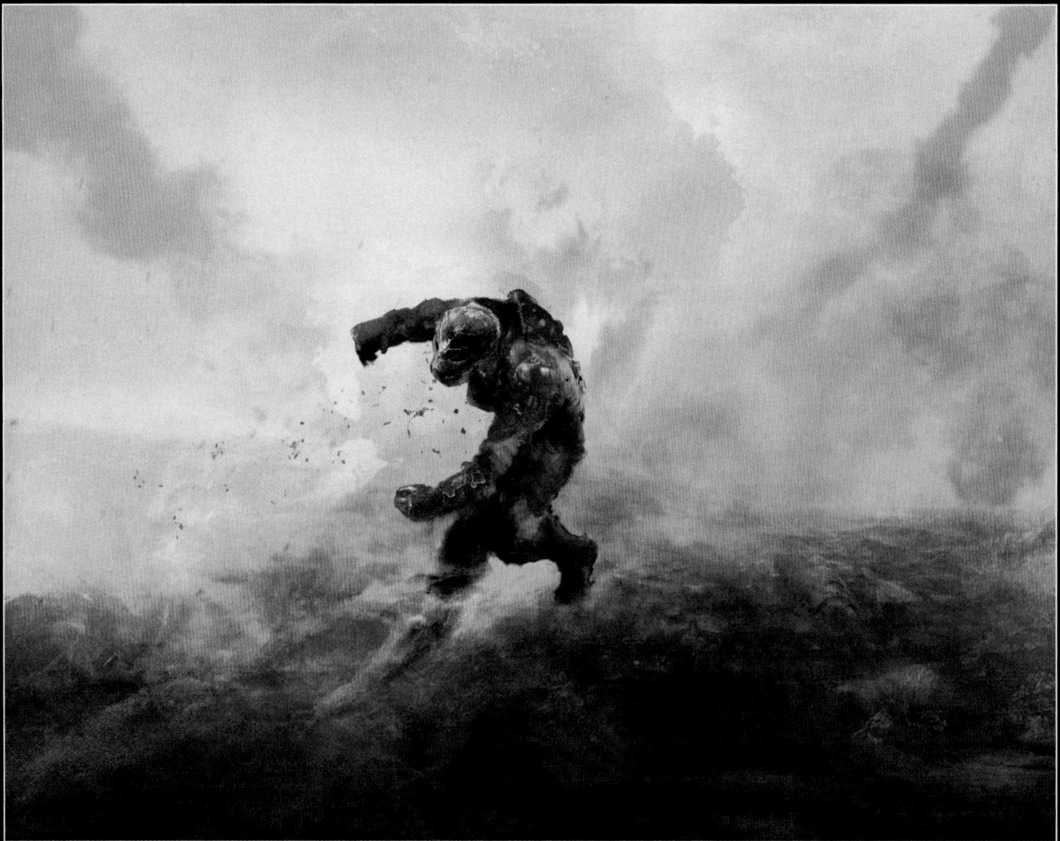

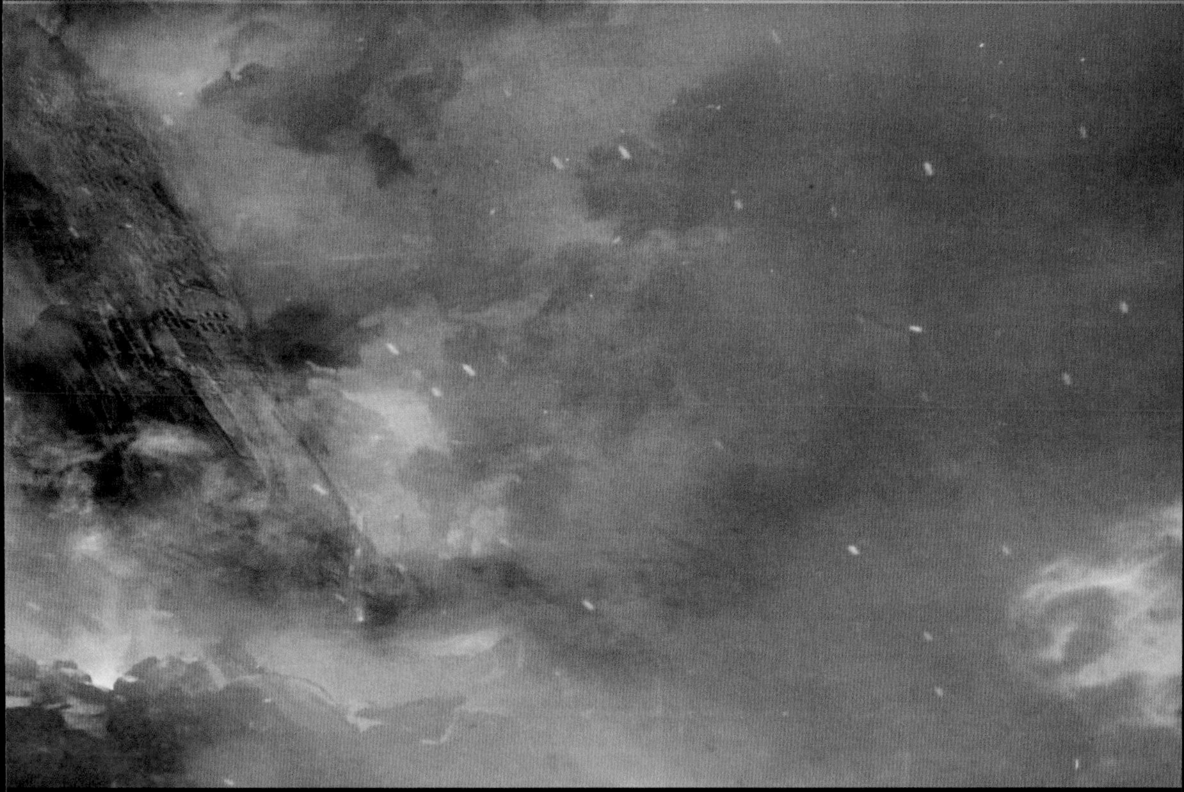

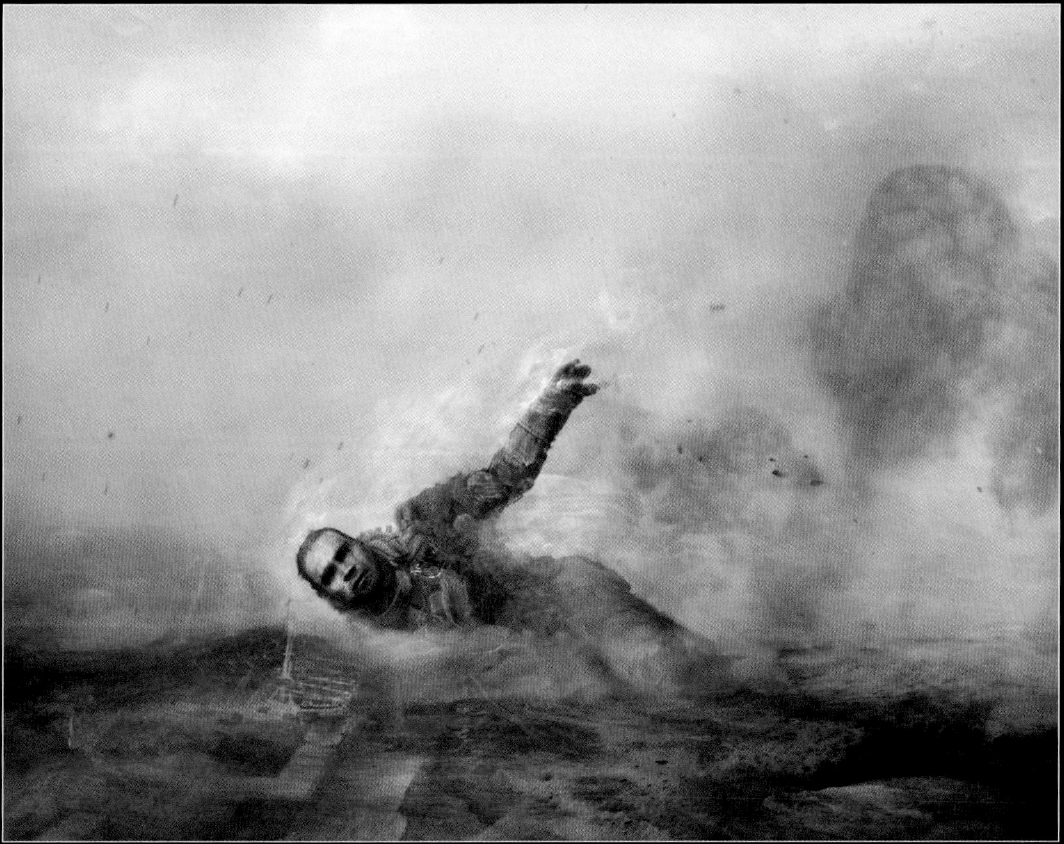

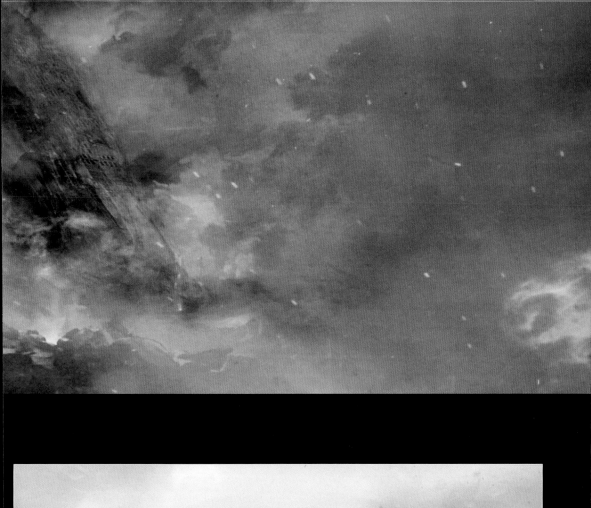

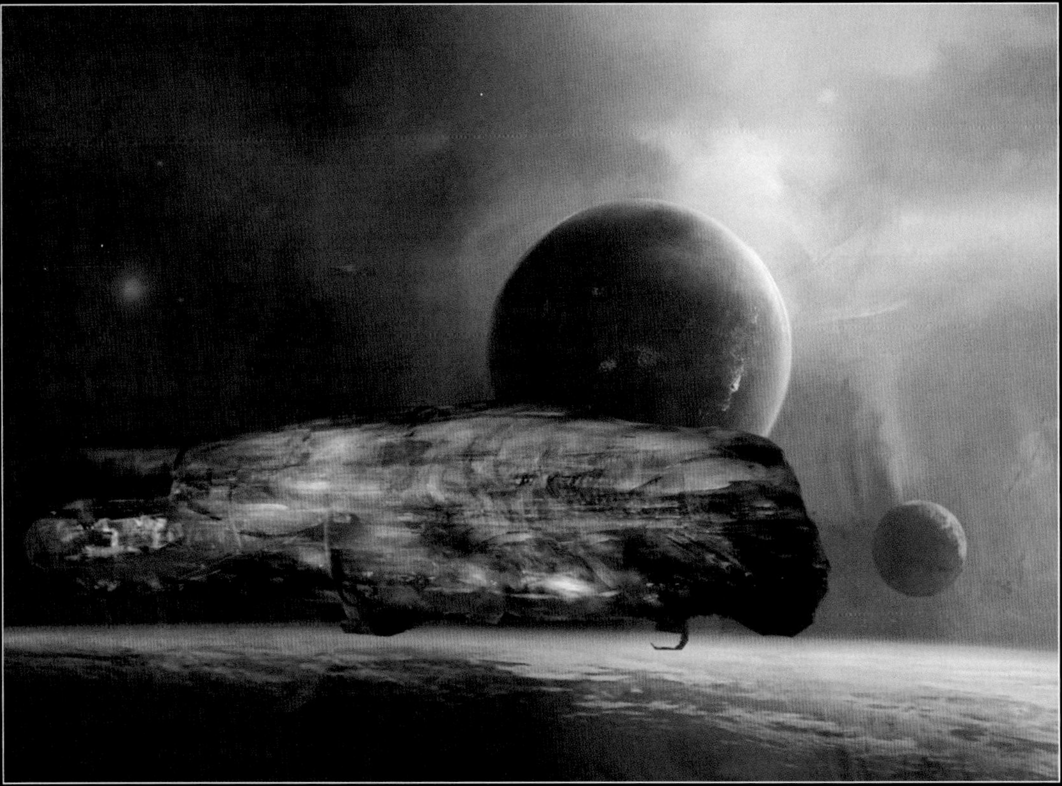

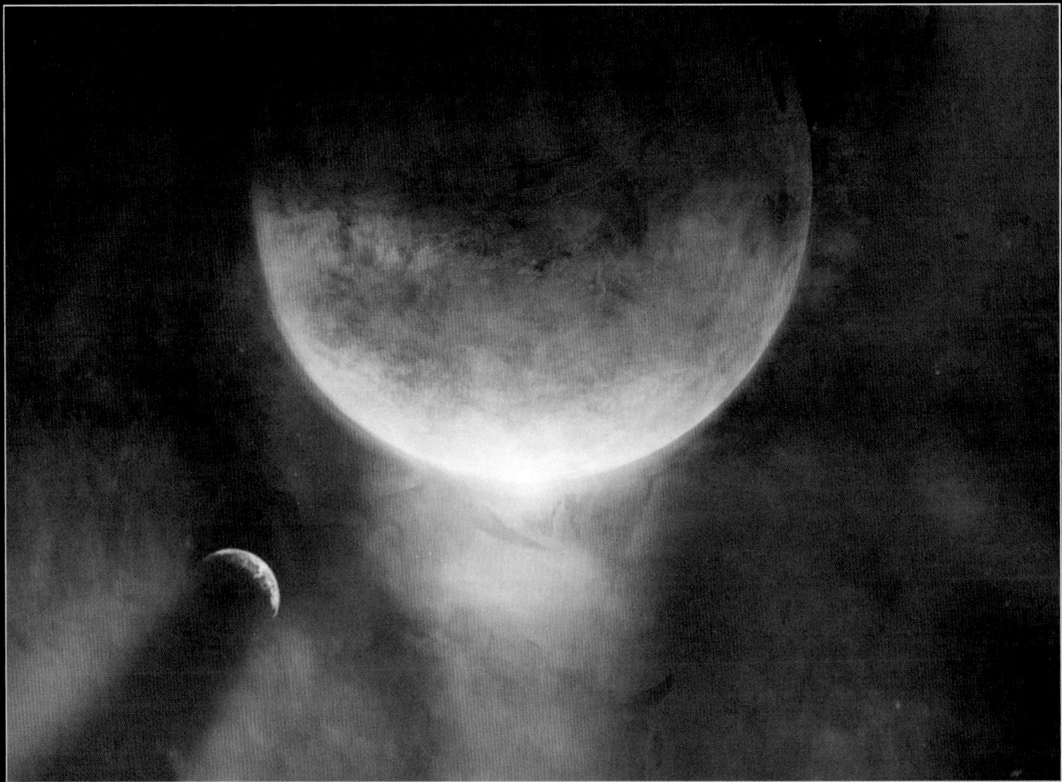

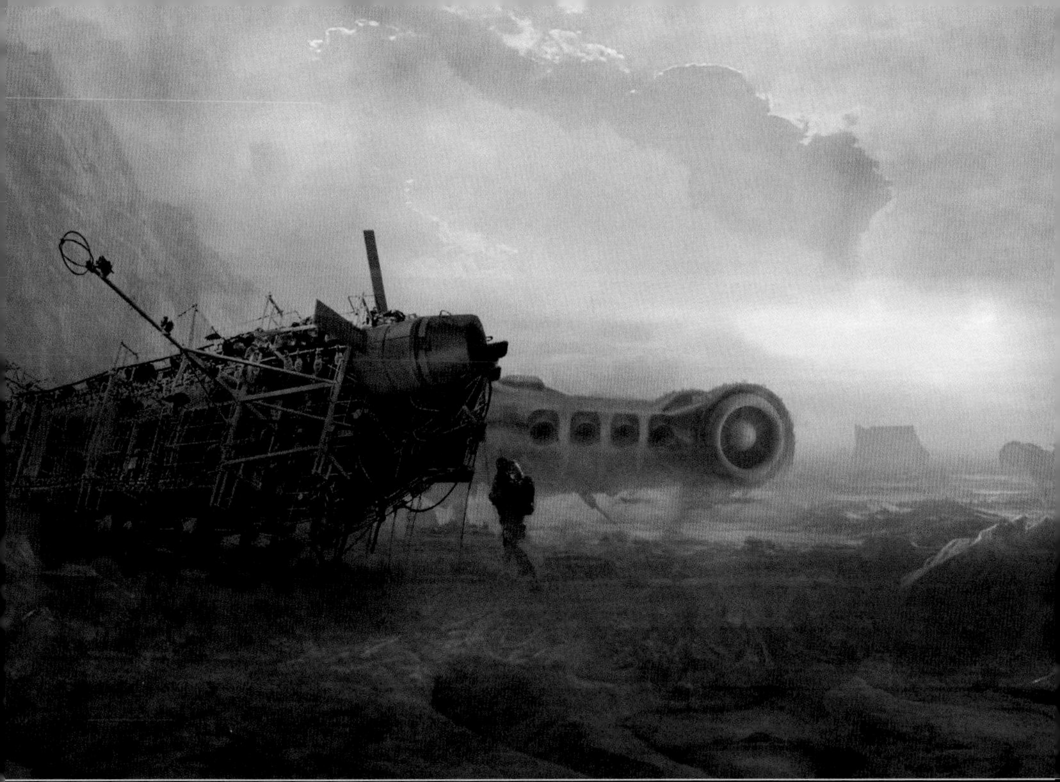

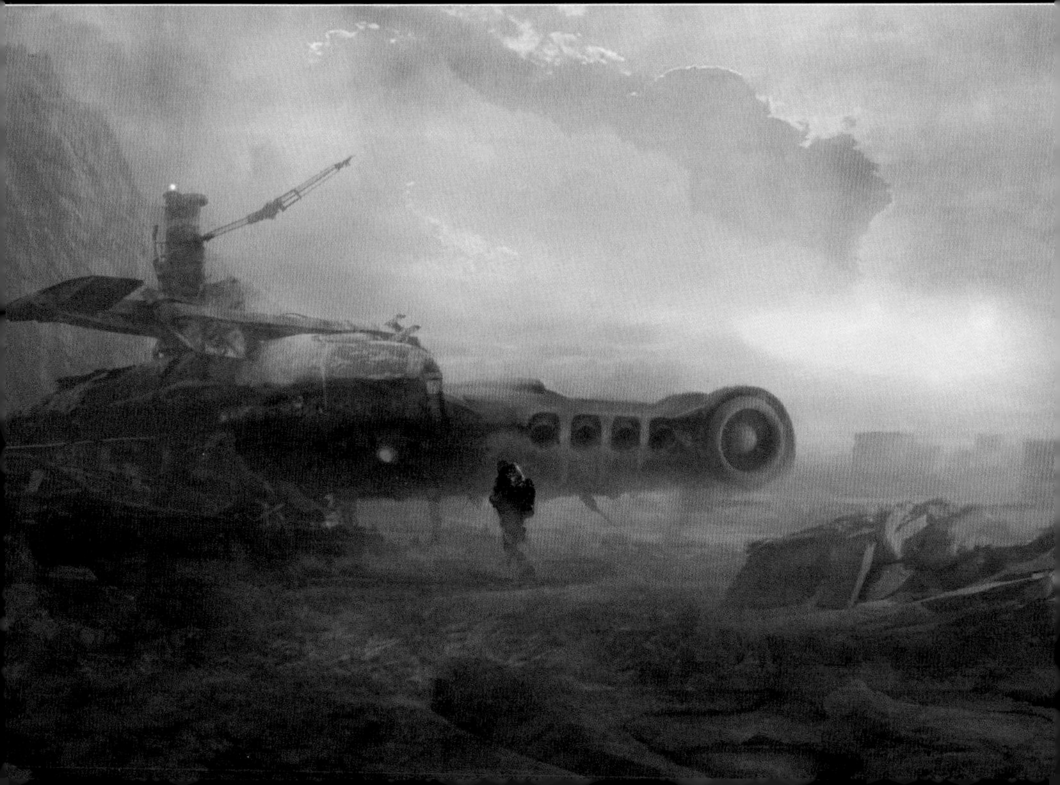

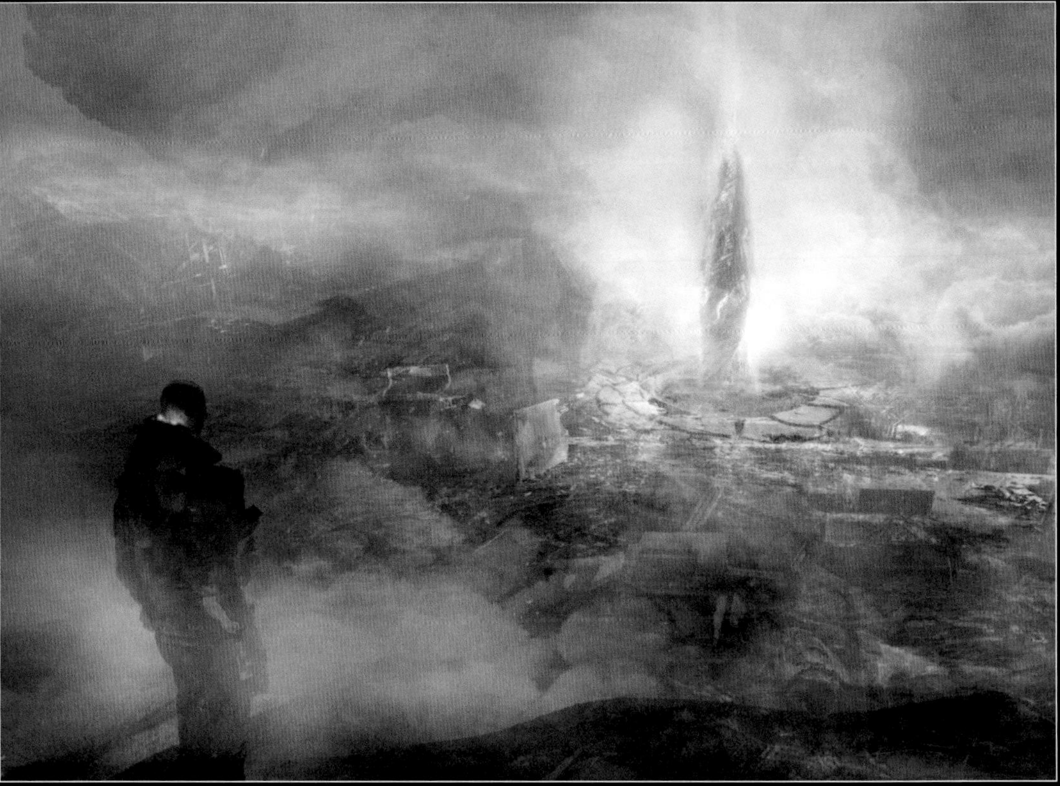
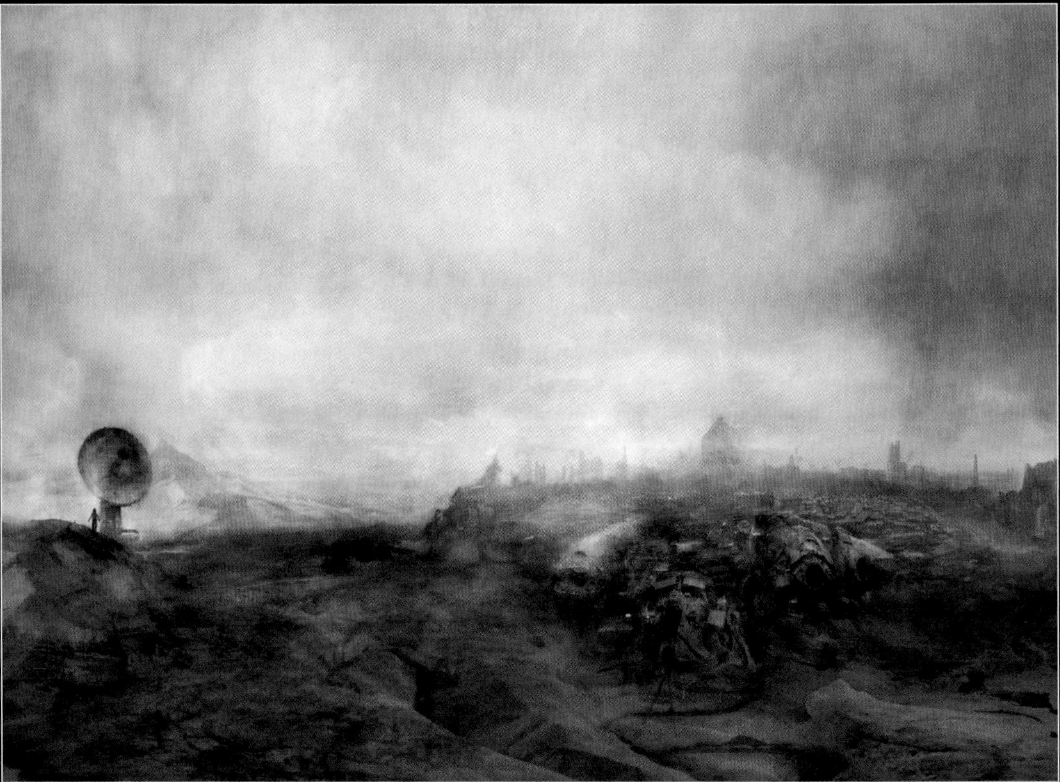

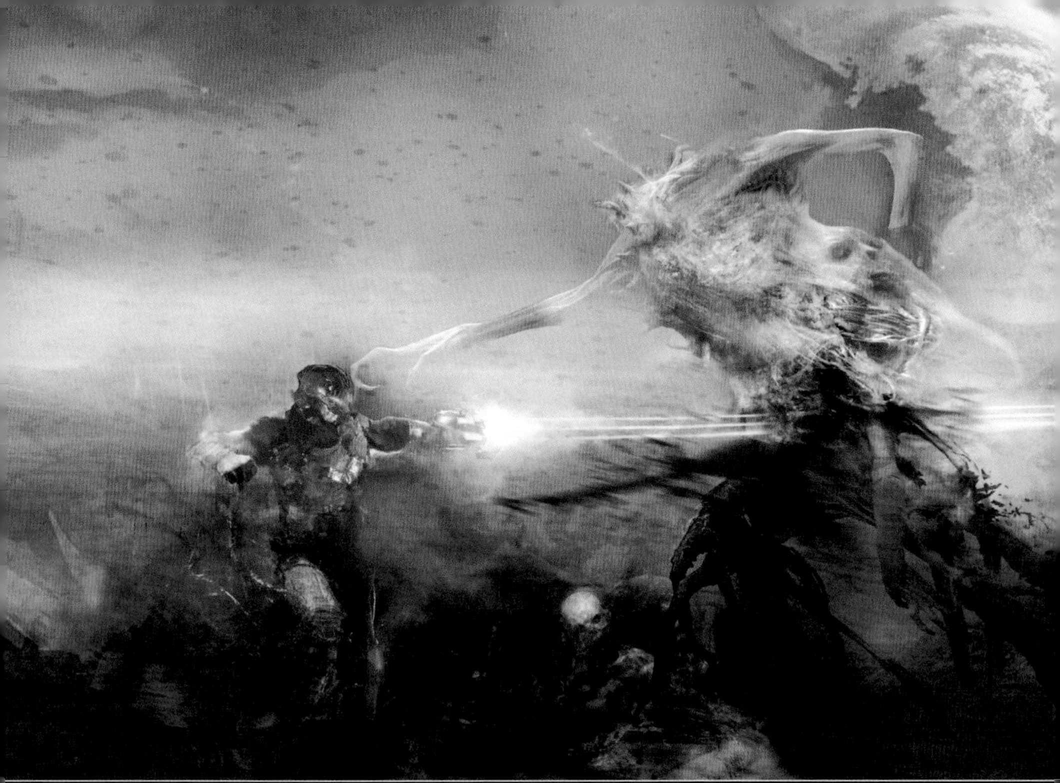

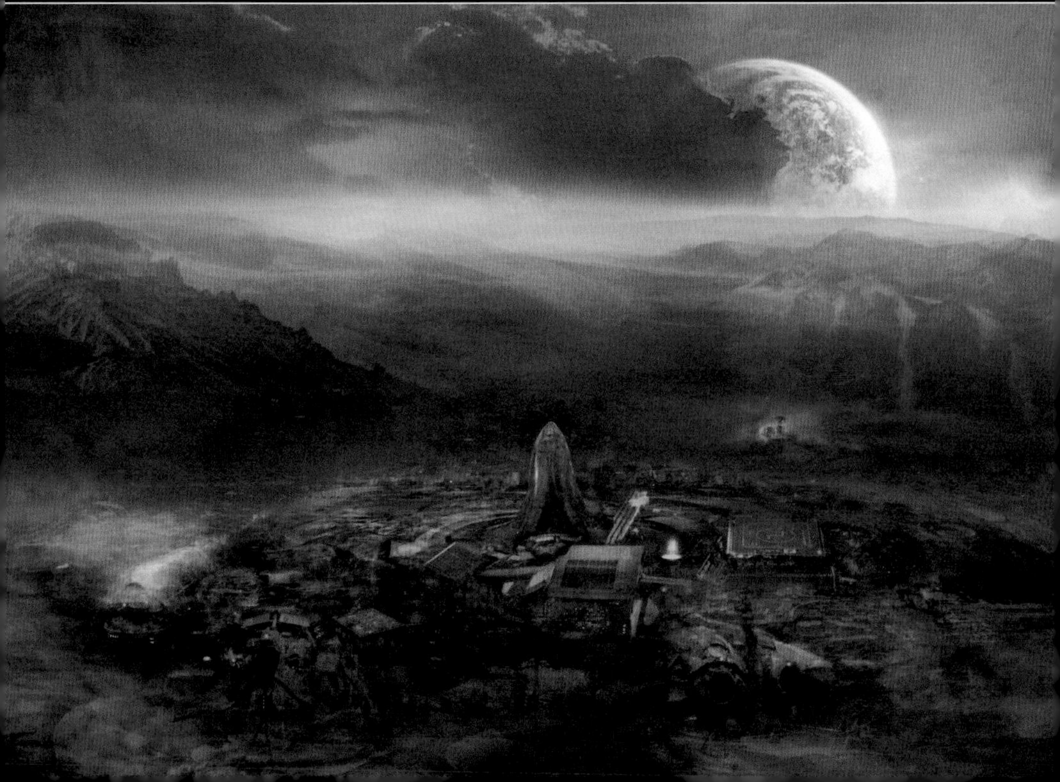

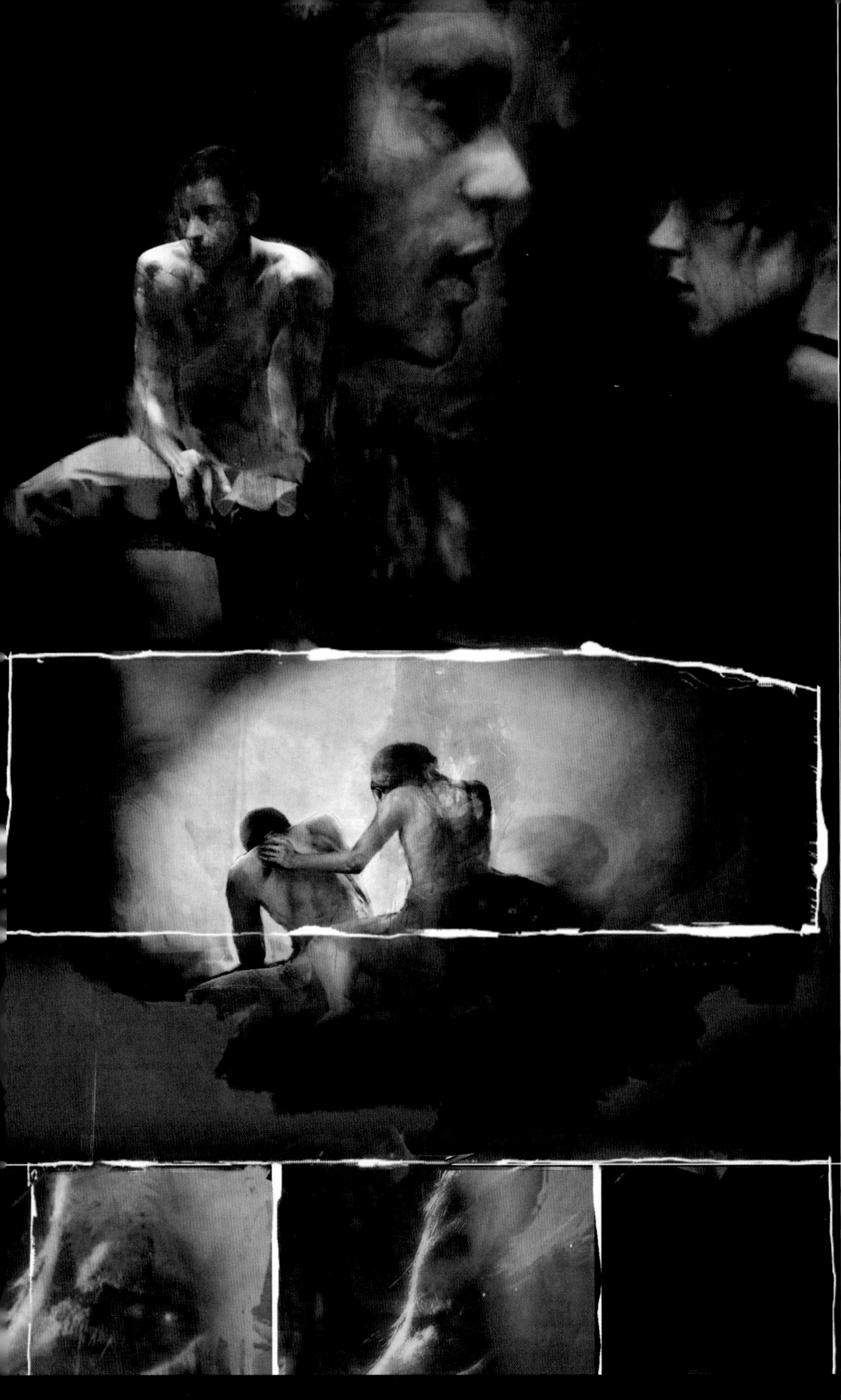

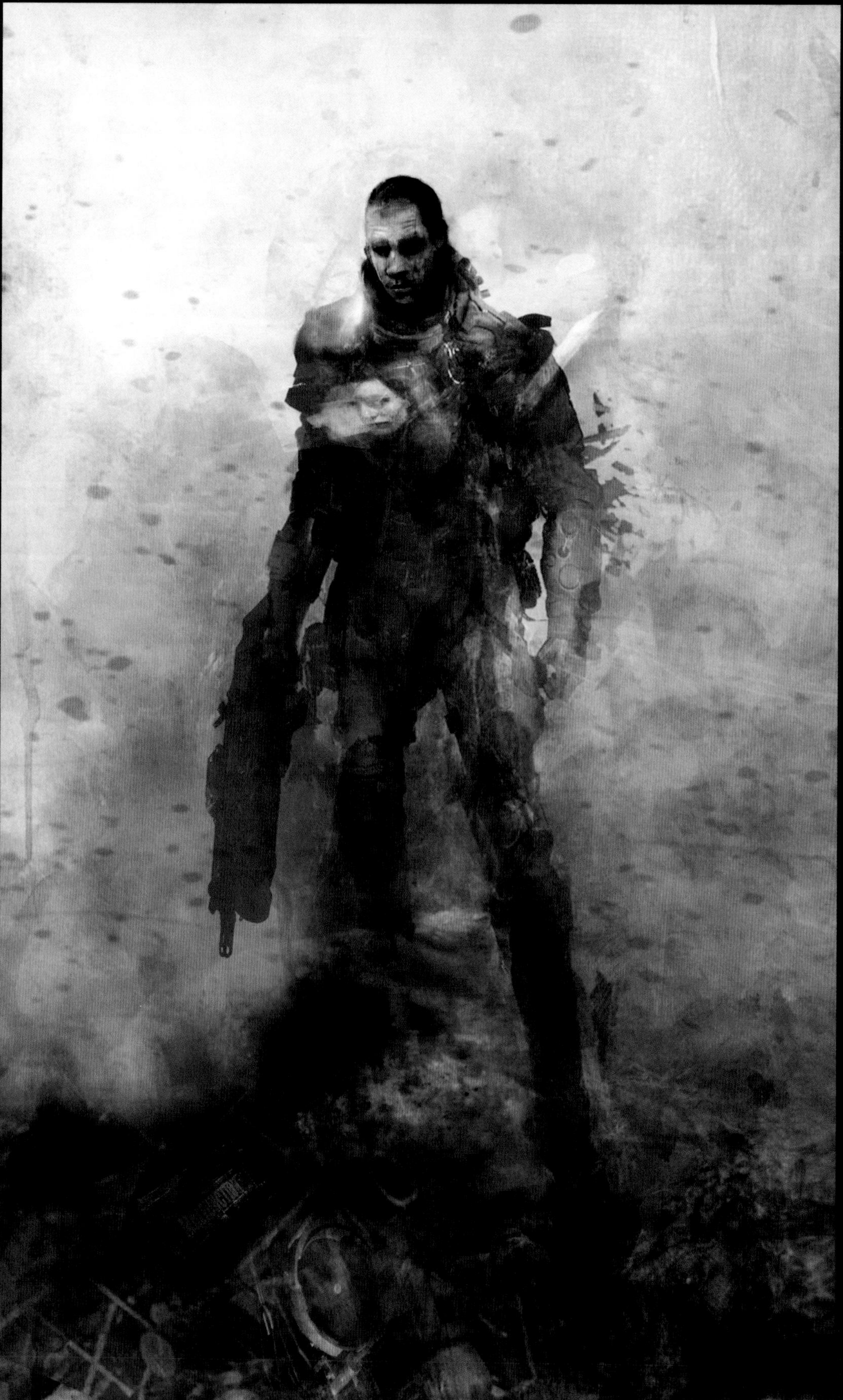

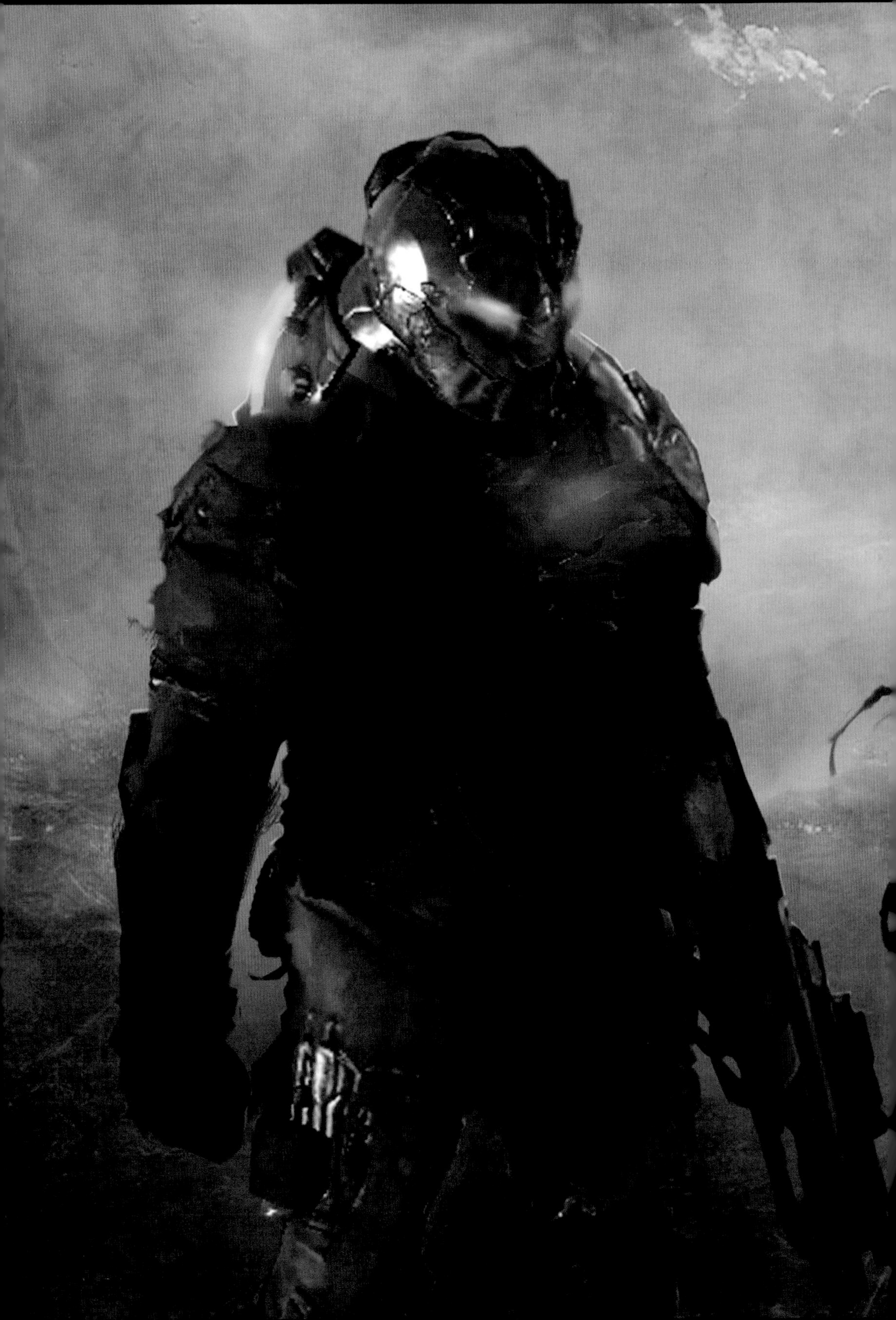

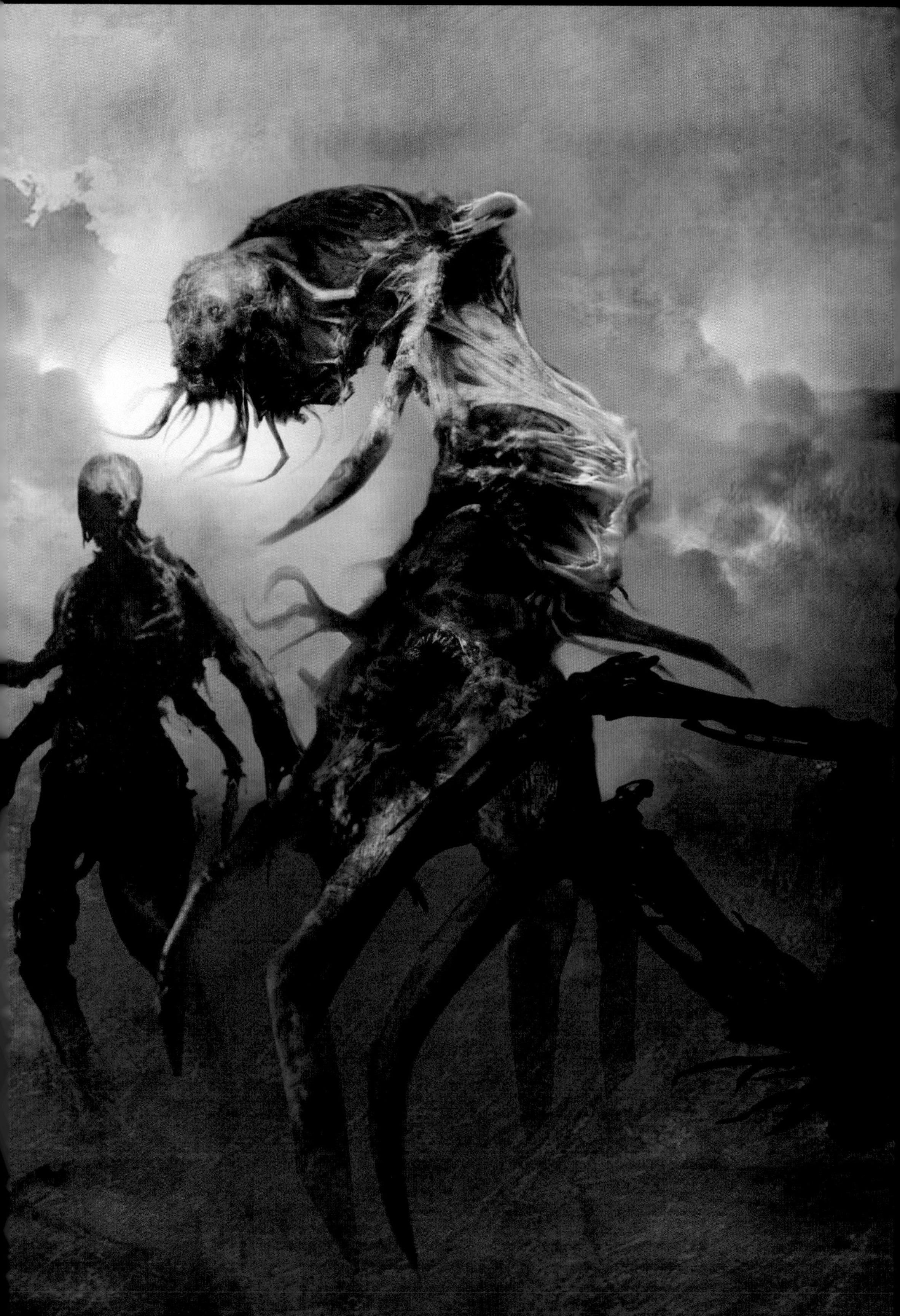

DEAD SPACE ™

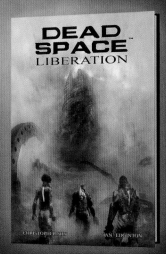